From Tokyo To America

Seven Times Down, Eight Times Up

七転び八起き

a memoir

by

Kumiko Olson

Copyright © 2014 by Kumiko Olson.

All rights reserved. No part of this publication may be reproduced, distributed or transmitted in any form or by any means, including photocopying, recording, or other electronic or mechanical methods, without the prior written permission of the publisher, except in the case of brief quotations embodied in critical reviews and certain other noncommercial uses permitted by copyright law. For permission requests, write to the publisher, addressed "Attention: Permissions Coordinator," at the address below.

Circle of Light Books, LLC
Regarding: Kumiko Olson
2001 NW Aloclek Drive
Suite #7
Hillsboro, OR 97124

From Tokyo to America: Seven Times Down, Eight Times Up
ISBN 978-0-9890681-1-6

The material in this book cannot substitute for professional advice.

Dedication

I dedicate this book to my parents who were my motive for writing this story. My parents always stood by me to help me fulfill my dreams, even letting their only girl emigrate thousands of miles away.

Contents

Preface 1

I Melbourne, Florida *Dream Land* 5

II Atlanta, Georgia *Adult School* 34

III Sebastian, Florida *Hamlet* 42

IV Tullahoma, Tennessee *Hello Kitties* 48

V Atlanta Georgia *Traveling with Two Cats* 60

VI Plano, Texas *Tokyo Friends* 67

VII San Francisco, California *Life in The Big City* 75

VIII Seattle, Washington *Communication Breakdown* 103

IX Portland Oregon *New Turn in My life* 112

X *Turbulence* 126

XI *Back to School* 138

XII *Online Date* 152

XIII *Moving to His House* 173

XIV *Déjà vu* 209

XV *Communal House* 229

XVI *New Beginning* 259

Acknowledgments

I would like to acknowledge my precious friend, Rhonda Bear, who not only encouraged me to write but also helped me with my English over the years.

I also sincerely thank my dear friends, Richard Logan and Ann Casper, who gave me valuable guidance for this book.

The completion of this project could not have been realized without the continual support and vision of my kind editor and publisher, Linda Stirling.

I profoundly appreciate my caring, loving, and supportive husband, Steve, who helped me throughout this writing.

From Tokyo To America

Seven Times Down, Eight Times Up

七転び八起き

a memoir

by

Kumiko Olson

Preface

"Stop it! He is crying. Eru is just a puppy!" Mom shouted from a sliding corridor window that faced the backyard. I dropped Eru. He hit the ground and dashed into the crawlspace under the floor. I sat there. In a moment, Mom showed up and squatted face-to-face with me. Grabbing my arm, she said mournfully, "How can you be so mean? That poor puppy. You can't throw your tantrum on the dog. I've seen you, many times, swinging him around in the air!"

I kept quiet. When Mom could no longer wait for my apology, she left and went inside the house.

With not much reflection, I soon reached my tricycle. As I flung my leg over my bike, Mom returned, holding a brown sack. I thought it must be filled with candies. She thrust the bag at me, saying, "I can't have such a mean child in this house! You can go live at the train station. Here is some rice. You can ask the stationmaster to cook your meals."

Instead of crying, I bit my lip, clenched my fists, and then crossed my arms over my chest. I stood in place, not moving, but Mom carried me outside our gate and set me down. The gate shut behind me.

With a fluffy pink infant's hat squeezed onto my four-year-old head, and the sack of rice in my hand, I started off toward the train station in Ohanajaya. I wasn't sure how to get there, but knew the general direction. *Station people wear blue clothes and blue hats*, I recalled. A vision of stern-looking people came to mind. I halted. *I don't want to go!* I glanced over at the flower field that ran alongside the road—white butterflies and blue dragonflies hovered over the mustard-flower field. I wished to be there, instead. As I turned my head, I saw Mom in the distance, racing towards me. Out of breath, when she caught up with me, she scolded, "Silly child." She lifted me off the ground and perched me on her hip. "Will you behave yourself now?"

I leaned my head on her chest.

Despite her frustration, Mom popped some sweet rice into my mouth as soon as we got back inside the house.

Mom was worried about my conniption fits and seriously wanted to stop them. I was a stubborn child, and if things didn't go my way, I sulked. That was why my two brothers left me alone. In my childhood, I did not play with the neighbor children much at all. I followed my mom as if I were her shadow.

One of my best buddies was my dad. For countless hours, I would sit next to him in his workshop, watching as he hammered with his steel tools.

Half of his shop floor was covered with *tatami* mats. We would sit on a cushion in front of his workbench. Dad would put goggles on me to protect my eyes. He told me funny stories while he sculpted metal to make prototypes of European plastic doll's eyes that opened and closed. He often said, "Little one, what are you doing here when you could be playing with the other girls?" But a stubborn child will sit for hours.

My parents never gave up urging me to play with other children. When I was enrolled in kindergarten, my parents held great hope, but other children bored me. *They aren't likely to be good playmates*, I thought. I preferred solitary play: to draw or read. My lack of social skills made kindergarten difficult.

Shy and withdrawn, I only made a couple friends during my school years.

A few years before entering college, I began to consider which major to pursue. I was good at artwork. While still in elementary school, my calligraphy had been hung in the National Museum of Western Art, and my watercolor painting of a Buddhist temple received a silver award from the Katsushika School District.

With those successes behind me and the need to choose a career, I said one day to my father, "Dad, I want to go to an art college."

"Ummm . . . not a bad idea, but an artist's life is full of hardship," he said.

Dad had an antisocial friend who was well-known for his paintings of tigers, but he often recounted to my dad how difficult it was to be an artist. Dad didn't want me to have such an arduous life, but he was concerned about me becoming more aloof and shy around other people, if I continued to live in my own world. He never said, "No," outright, so I finally asked him to share his thoughts.

"Well . . . it's sort of a solitary life. You won't be as exposed to other people like you would be in a corporate job. Besides that, you can't expect money to come in always, which limits what you can do."

When I heard his words, I said to myself, "Hmmm . . . but I am a woman. I am not thinking about making money. I will marry and not need to make a living." This was typical thinking for Japanese women in the seventies.

Even so, Dad's words resounded in my ears. I didn't want a solitary life.

In the back of my mind, I had often thought it would be cool to speak English. I imagined myself speaking to foreigners, whose hair, eyes, and skin colors were all uniquely different from mine. How internationally sophisticated I could become! I expressed this thought to my dad.

"Good! You can meet all kinds of people. The world is getting smaller. You are now living in an era where learning English is important. It can open new horizons for you," he said.

"Dad, I want to travel to foreign countries."

"If I were young like you, I wouldn't mind doing the same thing." He grinned, happy about my decision.

So I enrolled in a private junior women's college that specialized in English. A few of my classmates had been *kaigaishijo* (children of

Japanese expats) in the U.S., and those ladies painted their years in America as the most wonderful time of their lives.

My first job after finishing school was to work in the foreign department of the Industrial Bank of Japan. My co-worker and friend, who often visited Vancouver, Canada, raved about how beautiful that part of the world was. My dream of going abroad grew stronger. I saved money, left the company, and went to England to go to school. But a few months after I was enrolled in a technical college, while I was strolling on the sidewalk near Piccadilly Circus, a drunken driver in an English Austin taxi hit me. Luckily, my only injuries were a few cuts and bad bruises, but I was bedridden for a week with severe pain in my back and neck. This accident discouraged me from staying in England any longer.

Returning home from London, I soon found a job at a language school as a Japanese teacher. In the school, I met my future husband, Thomas, who was working in Japan as an English teacher. We married within two months. After three years, we moved to his hometown in Florida. Our decision to move to the U.S. was a dream come true. Although I had expected to experience cultural differences, I had never anticipated that so many life changing events would await me. My story unfolds the day I landed at the Orlando Airport in Florida.

I

Melbourne, Florida

Dream Land

It was midnight on August 10, 1984. After a month of separation, I was rejoining Thomas to start our new life in Melbourne, Florida. As I stood at the doorstep of the airplane that had just landed at the Orlando airport, damp air streamed onto my skin. Walking a few steps further, I saw my husband standing by the door, smiling radiantly. He must have persuaded the airline people to give him permission to come inside the passenger dock. *It is very you,* I thought to myself. He always liked to surprise me.

"I missed you," said Thomas.

"I missed you too." I said, lowering my eyes, then looking up at him from beneath my lashes in the manner I'd learned he appreciated.

"Ken is here, waiting outside in the pick-up lane to welcome you."

"That's very nice of him," I said, fuzzily recalling Ken's small, oblong face. I had met him once, two years before, on our belated honeymoon. Ken was Thomas's high school friend.

"Hi, Kumiko. Welcome to the U.S.!" Ken bent over me and hugged me lightly. He was standing still, but his upper body moved like a tree nodding in the wind. With his short, wiry body and scant hair, he reminded me of Woody Allen.

Ken opened his old station wagon door and I hopped in. As the car cruised down the highway, the spotlighted palm trees lining the highway gave me a tropical feeling. I'd felt fatigued, but having my husband back and being in his arms helped my mood. I perked up considerably. Although I had neither a strong knowledge of the American culture, nor enough English to feel comfortable, I believed our new life looked promising. An hour-and-a-half later, we arrived at Thomas's parents' house in a suburb of Orlando. We thanked Ken and wished him a good night.

Thomas unlocked the door of his parent's house. We had stayed for a week during our one-year-late honeymoon in September of 1982. Once inside, we tiptoed through the dimly-lit hallway into the room that had been Thomas's bedroom when he was a child. Though no lights were on, I recognized the house by its faint but distinctive smell, a smell that instantaneously took me back to my first visit. We stepped into his childhood room and Thomas turned on the lights. As I glanced around, I saw his self-portrait drawing, a large world globe, and his high school speech trophy. I could tell they evoked nostalgia in my husband.

"I'm glad you made it," he said with a relaxed smile.

"Me, too," I said, smiling back.

"It's 2:00 o'clock. You must be very tired. Let's get some sleep."

As I slipped between sheets that had been chilled by air-conditioning, I felt cold, but his soft kiss and gentle touch ignited my passion. In closing my eyes, his smell, absent for a month, intensified the love, and I felt ecstatic.

The next morning, I woke up with the sun. I was anxious to see Thomas's parents, Jacob and Sophia, but I gave myself plenty of time to do my makeup. While I was putting on my makeup in the bathroom, I saw something familiar: a large, flat case with a partitioned shelf that rose as the lid was lifted. I remembered from our previous visit that the aqua-colored case held numerous cosmetics. It had impressed me a great deal because I had never seen such a pretty multi-layered cosmetic kit. I opened the lid and gazed at the pink, red, plum, and many other shades of lipstick. The eyeshadows, too, came in a full selection of colors. I was tempted to use them, but realized it would be safer to stick with my own cosmetics, so as to be myself in front of Thomas's parents.

As I came out of the bathroom, I saw a light on in the living room. I took a deep breath to gather my nerves, then exhaled slowly as I walked toward my father-in-law to say, "Good morning." He gave me a big hug with a tiny kiss on my cheek. Sophia was reading the newspaper. She took off her glasses and stood up to give me a warm, friendly hug.

Thomas joined us a half-hour later.

"Good morning, son. I made cornbread. Hope Kumiko will like it," his father said.

We shifted into the dining room. The table was already set for breakfast. Once we sat at the table, Sophia poured coffee and fresh orange juice, then served us eggs, sausages, and cornbread. To show Thomas's father appreciation, I tried his cornbread first. The melted butter deepened the canary-yellow color of the bread and the aroma stimulated my appetite. I took a bite.

"It is delicious, Father," I said.

"I'm glad. It's a southern-style cornbread," he said.

My heart warmed from his family's welcome.

Soon after breakfast, Thomas and I left for our new home in Melbourne. He had told me earlier that he had found the apartment while staying at his parents' house. As he drove, he explained it all to me in a confident and subtly showy manner, for this was his home ground. Although my eyelids drooped and my head operated in a fog from lack of sleep, I felt overjoyed at the sight of rich-looking Mediterranean-style houses with landscaped yards filled with all sorts of both tall and short amusingly-shaped palm trees . . . and the crystal clear sky—so beautiful, unlike the polluted Tokyo sky.

As our used 1982 Toyota Cressida passed through the gate of our apartment complex, I saw the name, "Whickham Village," carved on an oblong wooden board. A few lanky palm trees and a dense growth of tropical caladiums with pink spots, charmingly planted in the small flowerbeds in front of the gate, adorned the two-year-old apartment complex. As the car neared our apartment, my heart started pounding fast with glee. I'd soon see my American home.

Right away, I caught sight of a swimming pool surrounded by a tall wire fence. Inside the pool area were a few overweight old ladies lying on reclining chairs by the pool in their flamboyant swimwear. There were a few young blonde moms playing with their small children in water that reflected the blazing sun. No one had a private swimming pool on their own property in Japan, at least not to my knowledge. If there were any private pools, I imagined they must be few in number and that they would be owned by wealthy families. Next to the swimming pool, there were two green tennis courts. I felt rich and elated.

Thomas parked the car in a wide space in front of the apartment. He opened the apartment door with a key on a chain that had no other keys attached to it yet, and let me in first. I took off my shoes, a Japanese habit, and felt the coolness of the floor tiles. The entrance led to beige carpeting that spread over into the rest of the rooms. This thousand-square-foot two-bedroom apartment had many windows as it was located at the end of the row. Vertical blinds blocked the daytime heat of the scorching Florida sun.

First we entered the master bedroom. A dominating tall king-size bed, which set in the center of the room, astounded me.

"Is this the waterbed you were talking about on the phone? It's huge," I said, recalling the conversation we had before I came to the U.S.

"Yes, lay down and check it out," he said.

As the height of the bed came up to my stomach, it was a bit hard to do so. Instead, I placed my hands on it, then pressed down on the mattress.

"Wow . . . it's soft," I said, wondering if it would make me seasick.

"You'll sleep like a baby," my husband assured me. I walked into the bathroom. I stroked the countertop of the double-vanity with its two shiny faucets, then looked up at the large mirror. Smiling, I thought, *I will enjoy using this room a lot.*

The kitchen fascinated me, too. A huge refrigerator, a dishwasher, and an oven—typical Japanese households didn't have an oven, and used a gas stove with an integrated broiler. I thought I could adjust to this new living style effortlessly and agreeably. Everything I had been experiencing so far was like being in paradise, where no reality intruded. This was America and everything was big and wonderful!

Later that evening, lying on the unfamiliar waterbed, I thought back over the day. I realized Thomas had worked very hard. He had to have been extremely busy all month preparing countless things, finding his job and our apartment, and getting our car and waterbed. He fell asleep holding my hand, but, having jetlag, I stayed awake for hours, my mind traveling back over all the things that had happened since I had met him. The three years in Tokyo with Thomas had passed very fast. I could not believe I was in the U.S. I remembered the first day we met . . .

The first time I saw Thomas, he was in the teachers' break room of the language school. He stood out, as he was 6'4", a brunette with blue eyes, a slender, handsome young American who wore a well-cut brown business suit. I didn't want to stare at him, but because of his height and appearance, I couldn't take my eyes off him easily. A few days later, he approached me with the school manager while I was chatting with other Japanese teachers in the break room.

The manager said, "Kumiko-san, this is our new English teacher, Thomas-san. He has suggested that you and he tutor each other in your own native languages."

I thought his approach was a little presumptuous, as we had not properly met each other, but I could not refuse my manager.

In my first English lesson, Thomas started drawing the outline of the U.S. map on the blackboard, then he filled in each of the state's borderlines as if we were in a geography class. When he finished drawing, he pointed to Orlando, Florida with his slender finger. "This state is my home town. My parents live here," he said, then he shifted his finger a little north. "This is Georgia. My college is in Atlanta, the capital of Georgia."

For the entire forty-five minutes he rambled on about his personal background. At the end of the class, he abruptly asked me if I could show him around Tokyo that weekend. His boldness amazed me, but I agreed, thinking about how hard it must be to live in a foreign country.

The following week, he asked me out on a date. Although I still thought he was conceited, I had noticed how caring and sweet he was when we were walking around Tokyo. He walked on the street side of the sidewalk, while listening to me attentively. His sensitivity appealed to me, so I agreed to a date.

He took me to the Disney movie, *Fantasia*. He thought we both would enjoy it, but I fell asleep in the middle of the movie. Classical music and slow-paced movies have a hypnotic effect on me and often put me to sleep.

After the movie, he invited me to dinner at his place. The menu was salmon and stir-fried vegetables. He spiced the curry pilaf with all sorts of unfamiliar seasonings (cumin, oregano, basil, and other unfamiliar things) and raisins. The curried wild and brown rice mix with raisins was spicy and sweet, but also quite savory.

After cleaning up the table, he served a fruit cup of apple, orange, and banana. I realized how thorough and thoughtful he was, and his kind gestures gave me the impression he was a good person. When he saw me off at the station, he asked me to meet him the next day after our classes.

We started seeing each other daily. The following Saturday, we visited the National Museum of Western Art, where we played a little game.

He said, "Let's choose four paintings that we like from this room. After we choose four paintings, we'll tell each other what we chose."

"Anything I like?" I clarified.

"Yes, anything you like."

I moved like a crab, sideways, observing one-by-one the European paintings on the walls. I took more time than he did. While waiting for me, Thomas stood at the center of the room that held over fifty paintings. Knowing his eyes were following me, I tried to deceive him by staring at some of the paintings I had no interest in a bit longer.

Forgetting about being in a museum, I said, "I'm done," loudly as I walked toward him.

He mouthed, "All right", and waited for me to get to where he was standing. Then he said "You go first."

I told him of my selections. He was flabbergasted. We had chosen exactly the same paintings.

Within five weeks, Thomas had decided to marry me. Even though we had only been dating for a little over a month, I didn't hesitate to agree. I liked his caring personality and proactive approach. In order to receive my parents' permission, he immediately changed jobs and became a technical writer at an electronics company, to prove he was capable of earning a respectable income and being a good provider. As concerned as he was about my parents, he only called his parents to announce he was getting married. I was surprised, but glad his parents were happy about our engagement.

We were married within two months of the day we met. His parents flew from Florida to Japan to attend our Shinto wedding. Traditionally, the religious wedding ceremony is held at a shrine, and in our case, the shrine was located inside a hotel. A Shinto priest always conducts the ceremony, which is attended by only the close family members of the couple. In keeping with this, only his parents and my family were there. In the ceremony, following the Shinto rites, we drank *sake* using a special cup, and we took turns taking three sips each of three different bowls of *sake*, each one larger than the last. Thomas was in *hakama* (Japanese traditional clothing) standing next to me. He, especially in the *hakama*, reminded me of Richard Chamberlain in the movie *Shogun*. I was in a red silk kimono with a crane design, when we took our vows. His eyes were on me, while my mind was focused on the priest's words. Thomas remembered the whole oath. My parents were greatly impressed, and I, too, was pleased.

After our marriage, my life became busier. Thomas had already learned some Japanese and knew about Japanese culture before arriving two months earlier. Even so, living in another country demands a higher level of communication skills, and he needed my help.

Thomas had become a member of a *Go* club before we married, and had been playing the game in his spare time. But a few months after we got married, he found a new hobby and spent less time playing *Go*. His boss, a fellow American, had built a computer from scratch, and he helped Thomas build his own computer. For a while, we spent every weekend in the Akihabara District. Thomas's Japanese wasn't good enough to shop by himself for specialized items that required detailed knowledge, so I had little time for myself on the weekends.

Akihabara, known as Akihabara Electric Town, is famous worldwide as the center for electronic and electronic goods. A visitor to Akihabara will be overwhelmed by the buildings lining the main street, whose walls, roofs, and windows are covered with all kinds of colorful shops' names and signs. Walking into the alleys, one finds small shops that specialize in electric parts, wires, and tools. We spent many hours there looking for computer parts such as chips, registers, capacitors, and circuit boards.

I also helped him do painstaking jobs like using a soldering iron to place memory chips onto a motherboard. This was a task I disliked. One early afternoon while sitting at a table soldering memory chips, I placed the soldering iron next to me on the floor pillow on which I sat. While I was intensely involved in doing my job, I smelled something burning. I glanced down at the cushion. The hot tip of the soldering iron had penetrated the cushion, making a sizable hole. I jumped up and beat the fire out with a magazine.

The incident stressed me so much that I was haunted by a dream later that night. I dreamt about burning a bunch of holes in a cushion with the soldering iron.

The next morning, Thomas looked at me with a curious face and asked me, "What about your dream last night? In your sleep you said, 'It's big. Be careful.'"

He thought I was having an erotic dream about a giant penis. I had to disappoint him by telling him the dream was about a soldering iron burning a big hole in a cushion.

"*Eh? Ah, Sou*" (is that so?) he said, with the subtle nuance that he was a bit disappointed.

Six months later, to my great relief, he finally finished building his computer.

Using his own self-built computer, he started to learn programming. His first program was a horseracing game. He tried to teach me programming, but his learning pace was faster than mine, and soon he wanted to be a professional programmer. However, his realization that he would not be able to find a job as a software programmer in Japan led him to look to his own country, where the software industries were way ahead of the curve. Thomas decided we would move back to the U.S.

The jet lag, the excitement of a new American home, and the sinking sensation of the soft waterbed kept me awake for a long time. Despite getting only a few hours of sleep, I woke up with a fresh mind, ready to take on the day. Our new life in Florida had begun. After breakfast, Thomas took me to a grocery store called Albertsons.

As I entered the huge supermarket, enormous vegetables piqued my curiosity. I had never imagined vegetables could grow this big. Onions, eggplants, cucumbers, green peppers, and potatoes were giant-sized, easily three or four times bigger than the ones grown in Japan. Moving to the fruit section, I was amazed by the wide variety of fruits. In Japan, imported fruit prices are very high because the Japanese government protects its own industries from foreign competition. Inside Albertsons, there were fruits I had never seen before, such as mangos, lychees, star fruits, durians, and passion fruits, but even fruits I recognized, such as apples, came in many varieties. They were colorfully compartmentalized in sections on the counter like apples on parade.

They must be imported from all over the world. How lucky Americans are, I thought.

Another eye-opener was the meat section. The big slabs of pork and beef were lavishly laid in the large window case. The amount in the packages, I thought, could serve a dozen Japanese people. Everything in the supermarket looked oversized, including a great number of the Floridians whose colorful shoes and clothes didn't cover much. Pushing the shopping cart, I heard Thomas saying behind me, "Are you gonna be here all day? I want to go home."

He didn't mind explaining to me what things were, as my face was beaming with excitement, but after showing me practically everything in the market, he finally got tired. The shopping cart was heaped with enough food for a week or more. I felt as if we were stocking up for an emergency; most Japanese homes have small refrigerators and the majority of people shop for groceries daily.

Thomas's work started a week after I arrived in the U.S. I had not even recovered from my jet lag when he told me I'd need to get a driver's license because he would be taking a two-week business trip soon, and I would get hungry if I could not get out for food. Although I knew I would need a license, I felt stressed that I had so little time to practice before the driving exam.

I had already had a couple of driving lessons with my older brother, Shohei, before coming to the U.S.—just enough to be able to move a car forward and backward at a slow speed. My brother was patient, and kind enough not to shout at me, although one time he commented that I had slow reflexes. It hadn't been easy for me to learn how to control the amount of pressure to apply to the brake or gas pedal.

"Easy . . . easy, don't stop abruptly," my brother said in our first lesson.

"I know. I'm sorry," I said, but in a second, I did it again.

I noticed the strained look on his face. I didn't blame him though, because his car was brand new. All I wanted at that point was to grip the steering wheel, and at least get some idea of how cars maneuvered, even if I didn't fully understand everything.

The next Saturday, Thomas took me to Winter Park, Orlando, near his parents' house, to teach me how to parallel park. On the highway, he had me take the steering wheel. I had only the minimum skill gained in the forward and backward practice with my brother at ten or fifteen miles per hour on an empty road near my parents' house. Driving on a U.S. highway was terrifying! When I was driving, I felt the speed was two times faster than if I was a passenger, and my heart seemed to beat twice as fast as well.

At Winter Park, Thomas showed me how to park a car by a concrete curb. He picked a place where there were two oak trees overhanging the roadway, just far enough apart for me to practice parallel parking between them.

Sticking his head out the window, telling me how to cut wheels, he said, "Are you watching me?"

"I AM WATCHING YOU," I said impatiently.

"Okay, it's your turn," he said, coming out of the car.

In spite of his instruction, I had in my mind how I would park. I tensed up, knowing that if I didn't park the way he showed me, he would lose his temper.

I moved the car slowly and cautiously, past the big tree. *Far enough,* I thought, and started to back up to park in that space, but his strident voice broke my concentration. All I could hear was his shouting. "Cut the wheel sharply! Not that way! Don't go that way!" I decided I would be a lot better off if I learned by myself.

Early the next morning, I got up before Thomas woke, so I could practice alone. No one was on the road; only a few cats dotted the edges. I started the car and eased forward at a slow speed, then made many circles around our apartment complex. I had already purchased a thick blue cushion at Kmart, to raise myself up so I could see well. I drew the seat as far forward as I could, leaving minimal leg space, so I could control the pedals without stepping on the wrong one. In the evening I practiced as well, but I realized I didn't have enough time to complete my lessons. I asked Thomas to take me to his office, so I could use the car while he was working. He was a little hesitant, but kind enough to agree.

The next morning, Monday, I put on walking shoes and grabbed the blue cushion, (which became my security blanket), and two brown Albertsons' paper bags. He took me to his office building. As he disappeared inside, I began practicing parallel parking between the two bags. After about ten or fifteen minutes, people started coming out from the building and moving their cars away from the area where I was driving.

One night a few days after Thomas had started taking me to his office for my driving practice, he said, "Let's go get your driver's license tomorrow."

"To-to-tomorrow?" I whined.

The DMV office was not crowded after one o'clock on a Thursday, so my name was called quickly. When I was directed by an officer to go outside, I went out and scanned the area to look for my examiner. A tall woman stood next to my white Toyota, so I assumed she was my examiner. As I got closer, I noticed her physique was manly and she looked stern. I was already nervous, but her formidable manner made my body stiffen. Remembering I was a brand-new immigrant, I approached her with my best manners to try to open the passenger-side door for her, but she scowled me down, saying, "Get in your car." Intimidated, I forgot about being kind, and focused on listening to what she instructed me to do.

Incredible! I passed the driving test!

In the same month I moved to the U.S., I had a great opportunity to see a space shuttle launch which was originally scheduled in June, but had been delayed three times. In the early morning of August 30th, taking scenic A1A Highway, Thomas and I headed to one of the off-site viewing locations (the causeway over the Banana River Park) near the Kennedy Space Center. We reached the site around at 7:30 a.m., and there were already many people anxiously waiting to see the shuttle. About ten minutes before nine, I heard someone shout, "The launch is soon." A few minutes later, I saw a white cloud bellow from the rocket engines, momentarily followed by an immense blast of noise as the shuttle lifted off and sputtered skyward. I was emotionally taken by the smoke, fire, and the ground-trembling noise. This was an event I had never imagined being able to witness.

Although two weeks had passed since I got my driver's license, I hadn't driven anywhere alone except to the grocery store. One evening before we went to bed, Thomas said, "By the way, you have a dental appointment next Monday."

"What?" I asked.

"I heard you complain that your tooth hurt. Remember? You said your back tooth hurt when you ate dinner last week."

"You're gonna take me there, right? 'Cause I don't want to drive by myself," I protested.

"It'll be good practice for you. I'll teach you how to read a map."

I had some difficulty reading a road map. Like most Japanese, I had never used a road map to navigate. In most of Japan, streets are not named except for the main roads, and blocks are numbered. Mailmen have to know the area well. Japanese have to know the city, the name of the ward, and the block number in order to find a place. Beyond that, most Japanese ask for directions. When you ask for directions, people usually give you some landmarks. You'll hear something like this: "You go straight that way for three blocks and at that intersection you take a left turn. There is a tall white building. Pass that building, and in a distance of ten feet, you will see an elementary school on your right. Pass it, then turn right into a small alley, then follow it for a while . . ." In any event, I studied the directions before I took off for the dentist. But even though I had looked at the map, it was quite a challenge to drive to an unfamiliar area. I surely had a guardian angel.

Thankfully, I managed to get to the dentist a few minutes before my eleven o'clock appointment. *My word! Is this a dental office?* I thought. The waiting room looked like a small-scale hotel lounge. As I finished the paperwork, which was filled with a great deal of consent forms, an assistant took me to one of the rooms. Unlike a Japanese dental office, the patients' rooms were all individualized. The room I was taken to was equipped with all sorts of hi-tech machines. *A decade ahead of Japanese dental technology*, I thought, feeling good about receiving treatment. But when the dental assistant said, "We have to take X-rays of all your teeth first," I was troubled.

I said, "I know which tooth hurts. I pointed it out."

"We have to take pictures of all your teeth. I'm sorry, but that's our policy," she said.

"Twenty-three times!" I cried out in surprise.

Feeling helpless, I let them take the X-rays. Not only did I have to bear the pain of having X-ray films pinch my relatively small mouth each time, but I also dreaded being exposed to so much radiation. In a strange way, I discovered in myself a resistance to following the American way. Nonetheless, I realized I simply needed to adapt to the U.S. system in order to fit in.

There was another thing I had difficulty adapting to. When nearly two months had passed, Thomas wanted me to pay bills and balance our checkbook. That was a struggle. The majority of Japanese people use cash and don't write checks except for business purposes. Even fewer carry credit cards. To this day, many Japanese people prefer cash. Consequently, I found it difficult to manage money using plastic cards or checks. I needed to learn how to pay bills from scratch.

I told Thomas, "I don't like carrying credit cards."

"Too bad . . . you are in the U.S.," he said.

"But the risk of getting into debt is high," I snapped back.

"Unfortunately, if you don't use credit cards, you can't establish your credit here," he said.

Japanese highly value saving money. I liked the idea of using cash because you could see visually how much money was in your wallet. The virtue of saving money and the virtue of borrowing money to build credit are totally different concepts. I didn't know which system was sound, but since Thomas told me to use credit cards, I did so, regardless of my concerns.

As autumn came to an end, there was an incident that drove me to look for a job quickly. Normally a jar of orange juice sat in our refrigerator, but there wasn't any one day and Thomas wanted some.

He said angrily, "Can't you make orange juice? You have nothing to do all day!"

"Sorry! But you don't need to get upset like that!"

It was true I had nothing to do. I was kind of swimming around like a betta fish does when it is poured into a bigger fish bowl from the tiny see-through container from a pet shop. But his complaint made me ready to take action. I said I was sorry, but almost at the same time, fuming, I yelled, "I'll find a job TOMORROW!" Perhaps he wasn't that angry, perhaps he was just tired, but I was a sensitive person and didn't take reproach lightly.

The next morning, I drove to the Melbourne shopping mall and roamed the inside of each shop. At every business, I asked of any salesperson who was available at the moment, "Can I apply for a job here?" Many of them looked at me as if to say, "What are you talking about?" but I wasn't hesitant, and continued to search for a place to make a strong appeal. Though I was a genetically shy person, when the time came to achieve something, I became adamantly persistent. My smiling face and a conservative, but chic, outfit helped me to finally get the attention of a manager of the Jordan Marsh department store. He was standing at the main door, amiably greeting the customers. I didn't know who he was until he took me to his office. He sat down in his executive high-back leather chair, leaned back, and loosely folded his arms.

"Have a seat. How can I help you?"

"I would like to work at this department store."

"Any experience working at retail stores?"

"In Japan," I said confidently, back straight, hands stiffly crossed over my lap.

"How long you've been in the U.S?"

"Two months."

He rested his elbow on the armchair, held his chin in his hand, then looked at me, knitting his eyebrows a bit. His eyes were riveted on me and, for a long moment, he was silent. I felt awkward under his stare.

He finally said, "Okay, leave your resume, and we'll let you know soon."

I bowed deeply and left the office.

I waited for his answer each day. A week passed then another, finally in the third week, I received a call from the Human Resources Department, asking me to come back to take three days of training. I was exultant as I had almost given up all hope of getting the job.

I showed up in the classroom at 7:45 a.m. with a bulky Sony tape recorder, sat down in the front row, and nervously waited for the instructor to come in. Register machines had already been set on our long narrow rectangular tables. Until our teacher showed up, fifteen people—a few old, chatty women, several young ladies, and a few young men—talked with their neighbors. But I was quiet, so quiet I could even hear my own heart beating noticeably faster than its usual pace. I hoped the instructor would be nice and understanding.

A petite young woman in a short, tight navy blue skirt and white silk blouse, with a thin red bowtie ribbon around her neck, stepped lightly into our classroom.

"Good morning, everyone! My name is Susan," she said enthusiastically.

"Good morning Susan," we said in chorus.

"We have a three-day training. It's important for you guys to show up for the classes on time and learn all the procedures," she said in a serious voice, then added, "If you fail to learn all the transactions taught in the class, then you'll need to take another class."

No one said anything. My heart started racing even faster. I was starting my first job in this country!

Every so often, Susan stood behind me to make sure I was following the procedure. For two nights I reviewed the tape recording to catch up for the next class. I managed to pass the training and was assigned to work in the gift-wrap department around the busiest time, the

Christmas season. In a dimly-lit back room, I had no contact with customers except when my co-worker needed to take a break. All day I wrapped boxes that held all sorts of different items. Odd shapes of boxes significantly slowed my work and made my fingers weary. This was the most boring job I had ever worked. Only soft rock music playing from my co-worker's radio sustained my mind.

"I wish I could work on the floor and not back in a dark room," I said to my husband one day.

"Oh, you know, I had called HR to get you in there because they had been taking time getting back to you," he said, then added as if he just remembered, "They said they had been waiting to find a suitable position for you."

I recalled they had taken a long time to get in touch with me, and I had been peeved and often took out my vexation on Thomas. Nonetheless, I hadn't asked him to do anything. He thought he had done me a favor, but I reproached him, saying, "I can handle those things by myself, just as I found the job without your help."

Towards Christmas, the manager of HR came into the room where I was rushing to wrap a whole bunch of boxes piled up around me. He made his way around the tables to my place while looking around the room as if he were counting the boxes.

He said, "Hi Kumiko. You are doing a great job! You know, soon you'll have a chance to get on the floor." He tapped my shoulder lightly in a gesture of approval.

"Thank you very much," I said, and bowed.

Finally my day came to work on the floor. I started out in the dress department. Though unfamiliar clothing brand names overwhelmed me in the beginning, I hastily familiarized myself with them. What scared me most was answering calls from customers who asked me to check to see if we had a particular item. I listened carefully to the descriptions and jotted them down. For instance, a customer would ask, "Can you see if you have Dockers' pants? Khaki color and slim fit . . . cargo style. My size is fourteen." I would puzzle . . . *What is Khaki color? What is cargo?* I had to at least attempt to find the item. I detested running around like a chicken with its head cut off. I often ended up looking for another salesperson and showing them my scribbled notes. A lot of times I managed to run away from the phone calls, but at times I was assigned to work on the floor by myself. When I stood alone, I kept a low-profile, hiding myself among the hanging clothes, far from the telephone.

It was sometimes a challenge dealing with customers. One evening when I was in the lingerie department, I was shocked to have to deal with a middle-aged woman in a muumuu dress who brought in a gigantic bra to return. The bra, once white, looked worn out, and she told me she wanted to exchange it for a new one, because it simply didn't fit. I was perplexed and stared at it for a while, but as I looked up and saw the customer's impatient countenance, I suddenly remembered I wasn't supposed to argue with a customer if the price was less than fifty dollars. I processed it as damaged goods.

In Japan, I had worked in the dress department of a large department store during my junior college summer vacations. No one brought me a return. Returning items is rare in Japan unless they are damaged or broken at purchase. In general, dealing with customers is easier, because most Japanese pay cash. An important attitude in the Japanese retail business is to treat the customer like a god. At large stores, when you arrive at the opening time of 10:00 a.m., sales people are standing in a line to great you. While bowing slowly and deeply, they all say in unison, "*Irashai mase,*" (welcome) in enthusiastic voices.

In early May, fortunately or unfortunately, I fell down a staircase inside the mall as I hurried to the parking lot after work. I thought the injury wasn't bad, but I couldn't walk. Thomas immediately took me to a doctor. The doctor said I had a greenstick fracture in my left shinbone. I ended up using crutches for almost a month. I quit the job, feeling justified in doing so, because I couldn't work on crutches. Frankly, I wasn't prepared for that sort of job, so I was perfectly happy not working. I felt relieved. *Well, it's time to rest!* I reasoned. But my injured leg made even simple tasks unimaginably hard and tiring. Even bathing wasn't easy. I had to lean forward to hold up my upper body, and hang my left leg over the rim of the tub to wash. *Well, then again,* I thought, *it could be worse. If I had damaged my right leg, I wouldn't be able to drive a car.*

Towards the end of the treatment, I mentioned to my husband how uncomfortable I was about the way my doctor had been treating my leg.

"I don't like my doctor, Dr. Chan. He always soaks my foot in warm water to give it a massage. But often he raises my leg up high, trying to look up my skirt," I complained one day. "You know I can't wear pants because of the cast."

He rubbed his chin and frowned, then asked, "How long have you been going?"

"About a month," I responded.

"You know, Kumiko, you'd better be checked by another doctor," he said.

The next evening after work, Thomas took me to an orthopedist. The new doctor removed the cast. The X-ray showed the tiniest hairline fracture. When the new doctor told us I hadn't needed a cast, I got agitated, and Thomas was furious. When we got out of the office, he cursed. "I'm gonna call that quack doctor tomorrow and chew him out!"

My leg muscles had atrophied. When I tried to stand, my knee couldn't carry the weight. If I tried to use my knee, I thought I would topple over. I immediately started to rehab my leg by swimming—

breaststroke, dog paddle, and backstroke for many hours. It took days to be able to use my left leg in a normal way. I learned by this experience that the human body is meant to walk. "Use it or lose it," is true. After swimming, I sat in a Jacuzzi and rubbed my legs. I saw the bubbles streaming up from the jet ports, and this triggered an image of a hot spring. My thoughts then turned to my parents. *Ah . . . almost a year has passed since I left Japan.* I remembered my mom saying many times, "Your dad and I want to thank Thomas-san's parents in person. You know they came all the way to Japan to attend your wedding." So that night, I asked Thomas about inviting my parents to our house. Thomas thought it was a great idea.

They visited in late July, just about a year after we had moved to the U.S. On their arrival day, I was anxious, as there wasn't a direct flight, and they needed to catch connecting flights twice, one in Atlanta and one in Orlando. Thomas and I hurried to the Melbourne International Airport a little earlier than their scheduled arrival time. But as we proceeded toward the gate I saw my parents already walking towards the baggage claim. I immediately recognized my mom's blue-striped dress, which I had bought using my employee discount when I worked at the Jordan Marsh department store.

I called out, "Otosan! Okasan!" which means mom and dad in Japanese.

When they saw us, they grinned as if their facial muscles couldn't stretch any wider. Dad raised his right hand up to his shoulder. Mom stooped a little, attempting to make a greeting gesture. We trotted towards them.

When we met, my dad let out a big sigh of relief and said elatedly in Japanese, "You know Kumiko, when I saw the clock in the Atlanta airport, I noticed the time was different than on my watch. For a while I didn't understand." He took a quick breath and continued, "But I soon realized the time difference between Japan and the U. S. I adjusted my watch there, and hurried up to catch the next flight. If I hadn't realized the time difference, I tell you, we wouldn't be here."

"Oh-oh, I didn't even think about the time differences. Sorry. I am very glad you noticed," I said.

Proudly, Mom said, "I just followed your dad. If I were alone I would never, ever be able to come to the U. S. Your dad can read English, you know."

Changing planes in Atlanta and Orlando must have been quite a challenge for them, I thought, recalling my own travels. I was glad my dad was travel savvy.

We arrived home. I was tickled about showing my parents around.

"Wow . . . it's cool inside!" Mom said.

"Central air conditioner is on," I replied.

Mom started roaming around. Dad and I tailed after her.

"Wow . . . the rooms are spacious," she said.

"It feels good walking on the soft carpet," Dad noted with pleasure, as if the carpet could take away his leg and foot fatigue from their long journey.

In entering the kitchen, I remembered to explain how dangerous the garbage disposal could be. When I turned the switch on, they threw their heads back in astonishment.

After showing the kitchen, I took them to one of the bathrooms to show them how to use the shower over the tub, because the layout of Japanese bathrooms and western ones were quite different then. In the U.S., a bathroom is usually a single room with a toilet, a washbasin, and bathtub or shower. However, in Japan, the toilet has its own separate room. The actual bathing room has a tiled floor with a drain and it is equipped with a sink and deep tub. The previous apartment Thomas and I had lived in had a hand-held shower fixture that was hooked up to a waist-high attachment on the wall in the washing area, but the shower hose wasn't long enough for us to stand up, so we used the shower while we squatted on a little stool. When I lived in Japan, quite a lot of people didn't have bathtubs, especially the ones who lived in apartments. They went to a communal bath house, called a *Sento*. We used to have a *Sento* near our home, but our traditional cultures have faded away and there aren't many of those public baths nowadays.

The next day was a big day for my parents. The main purpose for their trip was to return the honor to Thomas's parents who had crossed the ocean to attend our wedding. They carefully carried a Hakata doll of a Samurai figure (traditional Japanese clay doll) in a glass case that was twice as big as a man's shoe box. Trying not to bump the box against anyone or anything, they had been watchful all the way from the time they left their home in Japan. My mom said that at times they needed to put the doll on their lap in the airplane. They hadn't relaxed until they finally saw Thomas's parents open the package. The Hakata doll was in perfect shape. Another of my parents' gifts was a vintage ivory necklace for Thomas's stepmother, which wasn't a good idea, as she was a high-school biology teacher and didn't like the idea of wearing ivory because of elephants being an endangered species. Of course my parents hadn't been aware of that, and handed it to her as an honorable gift. But Thomas's parents showed great appreciation, so my parents felt a great release from their obligation to say, "Thank you," in person, and relief that all had gone well. Japanese are tangled with *Giri* (moral obligation.) They won't feel comfortable until they return a favor, whatever it might be.

Before my parents came to the U.S., Thomas had told his boss, Steve, how much my dad liked playing golf. Steve was kind enough to ask his father, Roy, to play golf with my dad. One weekend, Roy took my dad to the membership-only country golf club in Melbourne to which he belonged. On that day, the four of us appeared at the golf course in the early morning and we met Roy. Thomas introduced us to Roy, and then Roy introduced the couple of friends he had brought along. Thomas and Roy chatted in a light mood for a while before Roy turned to speak to my dad. Roy had a chiseled, tanned face and stern look, but when he talked to Dad, he softened his expression and very slowly enunciated, "Hi, Kiyoshi, do you like playing golf?"

"Yes, he does," I answered reflexively.

"Well, shall we start playing golf?" Roy said gently to my dad.

"Yes," Dad said in English, without waiting for my translation. He understood "play golf" and his facial muscles relaxed after he realized the ritualistic conversation was over.

As Thomas, Mom and I were leaving, I turned and glanced to see how Dad was doing. He was laughing. I can vividly recall when we first entered the golf course. My dad's wide eyes had scanned the whole course. He said, "Wow . . . how beautiful the landscape is! I cannot wait to play." But it wasn't the golf course that caught my eye first. I was looking at the houses. Along one side of the golf course, there was a line of Spanish-style houses. They were very striking with whitewashed walls and terracotta-colored roofs. Because I was facing the houses while talking to Steve's dad, I pondered if the golf balls might hit the houses. This was my first strong impression, but the course was picturesque. On the manicured green grass, there were soaring spindly palm trees standing around the small lakes. The course looked tropical and paradise-like under the sapphire sky.

When Thomas, Mom, and I returned to the golf club, the group had already finished playing golf and stood waiting for us. Dad had barely noticed us walking toward him, when he ran to me. Hastily, he asked me to translate how impressive the golf course was, and how thoughtful they were. When Roy and his friend caught up to us, Dad turned his head back to give a big thank-you smile to them.

As soon as I finished translating, Dad jumped into our conversation before letting Roy respond, "Roy-san sang an old Japanese love song, 'Shina No Yoru' (China Nights) and we both sang together."

When he said this, for a moment I wondered whether or not they had evoked the memory of World War II. *Well . . . I hope not.* After all, Dad was in seventh heaven. Tapping on my dad's shoulder, Roy-san praised him. "Kiyoshi is very good." Roy's two other friends flattered my father further, saying, "He's a Japanese Arnold Palmer." Scratching his head, Dad smiled bashfully.

This memory of the golf outing was strongly imprinted on his mind. He sent me a thank-you letter to give to Roy after they went home. I translated his long calligraphy, and gave it to Thomas's boss along with Dad's formal letter.

During the month of their visit, Thomas took us my parents to Epcot Center, Kennedy Space Center, and Vero Beach. On weekdays, I took my parents to all the places I could think of. One day, I took them to St. Augustine. I had been there with Thomas before and the memory of the historical Spanish architecture with brilliant shades of red was ingrained in my mind. Striking Renaissance architecture buildings sprawled across the landscape and the moss-draped oaks were ubiquitous; the timeless art in the Colonial Spanish Quarter utterly captivated me. Much to my regret, we had only three hours to spend there and needed to head home.

On the way home from St Augustine, there was a frightening moment. I stepped on the accelerator with the transmission in reverse after waiting for a traffic light to turn green. It took us backwards at top speed for roughly thirty feet. I immediately stepped on the brake. *Why on earth had I put the transmission in reverse!* That sensation was unnerving and nauseating. My heart pounded vigorously and my hands trembled. Luckily, there were no cars behind us. My parents did not utter a word, but looked at me questioningly. I didn't say anything and only thought *are they gonna trust me to drive further?* They didn't express any concerns about my driving, but they were quiet all the way home.

Despite the fact I scared them, they enjoyed riding with me till their departure day. Having fulfilled their mission to return their obligation and carrying loads of treasured memories, my parents returned safe and sound.

After my parents returned home, I became homesick. Many times, gazing out the window of our living room and looking at the sky, all I could think about was my parents. Thomas worried about me. One evening, he said, "I got this address from my co-worker. This church has activities and non-Christians, like you, can join there too. They do cooking and have art and craft projects, so I heard." Since he strongly encouraged me to go there, I used the Toyota during the day and visited the church. Nearly twenty people gathered for church activities. Mostly, they were immigrants like me. There were Chinese, Italians, and some Puerto Ricans. We each took our turn demonstrating how we cooked our national cuisines. Cooking foreign cuisines with the locals was quite entertaining and an eye-opening experience. Fried Plantains (fried banana) with creamy aji amarillo sauce (yellow hot-pepper paste mixed with mayonnaise) was *delicioso*. The twice-weekly meeting stirred my interest. November soon arrived and the intense sun softened. Life in Florida was becoming pleasant, but then one evening I heard Thomas grumble, "Why am I the one who needs to go to counseling?" His company was sending him there due to his bad behavior. I already knew about his discontent because he had been telling me how rude his coworker was—his coworker's chair was always left in his way, like a shopping cart parked in the middle of the aisle. Contorting his face with anger, he said, "It's annoying I need to move it aside all the time." Knowing his aggressive self-righteous temper, I had suspected something might happen. *Here we go,* I'd thought, when he'd first complained. He had finally kicked his coworker's chair.

No . . . that's the wrong approach, I thought to myself. In any case, at first I deemed needing the professional help of a counselor to be shocking and shameful. However, after some reflection, I began thinking that there might be a slight chance for him to better control his hot temper if he took enough counseling sessions. But a month or so later, another incident occurred between the same coworker and Thomas. This time, the company decided to dismiss him. He was furious, and I was disappointed.

This episode reminded me of several incidents that had happened in Tokyo. Whenever he spotted a smoker in a movie theater, he would get out of his seat, march over to the smoker, grab him by the arm, and point him to the door. Because he knew that smoking was prohibited, it greatly annoyed him. He would also become vexed when he saw people trying to cut in front of a line. He stepped towards the people and said in poor Japanese, "*Yamete kudasai!*" (Please don't do that!) He had no tolerance for what he thought was not right. But he was not a policeman: he only embarrassed me.

I had always been worried that his audacious behavior would get him in trouble. In odd contrast, however, he did many altruistic things. I saw him picking up soda cans, Styrofoam cups, and litter on roads. He often handed money to female panhandlers. Once he saved a stray cat. He had the cat washed, neutered, and given vaccines before finding its owner. After he found its home, he even visited to see if the cat was treated well. He didn't kill spiders or bugs wandering about in our house, but caught them in his hands and released them outside. In fact, I learned eco-consciousness from him. I started doing little things like carrying my own grocery bags.

He had shown me many acts of kindness, but I remembered that at the beginning of our marriage, he was oppressive. I knew his intentions were good, but it was unbearable being told no coffee, no alcohol, no junk food, no red meat, no trash magazines, and no high heels. He even tried to get me to jog every weekend. After a while, he gave up on the idea of trying to change my eating habits and preferences.

In any case, we needed to make a living, so he had to find another job. He suggested to me that we move to Atlanta because he had gone to college there. Moving to a different place didn't inconvenience me at that time since I didn't have friends or anything to tie me down. In fact, I thought it would be rewarding to get to know the different parts of the U.S. Right away, he began to look for a job in the Atlanta area.

II

Atlanta, Georgia
Adult School

Just before Christmas, Thomas was hired by a Japanese electronics company in south Atlanta. We moved into a townhouse we had rented over the phone. We hadn't seen the place, and when we got there, it was a big disappointment. The house wasn't at all what we expected. It was dark inside. The second floor received some sunlight, but the whole downstairs, living room, dining room, and kitchen, had almost no exposure to daylight because of the maple trees surrounding the townhouse. I sensed the energy in the downstairs was low and inauspicious. I hated dark rooms.

On the following day, the moving truck arrived, and the shipper unloaded our furniture. Thomas's best friend, David, came over to help us move. He brought me a Christmas sock monkey as a gift. "Arigato," I said, thanking him in Japanese. I hadn't seen him for over two years. He had visited us once when Thomas was in Tokyo, and he and I became good friends because his fluency in Japanese brought us close. His family spent some years in Tokyo while he was at a teenager, so his knowledge of Japanese culture and language was remarkable. Having such a nostalgic friend in an unfamiliar area emboldened me.

A few days after we had moved into the house, Thomas started his new job. After sending Thomas off to work, I began unpacking boxes. When I kneeled on the kitchen countertop to wipe all the cabinet shelves with a rag before putting away the dishes and cups, I got a whiff of mildew. The sunless, musty old apartment made me feel gloomy. Certainly, this was not like the apartment we had in Florida. I sped up my work to move onto the next task.

Unpacking took three days. Now that I was ready to take action, I went to the DMV. When I entered the office, I saw people staring at computer screens. *It's not a written test? Computer . . . will I be able to operate it?* Feeling a lot of pressure, I began the test. But once I understood how to use the computer, I found the visually-oriented computer test was better than the written test I had taken in Florida. For instance, I didn't remember which way to turn the wheels when parking on a hill, but the computer illustrated the scenario more clearly than the paper-test. I must have taken a very long time doing the test, for a couple of people who came in after me had already finished by the time I clicked "Done."

I didn't mind not having the Toyota in the daytime, as I had already heard that the MATA, the mass transit, was efficient. In Florida, I had learned three eminently important steps to take when I moved to a new place: 1) unpack; 2) get a driver's license; 3) find a job. But this time the car wasn't in my possession as Thomas was using it, so number three had dropped from the list.

Not having much to do, I felt lost and alone. A few weeks after we had moved, Thomas said, "You know, I heard from my Japanese coworkers that their wives go to an adult school. Why don't you go there?" The next morning I took the MATA bus to the adult school which was held in a large church building. There were six levels of

English classes, from beginning basic to very advanced. I was placed in an advanced class after succeeding at the placement test. In my class, there were three Japanese ladies who already had a good knowledge of English, but were inexperienced in speaking it. I'd noticed when among people from other countries, that they showed more fluency in speaking English. It seemed to me at the time that with more outgoing assertiveness, people learned a language faster. Japanese are less assertive by nature and that leads us to speaking with less fluency. Besides that, we don't have the English "r" sound in our language and we tend to fail to correctly pronounce words containing this letter. This discourages us when we compare ourselves to other non-native English speakers. I often mixed up the letters that had 'r' and 'l'.

Having a simple routine—going to school Monday, Wednesday and Friday in the morning from 9 a.m. to noon kept my mind occupied and I didn't feel lonely. The school was satisfying, but what I really enjoyed the most was the break time. The coffee time was the highlight of my day. During the coffee break, I chatted with my classmates, Shizue, Tamae, and Yuka. Shizue and Tamae, whose husbands worked at the same Japanese company, but not where my husband was working, always socialized together and didn't make much space for me to intermingle, but they were kind and polite. In Japan, Shizue was a junior-high school teacher of English, and Tamae worked at a major Japanese trading corporation. Their grammar was good, but they wanted to practice conversation. But as for Yuka, I didn't know anything about her except for the fact that she could provide us any information we wanted to know about movies, restaurants, events, and other fun activities. I didn't get the idea she was married, because she ventured out to many places by herself. She loved parties and always had stories to share with us about what had happened to her the day before. I was curious about the people she met, the food she ate, and what she did at the parties.

Spring arrived. Aromatic dogwoods and rhododendrons started blooming, embellishing our townhouse complex. Thomas had been telling me he wanted to introduce me to his coworker, Mr. Takamori, and his wife, Tomoko. Finally we dined with this handsome, notably Americanized couple. They expressed their opinions candidly with a lot of gesticulation. A couple of times, Mr. Takamori winked charmingly while talking. Their lively and humorous attitude fascinated me. Mr. Takamori had been sent to a different plant in Fort Lauderdale, Florida before, and he and Tomoko had lived there for five years. They seemed to have become accustomed to life in America, and enjoyed the benefits of being an expatriate family. They played tennis, went to concerts, traveled to other states, and dined out often. Their lifestyle was ritzy.

I soon learned that most Japanese expat families were well compensated by their companies, as the Japanese economy was strong at that time. Their companies paid the home salary, plus bonuses, and allowances for housing, transportation, food, children's education, and tax equalization. They could live in nice houses, and the wives had their own cars. Many of them traveled to places like New York, Las Vegas, Los Angeles and Orlando. I envied them, but of course understood their situation. I, too, would take advantage if I were in their place, knowing that once they went back to Japan, they would live in a small house, and most likely there would be little chance to go to foreign countries.

In Japan, many Japanese husbands devote their life to the company, giving less time to their families. Their kids are the same way, spending their after-school time at *jyuku* (cram school) till late into the night to assure entrance into a prestigious school. I heard from my Japanese friends that living in a foreign country brings their family closer together, so in addition to the luxurious lifestyle, their family life seems to improve. They also told me unanimously that their husbands became very cooperative—helping the kids with their homework, shopping for groceries, cleaning up the dishes, and taking the family on trips. I remembered my husband wasn't that helpful when he was in Japan. But when he moved back to his own country, he did the shopping, took the garbage out, cleared the dining-table, and many other things. I guess he followed the rule: "When in Rome, do as the Romans do."

In any case, the American environment and culture seemed to have helped my Japanese friends' relationships with their husbands. Those Japanese husbands, who were so isolated from their family when they were in Japan—because of spending many hours with coworkers, not only on the job but also in after-hours socializing, going to bars or playing golf—became more focused on their family's needs. It occurred to me their husbands might have some apprehension about losing their traditional positions within the household when they went back to Japan.

Even though I knew they had only three years to live their luxurious life in America, I was envious because our lifestyle wasn't as colorful as theirs. Thomas and I didn't travel. On weekends, we often strolled by the Dean's Mansion at Emory University, which stood on a little hummock at the end of the far side of the park. After our walk we'd dine at "Everybody's Pizza" on North Highland Avenue, a popular hangout among Emory's students. Once in a while, we sauntered about with our friend, David. David and my husband had met each other on the Emory campus, both being members of the Go Club. When David could come for a walk with us, we played Frisbee and stayed for a longer time in the park.

Jack was another old friend of Thomas's who we hung out with sometimes. His lifestyle was unique and unconventional. I was still new to America, so everything was novel and fascinating to me. While we lived in Atlanta, Jack was building a second house on his property. But this house wasn't a normal one. It was a large hut on a platform supported by stilts. It reminded me of a treehouse. The wide staircase that led up to the front door was flanked by two serious-looking wooden dragons, painted in deep green and trimmed with gold and red. I was struck with admiration for this free-thinking mentality. I never really thought about how a house could be a playful living space. I considered a house to be just a place to eat, sleep, watch TV, and do some private work. Certainly the majority of houses in Japan are not built for enjoying the space or to create the perfect environment to kick back with a glass of wine, or sit on lush carpet watching a fire in the fireplace, or hosting a party to show off houses. Most Japanese houses are too small for things such as these.

One day Jack and his girlfriend, Martha, took us canoeing on the slough of Bull Sluice Lake on the north side of metropolitan Atlanta. I was thrilled. While floating on the serene slough, I thought how America indeed had a lot of resources that enabled people to get close to nature. Jack spotted a huge bald eagle nest. The nest was as big as a bean-bag chair.

Jack and Martha presented me with another American lifestyle I wasn't familiar with. In his house, I saw beans, wheat, and herbs displayed in large heavy glass jars in the kitchen. In the bathroom there was sheep milk soap in the soap trays. I smelled the aroma of incense throughout the house, which triggered the memory of my grandmother's house with incense at the family's Buddhist altar. Furthermore, Jack and Martha were the first strict vegetarians I had ever met. I knew of people, Japanese Buddhist monks, who only eat vegetables; they eat only *Shojin Ryori*. Shojin cooking does not use fish, meat or other animal products such as eggs. I heard monks don't even eat strong-tasting vegetables such as leeks, onions and garlic, because it is believed that they will hinder the pursuit of discipline. In any case, Jack and Martha's lifestyle, which I had never seen the likes of in Japan, fascinated me.

Sundays, Thomas and I went hiking, just the two of us. One weekend, he took me to Stone Mountain. We hiked up the trail to the Confederate Memorial, and stayed to watch the laser show that night. Once the sky darkened, the temperature plummeted. The red, blue, and yellow lasers began to beam images onto the mountain rock that had a relief of three famous soldiers on horseback carved into its face. The climax of the show came when the mounted soldiers appeared to gallop out of the rock into the night sky. I felt chills up my spine. I threw a glance at Thomas each time when I wowed. Thomas remarked, "Americans love grandiose things."

About six months after Thomas started working at his Japanese company, his boss told him he was scheduled to go to Japan for a few months' job training. Happily, I was allowed to go with him. Excited by the great news, I immediately started preparing for the trip. I took the MATA bus to the Lenox Shopping Mall to buy souvenirs for all my family members. Then on Friday, Thomas came home from work and announced gruffly, "We aren't going to Japan Monday. The trip was canceled."

"Noooo way, they can't do that!" I shouted, but seeing his taut look, I realized he wasn't kidding.

He didn't reply, so I said, "I already bought souvenirs. What shall I do about them?" I looked into his eyes, lowered my voice, and continued, "What happened?" although I knew he wouldn't give me the reason.

"You can ship them," he answered sharply.

Hit by a sudden realization, I started thinking . . . Thomas had demanded that he would go only on the condition he could take me. I remembered that I pressured him, demanding, "Take me to Tokyo with you. I don't want to be left alone." I suspected he demanded more from the company than they were willing to subsidize, and for that reason the deal was off.

Soon after this happened, Thomas got the sack. I had already foreseen that he wouldn't stay long at the company. He found a new job in a desolate town in Florida where the nearest grocery store was forty minutes away. Too isolated, I thought, but after going through some mental struggle, I told him I would go as long as he would let me go to school. He agreed.

III

Sebastian, Florida

Hamlet

Sebastian, a seaside hamlet, had nothing to interest me, with little culture compared to any other place I had known. The coastal town, known mainly for fishing, seemed to be a forgotten place, sparsely populated and tranquil. The June temperatures were still in the eighties. The vast flat land, with few buildings, was filled with various palms, pines, oaks, and mangroves. Off and on throughout the day, you would feel the sea breeze. Perhaps older people would love this quiet little city, but for me it was too dull, especially having come from a crowded city like Tokyo.

We found a new home. Amazingly, the apartment was set near a small private golf course that was practically unused, but the cool pleasant sea breeze blew through our apartment, so that even on the second floor, we didn't need an air conditioner. At night, we were assaulted by the croaking voices of countless frogs. Their lovemaking sounds started around nine o'clock and continued until I fell asleep: they played hard. Sebastian felt remote and inconvenient and I felt isolated. However, the resort area of Vero Beach, adjacent to Sebastian, had good restaurants and high-fashion boutiques, and, as Indian River County, seemed to have strict building codes. The commercial buildings looked architecturally pleasing.

I learned soon that there was an internationally-known fresh orange juice factory near our apartment. Every weekend I took two empty one-gallon bottles to the shop to buy fresh-squeezed orange juice. The oranges were picked from an orange grove in the farmers' backyard. When living in such a dull city, a little event like going to an orange juice factory where you can buy gallons of mouthwateringly delicious orange juice can be the highpoint of the week. Every time I went there, I stepped outside the store, sat on a bench facing the impressive orchard, and sipped a glass of cooled orange juice. Purely decadent!

My routine: Step 1 - unpack. I had become more practiced at the routine of moving, and it took less time to unpack. Step 2 - get a driver's license. Luckily, as I had already gotten a Florida driver's license within the previous year, I didn't need to retake any tests, and only needed to report and pay the fee. Step 3 - job hunting. No need. I had already made a deal with Thomas to go to school.

There was a college in Vero Beach, approximately an hour's drive from Sebastian. After sending Thomas off to work, I could use the Toyota. One morning, I visited the school administration office to ask how to enroll. It was summer term and the building appeared to be empty.

"Hello," I said, peering into the little window of the admission's office.

A middle-aged lady in a pink floral print muumuu sat at a desk. She pushed her heavyset body to a standing position and then reluctantly approached the window.

"What do you need?" she asked.

I somehow couldn't respond quickly. Perhaps it was the way she looked at me. When she could no longer wait for me to open my month, I finally answered, "I would like to enroll in this school."

"You need to take an SAT test. Do you understand?" she asked, and then slightly knitted her eyebrows.

I was intimidated by her annoyed expression, so I stammered out, "I need an application."

"You need to take an S – A – T test first," she enunciated.

"I understand," I said feebly.

My SAT scores were pathetic. I was mortified and profoundly depressed to be placed in an English as a Second Language class, but I reluctantly enrolled in the class three days a week. On the first day in the ESL class, I made a friend. Her name was Margarita, and she became my first American buddy. Her trailer home was fifteen minutes away from my home and we could carpool to the school. She was eighteen, a pretty young lady with milk-chocolate skin. Margarita was as skinny as me, but a bit shorter. I don't know how she managed it, but she had a nice car. She worked at McDonalds and liked to have a coffee before we went to school. She never put her coffee down when she drove her new red coupe. Her little hand seemed to have a lot more power than I would have imagined, and her driving was quite impressive.

We usually didn't go directly home after school, often heading to a mall. Her fashion sense was fabulous. She had a terrific body and knew how to maximize her doll-like features.

"Kumiko, you should show your long legs," Margarita said.

"Really?" I said.

"Yes, definitely. You should show your figure. How about this miniskirt?"

"That's too short for me. Also the color is a bit shocking."

"Why not? It'll be cute on you," she said, then handed me a pair of boots, too. "That short skirt goes with these boots. Put them on."

It wasn't my style, but in the mirror, I thought I looked cool in that outfit.

On Saturday, that same week, I put on the striking red mini-skirt and ankle-high black laced-up boots, ones like Janet Jackson would wear. Thomas looked at me and rolled his eyes.

"My word, you look like a whore," Thomas said.

"What do you mean *whore*?" I asked, dejected.

He responded, "You look like a prostitute."

I kind of liked the outfit, but changed to a long flared skirt to go out with Thomas, feeling bad Thomas was so conservative about fashion.

My life in Sebastian was easy, and I took pleasure in going to the school with Margarita. One day in early November when the weather cooled down, I dreamed about a big ship on an ocean, floating in a strong current. The next morning I woke up, worried about moving as two things had jinxed us. One thing was, if I dreamed about a ship, then moving was predestined. The other one was if our watches stopped, that meant we were destined to move in the near future. Thomas knew about the jinx of a watch, but I didn't tell him about the jinx of the ship on an ocean. A few days later on a Saturday afternoon, he told me he needed to look for a new job. I felt a profound desperation. I couldn't stay in the house, and needed to be somewhere else. I left home and drove to the

Sebastian beach. Once I got there, I walked along the beach toward the fishing wharf. The sand pipers cautiously darted to and fro as I passed. A warm breeze stirred up small white caps over the blue-green water. As I ambled along, I tried to process my feelings. *I really don't want to move this time*, I muttered. After spending hours on the beach, I returned home with my mind still conflicted.

As I entered the apartment, my eyes met Thomas's. He said immediately, "Where did you go? I was worried."

I mumbled, "Ummm."

"You want to talk?" he said, escorting me to the couch, and then added, "I need to talk to you."

I sat on the couch, and he sat on the coffee table face-to-face with me.

"You know why I went to Japan? It wasn't just because I wanted to play *Go*. I planned to go to a Zen Buddhist temple so I could learn patience, but I met you right after I had moved to Tokyo."

I didn't say a word.

"I know I need to change my attitude and be more patient," he said.

I kept silent.

"Don't worry, I'll find a job soon, and you can continue going to school," he added, then squeezed my shoulder as a way of getting my okay.

Looking at his remorseful face, I couldn't be upset anymore, so I nodded lightly.

A few weeks later, he located two possible jobs. One was in Tennessee and the other was in New York. He asked me if I wanted to go to New York, but I told him it would be an amusing city to visit but not to live in. My notion was that New Yorkers were too aggressive, and I wasn't ready to deal with that. He decided to take the job in Tennessee, as he thought New York might not be safe for me. The company in Tennessee arranged for all the accommodations to relocate us. After the moving truck finished loading up our furniture, we headed to a temporary hotel in Tullahoma.

IV

Tullahoma, Tennessee

Hello Kitties

I wasn't happy about moving again. It was always hard for me to adjust to a new place where I had no friends and nothing familiar. Again it was cold when we moved, just before Christmas, 1986. The main road of Tullahoma City, Lincoln Street, was lit with lanterns and Christmas lights in an unsophisticated way. Tullahoma reminded me of the movie "Back to the Future," set in the late sixties. We stayed at a hotel for a few weeks until we could find a place to settle down. We first looked for a house, but chose an apartment for the location and convenience, since I didn't have my own car.

The Tennessee winter weather was cold and dry. The clouds often held lots of moisture, forming heavy gray blankets that dominated the sky, but it didn't rain. Thomas had started working already and I was alone in our new, silent, apartment. I meandered among the unopened boxes that sat scattered all over the house. Unwrapping dishes and cups made my hands even drier and they became painful. It took two or three days to unpack our relatively few belongings and situate them appropriately in the late 1960s, two-bedroom apartment.

Thomas used the Toyota for his government job in aerospace technology. I was lost, and didn't know how to begin my life in Tullahoma without a car or any public transportation. One Sunday afternoon, a few weeks after we had moved into the apartment, Thomas asked me if I still wanted to have a Honda Civic.

Of course I said "Yes." So he said, "Let's get you one."

We hurriedly got into our Toyota and Thomas drove directly to a Honda dealer. We consumed many hours deciding which one I liked. I thought I had known what I wanted, but in the shop, there were many choices to make—color, with/without radio, cruise control, or other interior choices. And lastly, we needed to negotiate a loan and fill out all the required forms. At the end, I signed the paper as the owner of the car. It was already dark by then. With a broad smile on his face, Thomas said, "This is your Christmas present!"

"Nice! Thank you very much!"

"I wanted to wrap it with a red ribbon on top."

I thought that was romantic. We followed the salesperson to the front door. He gave us two keys.

"It's your car. You drive it," Thomas said.

The new, navy blue metallic, Honda Civic, shining under spotlights, was parked at the front of the shop, waiting for someone to take it away. The engine was already running. I was scared and didn't want to drive this brand-new, unscratched car on unfamiliar roads at night, but somehow I couldn't refuse. The city lights reflected off the surface of the shiny hood, making me more nervous, and while my body experienced the unfamiliar stiffness of the pedals and wheel, I was also disoriented by the differently-designed interior. When I finally parked the new car at home, I needed to lie on the couch for a while. Thomas made tea for me.

The people we met in Tennessee were gentle and genuinely kindhearted. Every so often we encountered people who were delightfully friendly. One evening, we were taking our walk on our usual course that ran into a private airport with one runway and a couple of small simple hangers. The airfield took up only one-third of the vast field, and the rest of the area was a green field. Thomas and I often trespassed in the field. There was an old rundown fence with a makeshift gate under which we could easily pass. After a mile or so, the skinny path that ran through the wild green grass turned onto a pebble road. Within a few minutes' walk from that point, there stood an impressive house. Normally we passed by the mansion, but this time we stopped to take a closer look.

A slender, elegant lady came out and looked in our direction. I immediately said in a loud voice, "I was looking at your house because it looks just like a Japanese inn."

She approached us, saying in a southern Tennessee accent, "Would y'all like to come in?"

I looked at Thomas. He nodded, so I said, "Yes, I would like to."

The house had the look of a mountain lodge, but the low sloped roof reminded me of a Japanese inn. Their rooms were filled with classy furniture that enhanced the ambiance of the undeniably expensive house. Her husband, wearing a baseball cap, joined us. He kindly brought an album and suggested that we sit down on the couch. He began telling us the story behind each of the pictures taken with Japanese businessmen. They were hospitable to us even though we were strangers who had trespassed on their property.

When we walked around their backyard, we saw a cat cautiously coming out from an old barn. The lady of the house told us that the cat had just given birth to five kittens.

Thomas eagerly asked, "May I see them?"

"Come in the barn. I'll show you the kittens," she said in delight.

We followed her inside and to the back of the old barn. In the very back corner, we saw them.

"Cute tabby kittens!" Thomas said touching the kittens, which were tightly cuddled together.

"They are different colors," I said.

"The gray one will be my daughter's. And that one will stay here and that one will be taken," she said pointing her finger at each cat. Then she looked at us and said, "That black one and this orange one are unclaimed. Would you like to have one?"

No! I said to myself. I didn't like cats. I'd had some bad experiences with them, two of which I remembered clearly. Our family dog, a very obedient English Setter, Jess, once had his eye badly scratched by a neighbor's wicked cat when my dad and I were taking him for a morning walk. Then, when I was seven or eight, a wild cat chased me aggressively. I had already known the cat was crazy, so I had been avoiding that neighborhood. But one day, I needed to take a shortcut and walked through the narrow passage. Much to my consternation, I indeed encountered that crazy cat. We stood face-to-face for a moment, the cat arching his back. I turned and sprinted away at top speed. The cat was very close to clawing me as I jumped into a neighbor's doorway. So I had never liked cats. In fact, I hated them.

But I knew Thomas wanted a cat, and I also had been thinking about having a house pet. I knew that it wasn't at all practical for us to have a dog, as we were constantly moving. I needed to modify my thinking. Still, having a cat wasn't tempting. Of course, Thomas wouldn't say yes to the lady without getting my consent, so he told her we would think it over. For days, I pondered the idea, and finally decided a cat might be a good candidate to become my companion if I trained him or her to be nice and gentle.

Five days later, we went back to their house to tell them we would like to adopt two tabbies. Thomas thought it was a good idea for a cat to have a buddy to play with. I didn't like the idea of having two furry ones, but I realized Thomas had a point. The kittens were six-weeks-old at that time, so the lady suggested we wait for two more weeks before separating them from their mother.

Two weeks later, we brought them home. We named these tabby cats; Mickey-chan (gray and black) and Rosie-chan (brown and orange).

We got them into the house and the meowing began.

"Oh my word, they are crying so hard. I bet you they miss their mom," I said.

"Pick them up!" Thomas said.

"I can't pick them up. I can't even touch them."

"They are cute, aren't they?" he said, picking them up, and bringing them up to my face. They were cute, but I needed time to adjust to them.

On the first day, the two little kittens roamed about our apartment pathetically. I wasn't sure we had made a good decision to take them away from their mother so soon. But the next morning, they were crying for our affection, pacing around the bed to be caught by our hands. On the spur of the moment, I picked Rosie-chan up. She looked at me and purred. Amazing! They seemed to have already bonded with us. I felt my heart open to Rosie-chan. It felt strange to not feel a trace of discomfort about holding the kitten. The creepy feeling I had earlier about these tiny fragile creatures vanished. I soon discovered that life was more amusing with kittens. They were so comical. Their actions were unpredictable, precarious, and nonsensical, but always hilarious.

Now that I had my own vehicle, the car I had wanted, my life had taken a new turn. I needed to keep the momentum going. I needed a Tennessee driver's license, so I drove off to the DMV office. It was a tiny office and the workers were incredibly friendly, but I found the driver's test to be difficult. It was heavily focused on testing our knowledge of alcohol levels and I almost failed.

The next morning, I checked into schools and found a community college in the relatively thin yellow pages of the Tullahoma phone book. After finding out the directions from the newly purchased Tennessee map, I drove off to the school. When I opened the admissions' office door, it was already noon, and only one gentleman was at his desk, eating. As he raised his head, our eyes met. He immediately rose from his chair, and walked to the counter where I stood.

"How can I help you?" he said softly.

"I would like to enroll in this college," I said.

Handing me a catalog, he turned the page to the section on how to apply.

"Have you attended another college?" he asked.

"Not in the U.S., but in Japan," I answered.

"Then you'll be a transfer student. You'll need an official transcript from your school. Ask your school," he said, "but you have to ask them to give you a transcript in English."

"Yes, I will do that soon. Thank you very much," I said and bowed.

A huge sigh of relief slipped from my mouth the instant I left the admissions' office. "No SAT test," I said to myself. I felt the built-up tension in my shoulders smooth out like a wrinkled shirt being ironed.

I started attending the community college during spring semester, taking three classes: English Composition I, Math I, and Fundamental Speech I. Although school was quite a distance from my home, driving my brand-new Civic was therapeutic. The highway seemed to go on endlessly in a straight line. Douglas Fir trees flanked the highway on both sides. The ocean blue sky above me and almost no traffic put my busy mind at ease and transported me into a meditative state.

I took pleasure in driving to the school and enjoyed my classes, but my speech class presentations were daunting. Whenever I stood at the podium, I felt like a beginning skier challenging her first big slope. Mrs. Lindsborg taught us with an elegant manner, didn't joke around, and didn't get derailed from whatever subject she wanted to stick with. One day, she gave all of us an assignment. We were to talk about some famous historical person. I chose Blaise Pascal. I spent hours in the literary researching Pascal for the fifteen-minute speech. Jotting all the information down in my notebook, I summarized it into a few pages and practiced. I put a small cardboard box on the round dining table for a podium, and set two chairs across from the table for my audience, Mickey and Rosie. Mickey immediately jumped off the chair, and Rosie crouched. Standing up tall in front of the dining table, I read the papers over and over, until I had stored all the lines in my brain.

The next morning, after not getting much sleep, I nervously approached my desk. The other students were always very friendly and supportive, but my nervousness soared as my turn to speak approached. I remembered the advice one of my classmates, the only African-American in my speech class, had offered. His manners were charmingly mature for his young age of eighteen. He advised: "Kumiko when you are standing at the podium and looking at us, imagine we're a bunch of pumpkins."

I told him very politely that I appreciated his thoughts, but, I said, "pumpkins don't have eyes like people." He kept trying to encourage me, saying I should try to look slightly above my audience. I thought that was feasible, so I tried not to look at anybody and began my speech. I set my eyeballs above my classmates' heads and concentrated on what

I had memorized. In the beginning, I thought this was manageable, but after about ten minutes, my eyes accidentally dropped and met those of a girl in the middle row. Her eyes took all my memory away, and I became speechless, standing there like a child who had lost her mom. I couldn't sleep that night and I kept replaying my pitiful speech over and over in my mind.

A couple of days later, when I was in the library, Mrs. Lindsborg came up to me and said with genuine concern, "Kumiko, don't worry anymore. There is always tomorrow." She paused for a second and then in a firm little voice she added, "But don't try to memorize."

I bowed and thanked her sincerely.

The apartment complex didn't have a communal laundry room, so we went shopping for a washer and dryer. The store looked like a small warehouse and had only one middle-aged saleslady working there. It took us very little time to decide which washing machine and dryer to buy. The saleslady was chatty, and while preparing the paperwork for us to sign, she went on and on explaining about Tullahoma, knowing we were newcomers. Finally she put the papers on the counter, and I started to write my name. I hadn't even finished writing my surname when I heard the salesperson's piercing voice say, "I *know* a lady whose name is KU-MI-KO! She's very nice. I'll find her phone number for you." She opened the file cabinet and continued enthusiastically, "She's such a nice lady. You'll like her."

When she finally found the number, she wrote it down on the back of their business card and handed it to me with a big smile.

She said confidently, "She'll like to hear from you."

It was very Tennessean, this hospitable gesture, but I was surprised she would give out a customer's private information. But I took the card anyway, and I called this other Kumiko-san a few days later. She was just as the saleslady had described.

Kumiko-san invited me for lunch at her house. She had five cats, all much larger than most felines. They had huge round faces on enormous bodies, but their faces were endearing. Those huge roly-poly cats didn't move like the cats I knew, but rather more like cows (especially the white cat with black patches) and they all acted like they owned the house. I petted one of them. It didn't budge an inch, but closed its eyes. I left it alone.

As I entered the dining room, I saw five bar stools around the large oblong dining table, along with five normal chairs. As I was gawking at those high stools, Kumiko-san turned toward me, and explained with her eyes half-closed, "My husband, my kids, and I eat with our cats."

"Ahh . . . ," I opened my mouth and almost forgot to close it. Kumiko-san continued talking about her cats. I regained my sense of reality, which I had lost momentarily, and said to her, "It must be quite interesting to dine with cats."

Kumiko-san smiled and responded, "Yes, they sit on the chairs with very good manners. Once in a while, one of them cannot wait for the others to come to the table, but one of us gives them a look. They withdraw their paw from the table."

Wow! I didn't question her, but was wondering how her husband, a professor, felt about eating with mousers.

When Kumiko-san carried the last casserole dish from the oven to the table, we took our seats. The table was set with yellow floral-patterned dinnerware, and the creamy chicken and broccoli looked appetizing. She was a great chef and our conversation was lively. It was very nice knowing her. I was indeed glad the saleslady had given me Kumiko-san's phone number.

There weren't many things to do in the small-town of Tullahoma, Tennessee, so Thomas and I went caving. I had no idea what it would be like in a cave. Inside the first cave we explored, we discovered a different part of Earth: there were hills, cliffs, and a stream. Also there were some insects, which I tried to ignore. The temperature was noticeably lower. I had a light on my helmet and Thomas carried a hand lamp and beamed it at me with every move I made, but walking, crawling, and climbing inside a dark, muddy chamber was scary. My ninety-two pound, five-foot-four frame didn't take up much space, but it took my whole attention and all of my nerve not to fall from the narrow ledges. The next day I spent hours washing and brushing caked mud from our clothes and shoes. This was the worst part of caving.

Christmas was fast approaching and Lincoln Street, the main road of Tullahoma, was adorned with green and red tinsel. As I glanced up at the pole-mounted decorations from my car, I recalled how last year when we moved to Tullahoma, the tinsel artlessly hanging from the poles had given me a strong impression of a cheerless, desolate, yet somehow sweet and welcoming city. *Ahh, one year had passed.* I looked back upon that year. Tullahoma had been nice for me.

Thomas lost his job. Again. I was upset, but this time for the first time I worried about our finances. Of course, our finances had never been in good shape, but he had sent me to a dentist for braces soon after we had moved to Tullahoma. I felt like I had caused a financial predicament. This time, we needed to borrow five-hundred dollars from Thomas's mom to just get by. Within a month, we returned it, but I realized I couldn't expect him to always be the only one responsible for our finances.

One evening, a week before Christmas, I drove to the Tullahoma mall to look for a holiday job, but it was too late to find a seasonal job, so I had no luck. While I was heading home, I thought about Thomas. *What's wrong with him?* I had heard from his previous bosses how intelligent he was. In fact, many people said how smart he was. He was charming most of the time, but on occasion he could be very audacious, and impudent. Actually, I had noticed this propensity soon after we married, and it had worried me ever since.

Once in Tokyo, soon after Thomas got a new job as a technical editor, I received a call at night. The caller didn't even give me his name, but plunged at once into business.

"Are you Thomas-san's wife?" he asked me in a grouchy tone. I suspected he had consumed some alcohol. He was calling from a noisy place, maybe a bar.

I said, "I am."

"Please tell your husband not to give you love calls all day while he's at work," he blurted out.

I had been worrying about Thomas's frequent calling, five or six times a day. On some days he called ten times.

Wakarimashita, I said, which meant I understood.

"Pleeeese," he said, making a strong appeal, and then he hung up.

I later discovered the call had been from someone in the personnel department. Apparently, they didn't have the guts to tell Thomas directly. Thomas lacked common sense. Most employees wouldn't call home as often as he did. While we lived in Tokyo, I had thought his bold and audacious behavior was cultural.

It was unfortunate that all his good qualities were negated by this other side of him. Thomas had lots of enviable talents. He could sing like a professional (he had his own band in his early twenties and sang in bars and clubs), he could draw like a professional artist, he could design software programs, and he could write well. I even thought he had charisma. I often thought it must be difficult for someone like him, who created bad karma for himself. But for me, the worst part was the impact his actions had on my life. My future was often cut off like a bridge that had collapsed. I consequently had to give up whatever I had been doing and reconstruct my life. I hated this perpetual pattern of life change, but I had to follow, as he was, after all, the main provider. In any case, this time, before we went broke, he found a job in Atlanta.

V

Atlanta Georgia

Traveling with Two Cats

Time to move again! It was a snowy January day. Large flakes of snow started falling and made a mess of the passage at the apartment complex while we were loading stuff into the U-Haul truck. The cats had been enjoying the unloaded boxes, but on the moving day, Mickey and Rosie got confused. We confined them in our bathroom so they wouldn't get in our way. They started crying and their lamentations annoyed me. But soon my busy mind tuned them out; we needed to get to our destination before dark.

With the box that carried Mickey and Rosie secured tightly in the back seat of the Civic, I followed the U-Haul. This was the first time Thomas had driven a truck. For the first half hour, his driving was unstable and I watch in horror when his truck shuffled between the median and the white line a few times. But once we got on the highway, his driving got better, I thought. But *no* . . . Thomas tried to change lanes without looking to see if there was a car in the right lane. There was. The driver made a quick swerve to avoid a collision. A horn blared. As Thomas quickly veered back to his lane, the truck tilted dangerously to the right. I shut my eyes for a second, then drew a long breath of relief when I saw all was okay. While suppressing my queasy feeling that he might cause an accident, we finally entered Atlanta. The weather was slightly better than in Tullahoma—cloudy but not snowing.

Thomas and I had made a short trip to Atlanta prior to the move, and found an apartment we liked. The apartment had southern exposure. Recalling the previous gloomy apartment, we made sure to find a bright one. Moving into the second floor apartment was challenging without any extra help, but once our belongings were moved in we managed to finish unpacking in a week. I was ready to again begin a new life.

I started looking for a community college. The transition was smooth, for I now knew my way around. I enrolled for spring classes after transferring the credits I had earned, and registered in 200-level courses in math and history, and 100-level courses in economics. This urban community college served multiple and diverse groups in a wide age range. It was more of a "mixing pot" culture than the college I had attended in Tennessee.

Spring term had hardly begun when I realized economics was going to be a difficult class. The teacher was intimidating. She was a small old lady with hard features and a deep voice. Each time she gave me a look, I brushed away her image by flapping my eyelids a couple of times. After three classes, I finally decided to go to her office to tell her in person that it would be better for me to drop the class. When I entered her office, she looked at me with big, droopy eyes that deflated what pride I had left.

She said, "I agree." She added, "Don't worry. You won't get an 'F'." Then she looked away as if I didn't exist and continued what she was doing. I bowed mechanically at the threshold of her office even though she wasn't looking at me any longer.

U.S. history was interesting in the beginning. The class was seventy-percent lecture. But I realized that most of the instructor's lecture material wasn't in the textbook. When I heard his announcement that seventy-percent of the final exam would be from his lectures, I became seriously apprehensive. In my generation, school in Japan focused on European history and very little on American history. I had little knowledge of U.S. history.

My daily routine was moderately stimulating with studying, housework, and having occasional lunches with the friends I had made when we lived in Atlanta before. A few days before my thirty-fifth birthday, Thomas took a business trip. My friends celebrated my birthday with me. But on my special day, I was alone and feeling melancholy about not celebrating with Thomas, as he had always made my birthday fancy. My favorite birthday memory was when Thomas took me to Tokyo Disneyland which had just opened in April, 1983. On this day, I dressed up in a new outfit Thomas had bought for my birthday. A white cashmere half-sleeve sweater, a beige flared-skirt, and fashionable beige sandals added to my joy. I picked all the rides: the Small World, Jungle Cruise, River Railroad and also the Disney shows. As we moved from place to place, he shot pictures of me with Mickey, Minnie, Donald Duck, Goofy, or Cinderella—whichever character was present. That day was unforgettable. But understanding the circumstances this time, I tried to let go of my disappointment.

Then around noon, I heard a knock at the door. I wondered who it could be. I tiptoed to the door and got close to the little spyglass, peeked through the hole, and saw red roses. A tall man was standing there, holding a bouquet in his arms. I instantly knew the dozen roses were from Thomas. *He never disappointed me on my special day!* I felt his love.

I opened the door and accepted the roses. After closing the door, I put the bouquet down, scooped up the cats and danced around the room, hugging them tightly.

My life was proceeding pretty well, I thought, but in early June, a few weeks before my finals, Thomas announced, "Kumiko . . . I need a new job."

"I CAN'T MOVE! I need to finish school," I cried out.

"I understand," Thomas said. "I knew you would be upset. I'm really sorry to inconvenience you."

As I didn't say anything, Thomas continued, "You just focus on your studying, and I'll do the moving."

"I just want to finish my finals," I murmured.

His voice softened. "Kumiko, I totally understand."

No matter what the situation was, all I wanted at this point was to complete the spring term. Thomas promised to let me finish it. He immediately looked for a job. He must have become experienced at interviewing by then, for within a week, he had found a prospective employer in Plano, Texas. The company even invited me to Thomas's interview and we flew to Texas. After Thomas had successfully finished his all-day interviews, he and I attended the company dinner, which all the employees and their wives joined, to welcome Thomas to the company.

My classes were about to end for summer vacation. Thomas and I decided he would go to Plano first, and I would finish my schoolwork in

the empty apartment. Although his company paid for moving, Thomas drove the U-Haul truck to save some money. I kept only the necessary things to live for a few weeks and slept in two sleeping bags (bought for this occasion) zipped together. However, at the end of the month when the apartment lease ended, Mickey, Rosie, and I had to move out, so we relocated to a motel along Peachtree Road for a week. The room had an office-sized desk and met my needs, but I was so afraid the cats might somehow get out of the room and be lost. Seven days of confinement was an ordeal for the cats and for me. I had to be careful every time I went out and make sure I hung the "Do Not Disturb" sign in order to prevent the cats from escaping the motel room.

Then, finally, this temporary lifestyle ended. The leaving day came at last. I had planned to leave the motel around 2:00 a.m., considering the time needed to travel to Texas and arrive before dark, so that finding the address of our new apartment would not be traumatic. Surprisingly, there were a few people awake and making their inscrutable noises here and there, which made me uneasy. Under the twinkling starlight, I quietly made many trips to the car to load all my belongings. My little car was in the spotlight of the streetlamps in the pint-sized motel parking lot. The moderate June temperature was agreeable, and despite my long journey I was in high spirits, knowing I could join Thomas soon.

The car was totally filled up and very little space was left for Mickey and Rosie. At the last moment, I took the cat-carrier in which Mickey and Rosie were squeezed together. I carried the small but heavy carrier that tilted to one side—for Rosie was significantly heavier than Mickey—to the car, and placed it gently down onto the front passenger seat. Also, I put a travel-size litter box in a secure spot, down on the floor, behind the passenger seat. With all of us at last in the car, I said "Adios" to the motel and embarked for Texas to meet Thomas. The sound of the engine broke the stillness and I stepped on the gas and headed my overstuffed car onto Peachtree Road.

A minute or two later, Rosie started to cry faintly, and soon Mickey responded to her. Their cries went from soft to ear-splitting. So I parked the car to let them out of the carrier. They came out from the little box with great caution. Then they started walking, crouched low with their panicky meows becoming loud and throaty. Rosie lay down on the floor of the front passenger seat, crying in a stretched-out musical rhythm—with only one lyric line. "Meow . . . Meow . . . Meow." Meanwhile, Mickey kept crawling around with his whole body low, almost scraping anything that came under his abdomen, his pounding heartbeat shaking his body up and down. He sounded as though his life was about to end.

I was trying to find a way of getting onto US 20. My mind was busy figuring out how to get on the highway while the cats displayed their discomfort to the maximum. Mickey clawed his way up onto my shoulders, badly scratching my body. It was painful being walked over, his nails digging into my tender skin. I could even see streaks of blood oozing on my hands and arms. When the dawn broke, this odd spectacle inside the car became more visible to other people, Mickey sitting on my lap, looking like he was the one driving the car, Rosie sitting on the rear window ledge, looking like a stuffed animal. They entertained the other drivers while I winced in pain.

US 20 took us all the way to Texas through Alabama, Mississippi, and Louisiana. To drive through those states would give me an opportunity to learn the geography, but I had neither the mind nor the physical liberty to enjoy glancing at scenery because of the cats. I needed to drive as far as I could go without stopping, but nature called and I had to use a bathroom. Somewhere on the Mississippi-side of the Alabama state line, I stopped at a McDonald's restaurant. When I came out of the restroom, I bought an Egg McMuffin, so as not to feel bad about just using the free restroom.

When I returned to the car, I opened the door warily, so as not to let the cats out, but of course, Mickey, the sneaky one, sprinted out onto the parking lot and ran like a crazy cat. I was astounded and chased him breathlessly, but he was a lot faster and manifested his determination to not have to come back inside the car. I was putting on quite a show, but soon people realized I was desperate and needed some other hands, so they started to chase my errant cat.

Mickey raced in circles around the large parking lot for fifteen minutes until we cornered him under a pickup truck. I crawled under the truck and grabbed his neck. He didn't show any remorse, instead kicking me with all his force. I managed to put him in the car and then locked the doors. He was panting so hard he frothed at the mouth. I was very worried and wet his mouth many times, but he continued frothing. At this point, I wasn't sure I could get him to our new home alive. I drove as fast as I legally could, but the last six-hundred miles of the trip felt like an eternity.

At last, the Dallas sign in white letters on a green board appeared in front of my bloodshot eyes. I was finally in the state of Texas. The time was shortly after four o'clock in the afternoon. Traffic started getting congested, and it required all my attention to find the right way to get to Plano. A river of large flashy cars swiftly flowed along the highway. I got the impression there was a lot of wealth in Dallas, and attributed this sign of prosperity to the fact that Texas was a rich oil state. Unfastening my purse, I grabbed the paper that had the detailed directions on it, and clutched it in my right hand. I looked at it whenever I had the chance, and drove with caution. Luckily, both cats were in their chosen spots in mindless sleep. As I entered the gate of the Parkway Apartments and slowly approached the address, I saw Thomas walking toward my car, waving. I couldn't have been happier to see his smiling face. I could put all the ordeals I had gone through behind me.

VI

Plano, Texas

Tokyo Friends

Thomas and I held Mickey and Rosie in our arms and carried them inside our new home. They waddled unsteadily at first, but began to rove through the rooms, still crying sorrowfully. Meanwhile, I was grateful and relieved I had made it to Texas accident-free, and had only had the one challenging incident with the cats in the McDonald's parking lot.

The journey with Mickey and Rosie, my worst driving companions ever, had been an arduous experience. Nonetheless, and most importantly, I liked Plano, as did the cats. They liked the large two-bedroom apartment with lots of windows. They loved the awning-style windows from ceiling to floor that tilted outward, because those windows allowed them to poke out their tiny heads to breathe fresh air. They often stuck out their heads and stretched out, their paws resting on the window ledge, and watched the activity outside in their backyard.

There was a vast green field by a river, about a mile away from our apartment, where we took walks in the evenings. Although a great number of massive, galvanized steel electric power poles stood imposingly at intervals along the river bank, the space seemed to attract people to come and play, to walk, jog, fly kites, throw Frisbees, and run with their dogs. The image of this playground reminded me of Grandma Moses's paintings.

Thomas had done all the work: our furniture was arranged in the same way as in our previous houses. My clothes were put away and he had done some serious grocery shopping. Above all, he had remembered to buy me some wine. I felt his love. Under such conditions, I could quickly acclimate and be ready for action.

With high hopes, I visited Texas University, but my hopes were shattered by the high cost of out-of-state-tuition. My heart sinking, I drove back home, remembering all the sweating I had done over my classes. On the way home, my attention wasn't much on driving, and my head was muddled because of the bad news. But oddly, my mood was not as much affected as I had expected. Perhaps the brilliant June Texas sky counteracted my gloomy mood.

As school was too expensive for me at that time, I had to give up on my education and look for a job. During those first weeks, I read the job section in the Sunday newspaper, and then the first thing on Monday mornings, I called the jobs I had marked. One Saturday in July, when I was looking through the ads, bold fonts caught my attention: American Airlines was looking for a part-time security person. I particularly liked the part saying, "Bilingual is preferable." I got the job after passing the five days of intensive training.

The airline required all the passengers flying to London, Frankfurt, and Tokyo to have a strict security clearance check-in a designated area where there were five podiums lined up. Security agents had the authority to ask a long list of questions, which gave me a little feeling of superiority. The best part was that there were chances to meet celebrities, although I wasn't very familiar with most of them.

One day I heard my co-worker shout, "Sting!" I knew of "Sting" the singer because I watched MTV regularly, but to my great surprise, the "Sting" she was referring to wasn't the singer.

So I asked, "Who is that big guy?"

"He is a famous American professional wrestler," she answered with her gaze stuck on him as he vanished into the crowd.

"Is that so?" I responded with no interest.

I woke up at 4:00 a.m. to drive up to the Dallas-Fort Worth International Airport, but I didn't mind rising so early, nor did I mind the fifty-minute drive because I indulged myself in listening to George Michaels' songs: *One More Try, Careless Whisper, Kissing a Fool*. It was still dark when I left home and the air was undisturbed. I was enamored with his sexy soulful voice. As the city became gradually visible in silhouette in the blue dawn, his sweet resounding voice carried me away into a dream space.

A few months after we arrived in Texas, I became friends with a Japanese lady I met at the grocery store. It was an odd moment when we met for the first time. Our eyes met when I was about to pick up a lipstick from a cosmetic display. She stood about ten feet away from me. Strangely, though her eyes showed interest in talking to me, neither of us immediately started a conversation. Instead, we stared awkwardly at each other, probably for close to half a minute. I finally said, "*Nihonjin no kata desuka*" (Are you Japanese?) She replied, "*Hai soudesu*" (Yes, I am), with a light bow. Then we approached each other. Our conversation quickly became lively, and soon our phone numbers and addresses had been exchanged. Her name was Yoriko, and she lived only fifteen minutes away from my house.

Yoriko was a rather sad person. Although she had cute facial features with large round eyes and dimples, her expression was somehow despondent. One day she told me the shocking story that her American husband wasn't treating her well. She had met him in Japan, where he was working for a year as an expat, and married him. She thought he was a good man, but after he brought her to the U.S., he became abusive and dictatorial. Once, with a touch of embarrassment, she told me how she had had to host his business friend for dinner while hiding a bruise around her eye with a scarf. Her husband had hit her.

She said, "It was so obvious, but my husband didn't even show any remorse."

"Do you have money to go back to Japan?" I asked.

"He discovered all the money I hid from him and took it for his own use."

Yoriko didn't even seem to be trying to change her situation. I felt truly sorry that she was being held captive in a charming, brand-new house like a bird in a pretty cage.

Yoriko introduced me to her Japanese friend, Kyoko, who was bubbly and vivacious. The two of them presented utterly different images. Kyoko was slender and relatively tall for a Japanese woman, with soft, silky skin. She had large, beautiful, crystal-black eyes and abundant straight black hair that often cascaded over her shoulders. Her wide smile was appealing to me, more Western than Japanese. When she grinned, her full wide lips parted, exposing her bright white teeth, which were quite charming.

Kyoko often invited Yoriko and me for tea. Getting together with them was like being in Tokyo. We chatted for hours and reminisced about Japan. Kyoko always baked a scrumptious cake. Her cakes weren't overly sweet or too richly buttered. The thinly sliced cake with fresh fruit topping was always a great treat for Yoriko and me.

When I think of Kyoko, I think about her elaborately-designed home. Her stunning house had a huge entry that was almost like a den. In fact, at first I thought this was a small bedroom as Kyoko displayed a large Japanese mirrored vanity there. An impressive feature of this foyer was a big wide step made of a thick slab of cherry wood that was smooth as glass. The house looked expensive, and it was a bit intimidating for me to enter it the first time. Straight ahead was a fancy music room that showcased a Yamaha grand piano in the center. The room had French doors and glass walls. One time Kyoko played the piano for us. While the classical prelude floated through the house, I thought what a noble lady she was.

However, despite her elegance, her alertness and coordination in driving were poor. One time she said, "I can't face my neighbor. One day I ran into his car and damaged his license plate. Six months later, I ran into his fence."

"I understand. It must have been difficult to face your neighbor after that," I said sympathetically.

"Well, what did your husband think about those little accidents?" Yoriko asked.

"To tell you the truth, I had one more little accident which made me feel very awkward," Kyoko said, embarrassed.

Yoriko's gaze and mine were fixed on Kyoko, inquisitively waiting for her story.

Kyoko continued, "When the last incident happened, my husband showed no concern about my wellbeing, but was just concerned about the car."

"What was the last incident?" I asked.

"I hit my husband's workbench while I was backing into the garage. But can you believe what he said?"

"What did he say?" we chorused.

He said, "With your history of accidents, let's not bother fixing the car." And then she chuckled.

Having conversations with Yoriko and Kyoko was a great pleasure. We had two things in common that made us close: first, we were about the same age, and secondly, Yoriko and Kyoko were also from Tokyo. We found many commonalities, such as where we had hung out. In the course of one of our conversations, I learned Kyoko's husband went to the language school where I had taught Japanese. I had never met her husband in person, but his picture, placed on the refrigerator with a magnet clip, seemed familiar.

I had a familiar dream. It was sometime in early June, 1989. Almost a year had passed since we had moved to Texas. The dream foretold that another move was near. This dream was, as usual, in black and white, and I was standing on the deck of a big ship floating out on the ocean. I watched the waves, dark and surging. I wasn't afraid of those waves, but rather I simply felt like I was revisiting a familiar experience. *Here we go again*, I thought. A few days later, Thomas told me he had to find a new job. The dream had indeed been a premonition; something from beyond had informed me of the move before it happened.

I had never asked Thomas why he lost his jobs in the past, because I already knew why. I was sure his provoking boldness and egocentric personality had alienated others in his workplaces. So I hadn't questioned why he lost his job, but this time I demanded, "Can't you find a job in this area. Let's not move!"

He squirmed a bit and looked away. Then he said, "I'll try. But it'll take a longer time to find a job if I only search in this area."

This trend of always moving to a different state made me think . . .

Hmm. I guess nothing could anchor him. He was a lone wolf, solitary, not family-oriented, not even people-oriented. I was becoming immune to sudden changes, and not even mildly shocked, though I felt like a sailboat on an ocean, at the mercy of a storm and losing control over my direction. I knew from experience it would be just a matter of time until things would work out again, but I hated the constant change.

While I was reflecting on our past, an idea hit me. *Why don't I give him options for where to move?*

So I asked, "Can you find your job in California, so I might have a good chance to find a job I want?"

He readily agreed.

The very next day, he bought the *San Francisco Chronicle*, and started looking for a job in that area. Even though there was a great deal of turmoil in our lives, he listened to me. That was why I could follow him. He soon got an offer from a software company in Redwood City, California.

It was around four o'clock on a Monday in the early summer. We moved out of our apartment soon after the moving truck left for our temporary apartment in the City of Mountain View, a place arranged by Thomas's new company for a short stay until we found our own place. That moving day was hectic, especially for me, because I was scheduled for my last visit to the dentist to remove my braces, which I had worn since Tullahoma. With that on my mind, I was anxious, imagining worst-case scenarios. I hoped everything would go well at the dentist and nothing would complicate our moving.

Despite my apprehension, things did go pretty well, and we were able to move out without any hindrances. My Civic was transported by the moving company and I was happy we could all go together in the

Toyota. The cats were drugged this time. The days of our long journey to San Francisco were actually more of a vacation. Thomas seemed to be optimistic about his job, and I was excited about going to a cosmopolitan city.

Traveling from Texas through New Mexico and Arizona was rather monotonous, but once we got on U.S. Highway 101 from Interstate Highway 40, the ocean views were exhilarating. The Pacific Ocean gave us ebullient energy that took all our worries away and made us a happy boy and girl. When we came to Santa Monica, we decided to spend the night there. We saw a small inn that looked very pretty, with heaps of Shasta daisies in the front yard. Thomas parked our car by the sidewalk along the ocean, and asked me to stay in the car so he could see what the place was like. Excited by the scene of palm trees, roller-skaters, and joggers on the sidewalk and the orange twilight, I forgot what he had told me. I got out, locking the car with his key still in the ignition. *Oh NO!* Our cats were inside and awake. Returning from the inn, Thomas looked at my wide eyes and immediately realized the car was locked. I read his lips. "Shit!" he said. He reproached me, then called a locksmith, but once we got settled in the cute hotel we were happy again.

VII

San Francisco, California
Life in The Big City

Thomas had to start working for his new software company soon after we arrived in the fully-furnished corporate apartment in Redwood City. On Saturday of the same week, I was startled by a loud noise overhead in the apartment.

I asked Thomas, "What in the world was that?"

"Blue Angels."

"What's that?" I asked again, thinking that the noise didn't sound angelic.

"It's a military air show," he answered.

We were there around the time of the annual U.S. Air Show in Mountain View. I said to myself, "Wow . . . it's like *Top Gun*!"

I wished I could see those graceful aerobatic maneuvers once in my lifetime, but Thomas wasn't interested in seeing them. He disliked crowded places. A Tokyo girl, I was totally the opposite. I recalled one of the soundtracks from *Top Gun* "Take My Breath Away," with the scene of a handsome guy and pretty woman in their Navy uniforms having a romance. Tom Cruise acted like there was nothing impossible in this world.

Two weeks later, we found an eye-catching apartment in Foster City. The striking new apartment had lots of gables like the houses in fairytales. The attractive and well-designed city was actually an engineered island, built on a landfill in the marshes of the San Francisco Bay. We often took a walk along the manmade canals. Foster City never got too hot; the breeze coming from the bay cooled down the city to a comfortable temperature.

I felt at home in San Francisco. The city offered a few Japanese attractions. Japan Town, though not as big as Chinatown, was large enough to fill six city blocks. Inside the indoor shopping mall, specialized restaurants (noodle, sushi, tempura—battered and deep-fried vegetables and seafood—and more), a hair salon, a drug store and a U.S. branch of one of the largest Japanese bookstore chains, Kinokunia, created an ambiance of Japan. I was enthralled. Another attraction was the Japanese Garden in Golden Gate Park. Harmoniously landscaped Japanese native trees (black pine, maple, cherry, and wisteria), an arched moon bridge, *Koi* (carp) pond, and a tea house, transported me to Japan. A Japanese Tea House was nestled in the center of the garden. Every time we went to the garden, we had tea with rice crackers. Overlooking the beautifully landscaped pond, we rested our spirits. The best local diversions though, were Japanese programs on TV. Every Saturday I watched a drama series in which my favorite stars were featured. I hadn't felt as close to my country since coming to the U.S.

Furthermore, San Francisco was appealing for its proximity to many other captivating places to visit—Napa Valley, Pebble Beach, Carmel, and Mendocino. Soon after our phone line was hooked up, I called my parents and told them how beautiful San Francisco was. As a formality, I invited them to come over to see San Francisco. I was surprised to hear they would seriously consider my offer.

Within a few days, my parents had decided to visit us. My mom asked me if it would be all right to bring her seven-year-old granddaughter, Aki, because my older brother wanted her to have the experience of being in a foreign country. A week later, my mom gave me their flight information, so I postponed my job search.

It was midsummer when my parents and my niece, Aki, arrived at the San Francisco Airport. At my first sight of my mom and Aki holding hands as they emerged from the customs and immigration area, I thought, *Is that Aki?* She had grown so much, and there was no trace of the toddler face I remembered. Five years had flown by. She shyly clung to my mom and was hesitant to come to me, despite the fact we had often talked on the phone. But this strangeness soon dissipated.

While I was driving on U.S. 101 heading home, my dad suddenly extended his arm in front of my face and exclaimed, "Kumiko, a golf course!"

"That's the one you'll be playing on soon," I said, smiling.

"Really. . . I see people playing," he said, leaning forward to see the course.

He was an avid golfer and loved to watch PGA Championship tournaments on TV. He told me the Japanese golf courses were no comparison to even the standard U.S. courses, which were so much more beautiful. I had to agree with him. He must have gotten this impression from his previous visit to Florida. Having a small geographic size, a large population, and a high-cost economy, I assumed it must be hard for Japan to compete with America in the arena of golf courses, even though there were a great number of Japanese golf lovers.

Two things interested my dad while he was in the U.S. Number one was playing golf and the second thing was visiting antique shops. He loved collecting foreign products and valued Japanese products less. For many years I didn't understand his fascination for international merchandise, but he told me one day that there weren't any good-quality Japanese products when he was in his twenties and thirties, right after World War II. Japan had been pretty much ravished. Instead, he saw many fine imported goods. I remembered when I was a child, my dad drove an Italian Fiat and carried a Leica camera. His many machine tools for his business were made in Germany. He loved cars and motorcycles, and at one point, had planned to buy a used MGA sports car, but that idea was vetoed by my mom.

Although a plastic prototype maker by vocation, he was a motorbike racer by avocation until he married my mom. In 1960, my dad bought a Harley-Davidson. I was only seven at the time. The flashy tinsel on the grips of the heavily-framed motorcycle was burnt into my memory. With his thin body build, I was worried he would not be able to maneuver the massive machine. One day he took the younger of my brothers, Shohei, who was about eleven at that time, for a long drive. According to my brother, they went to a muddy place somewhere, and the motorbike slipped and fell sideways. Heavy rain started to fall and it was a cold day. My dad tried repeatedly to set the Harley upright, but it was too heavy for him. My brother told me he was miserable, shivering in the cold and heavy rain. I felt sorry for him, as he wasn't wearing a leather motorcycle suit like my dad.

But my father's affinity for Western products and Westerners worked in my favor. I was able to marry an American without any negative reaction from my parents. Some Japanese parents who were old and had gone to war weren't so agreeable when their daughter wanted to marry an American. As a matter of fact, I had a couple of friends who were disowned by their parents when they married Americans. My dad hadn't fought the Americans directly, but had worked at an aviation plant, fixing military airplanes. I wondered if this might have had something to do with his being able to be lenient towards Americans. I only heard good things about America in our home.

One time my dad said, "Japanese are glad that Douglas MacArthur oversaw the occupation. We needed to be rebuilt into a more democratic country."

Suddenly he laughed to himself and said, "Whenever an American military jeep passed by, I asked for chocolate. American *Heitai-san* (Mr. American soldier) threw us Hershey's chocolate bars. They were generous, and the chocolate was so gooood." It was as if he were back in that time, tasting the luscious melting chocolate in his mouth.

The first time my dad came to America, I remembered him saying he wouldn't mind living in the U.S., if he knew English. My dad wasn't a typical Japanese man of his age, he was a non-conformist.

He often said, "Live your life big. Do what you want while you can. But remember to take responsibility for your actions."

He indeed did what he wanted to do. He dabbled in many hobbies, but his biggest was hunting. He also did clay shooting. His rifle skill reached the point where he could have become an Olympic competitor, but he didn't pursue it and elected to be a family man.

I was blessed to have a dad whose mind was so open. But I thank my mom for her unconditional support. It must have been very hard for her to see her youngest daughter go off to a foreign country. She never discouraged me from doing what I wanted with my life, and always bolstered my desire. She lived in Tokyo during World War II where the B29 bombed heavily. Her family dodged the major air-raid. She saw countless people jumping into the Sumida River which was so hot from the incendiary bombing that they instantly died. Nevertheless, I never heard her say bad things. I was a very lucky child.

I didn't spend one day at home during the entire month of my parents' stay because I wanted to show them America. One of my dad's desires was to visit The Lodge at Pebble Beach to see the golf course. So with Thomas's consent, I took them for a two-day trip to Carmel. Having already been to Monterey, Carmel, and Pebble Beach with Thomas, I knew my parents, and even Aki, would enjoy it. They all exclaimed over the waves breaking against the sharp cliffs and the striking scenes of lighthouses along the Pacific coastline. My mom was quite impressed with the wealth displayed at the Hearst Castle in San Simeon. Aki liked the Monterey Bay Aquarium. On the weekends, Thomas spent time with my family, taking them to Sausalito and Golden Gate Park, places not so far away from home.

Finally, the whole busy month ended, and my parents and Aki departed with ample memories, but they left their shadows behind. For days, their faces haunted me. I told myself I had better find a job quickly. The Bay Area was unlike any of the other places I had resided, and gave me more opportunities in searching for a job. The Japanese population was large in this part of California. Consequently, there were more Japanese companies.

One Monday in September, I went to a Japanese-owned employment agency. In a few days, they found me a job at a Japanese travel agency in San Francisco. The city was full of vitality, which reminded me of the living conditions in Tokyo. I had to regain the fast pace I had been used to in Tokyo, but it was hard to wake up at five o'clock in the morning to be in the office by eight. I took the Caltrain, a bus, and then had a thirty-minute brisk walk. I undertook this endeavor twice a day simply because I didn't want to pay the monumental fee for a monthly parking permit in downtown San Francisco.

My office was in a building located in the west end of the Financial

District and was close to Union Square where there were major department stores—Macy's, Neiman Marcus, Saks Fifth Avenue—and specialty shops. Also, famous hotels were scattered throughout the area. Of course there were various restaurants I could go to for my lunch hour ... which was the best part of my day.

My job was to provide land services, which included reserving hotels, renting cars, chartering buses, and buying entertainment tickets. Hotel bookings weren't difficult, as we, in most cases, used hotels we had regular business with, but fulfilling all the detailed requests, such as arranging flowers, champagne, or special orders for a certain room at a certain time, could be a big hassle, since occasionally we had to reserve rooms for over fifty people in a tour group. The work required tremendous meticulousness so as not to make any mistakes in the customers' arrangements, but I reveled in it. I was thrilled to be making hotel reservations in English.

One day, when I was making a reservation with a hotel manager, he said, "You have a voice like Marilyn Monroe."

I laughed, but, excited about his compliment, I almost bungled the reservation.

This travel business was operated by a total of nineteen Japanese-speaking employees. The majority were women about my age, around thirty, and many of them had American husbands. We generally felt comfortable sharing our experiences in the U.S. Our common experiences brought us close to each other.

During lunch hour five or six people regularly ate in the break room. We talked freely about personal matters. Our most common subject was our American husbands. Hearing others' problems furnished information I was very curious about. I learned that many of their husbands lavished a lot of time and money on their hobbies. In Japan, in my generation, many wives managed the household money to ensure they could make ends meet every month, and their husbands received a monthly allowance, so husbands did not have much liberty to do what they really wanted.

Other common issues were similar to mine. One day, I complained about how often my husband and I had moved, though I didn't mention the reasons. The others jumped in.

"My husband doesn't have patience with his job. He moved to three different companies in five years, although he always found a job before he quit," one said.

"My husband doesn't mind changing to a different company if they pay better," our accountant added. A newly hired girl said nonchalantly, putting away her lunch things. "Well, my husband is not sure what he really wants, and often tells me all kinds of possibilities he can pursue. So I don't know . . . we might move somewhere. You know Americans don't mind moving."

At other times, many of my coworkers noted that their husbands weren't sensitive enough to understand them unless they explained every point extensively. This was their common complaint. I wasn't a good communicator, but at least my husband was; he could even read my facial expressions. Japanese use silence, subtle body language, and tone, all of which imply some meaning. This must baffle most American husbands.

A month had passed since I started working at the travel agency. I had somewhat accustomed myself to work and the commute when my routine was suddenly, literally, shaken up. It was October 17, 1989, sometime after 4:30 p.m. Every day after 4:30 I gathered everyone's work for the day and sent the information by email to the headquarters in Tokyo. Our computers were operated by DOS commands at that time, and there were loads of steps required to do the task; it took about twenty minutes to complete. My whole attention was focused on successfully completing this process without making any mistakes.

I heard someone screaming, but I didn't pay attention and continued to focus on my work. But the continuous screaming finally broke my concentration, and I heard the vice president, Mr. Tanaka, yelling at me to duck down under the desk. The moment I comprehended what was happening, I felt a big motion. Hurriedly, I ducked under my desk. The tremor continued. The scary rattling sound and the feeling of the strong motion terrified me. *What if I die here?* I thought about Thomas, the cats, and of course my family in Tokyo.

Within minutes, Mr. Tanaka made the decision to tell us to go home. We all rushed to the staircase. We squeezed into the narrow stairwell and hastened down from the 4th floor to get out of the old building. One of our agents, Hiromi, who was newly married, talked to me as we descended. She said she was going home to grab their wedding picture. She said all she needed was her husband and the wedding picture. I thought, *How sweet!*

In the meantime, I was not even sure how I could get home. While I was exiting the building, I was thinking it would be best to walk all the way to the train station. Once out of the building, I saw people running around in confusion. When I saw the big pile of shattered glass in front of Neiman Marcus and Saks Fifth Avenue, I recoiled. *I don't know . . . I don't know . . . Can I make it?* I mumbled to myself. I cried inside. The only thing I could think to do was to walk first to the station. I hoped it would be the best place for Thomas to pick me up.

By the time I got to the station, it was dusk. The city without electricity was eerie. Something bright hovered in the sky. I stared at it until I made out the word, *Goodyear*, and realized it was a blimp. Many people approached the station to wait for someone to pick them up. I called home fearfully. *What if Thomas wasn't home yet?* But he answered immediately, "Are you okay?" When I heard his firm voice, I believed I would be all right.

While waiting for Thomas to pick me up, I felt a chill, although the day wasn't cold. I hoped he wouldn't have much trouble coming to the station. As I spotted our Toyota approaching, I let out a big sigh of relief. I tried to make a smile, but it didn't come out naturally, for my face muscles were too tensed up from the frightening experience. Highway 101 was lit by emergency generators, which enabled us to see our way home. I glanced around the unlit buildings of San Francisco through the car window, thinking the city looked doomed. When we finally got home, I at once looked for the cats. Thomas said when he came home right after the quake, he found our cats hiding in the safest place of all, under the heavy-framed bed. Only a couple of things were damaged. Books and some framed photos, which had been sitting in the huge entertainment center, had popped out from it, and were strewn on the carpet.

The next day, my parents called and told us they had recognized the Oakland Bay Bridge when they saw the TV news of the collapsed section. They remembered this bridge very well because of its length. My parents and Aki had timed how long the bridge was while I was driving across it. So they expressed their sympathy with a good understanding of the situation.

It took days and weeks for me to get back on the normal schedule for going to work. But under the circumstances, people seemed to be handling the disastrous situation quite well, and I didn't hear many complaints other than the fact that it was inconvenient for everyone to go to work. The city's recovery was quick, except in the heavily damaged areas, and normal daily life resumed.

From then on, our life in San Francisco proceeded quite merrily. Almost every weekend, we spent our time either in the De Young Museum or the Japanese Garden, and once in a while we went to concerts. I saw Michel Jackson, Johnny Winter, Elvis Costello, and an English rock band, YES. Friday was our eating-out day. We went to the same Karaoke restaurant over and over, and always ordered *nabemono*—a meal with a variety of vegetables, fish, and shellfish in a soy-based soup. The *nabemono* simmered in its iron pot on a small gas stove right on the table. From time to time, someone would approach the little stage, grab the microphone, strike a pose and begin to sing. Thomas could sing a great number of songs in his mellow voice while I could sing only a few Japanese songs, a bit out of tune. Tone-deaf as I was, I enjoyed the relaxed time. Our routine was packed nicely with work and entertainment, and life was pretty good.

Time flew and spring was on its way. One February evening my brother, Shohei, called to announce he would be getting married in April. His settling down at the age of forty-one surprised me. I had thought he would never get married. He asked me if I could arrange their wedding, since I was working at a travel agency. My mom mentioned that Masako was very beautiful and kindhearted, in spite of being immersed in a competitive world for ten years as a fashion designer. I looked forward to meeting her.

In April, rain fell every day for almost two weeks, which was unusual. I felt anxious about the wedding. But in the afternoon on the day Shohei, Masako, my parents, and her parents arrived, the sky cleared and finally the sun showed up. The whole Bay Area became sunlit. I left work a few hours early and ran to their hotel, the Park 55 Hotel in downtown.

As the elevator door opened at the fifteenth floor, Shohei and Masako were right there waiting. My mom was right; she was indeed attractive and refined. He briefly introduced me to her in the hallway.

Hajimemashite . . . Masako desu (How do you do? My name is Masako). Bending from her waist with a straight back, she made a formal bow.

"Thank you very much for doing this for us," she said, and smiled gently.

"I'm very glad Thomas and I could attend your wedding," I replied politely, and bowed the same way she had.

I felt good about setting up their wedding arrangements.

The next day was the wedding day. There was no wind, and the April air felt fresh and warm. It was the most perfect day I could imagine for the wedding. Thomas and I arrived at the hotel around nine o'clock in the morning. I saw that the stretch limousine I had ordered was already waiting for us at the front of the hotel. *Oh no! A black limo!* At no time had I realized the color would be black. I worried what the family, especially Masako, would think of this limousine. Black limos are used for funerals in Japan. Japanese strictly divide the two colors of black and white, and the symbolism of black is for funerals. Masako didn't show any signs of unhappiness; she only expressed great appreciation.

Before heading to the church, we picked up the cascading white orchard bouquet I had ordered. After crossing the Golden Gate Bridge, the limo drove along a narrow winding road. The church, which sat on a hill in Sausalito, was small, but stately. Masako had brought a large suitcase, inside which her elegant wedding dress, designed by herself and sewn by her mother, was carefully folded. We rehearsed for an hour before the wedding, and everything went well, but in the ceremony, my brother missed one word; he was supposed to say "symbolic," but said "simple" instead. Thomas grinned a bit and the pastor smiled too, but let it go. After the pastor said, "You may kiss your bride," my brother happily kissed Masako. We all relaxed and smiled at each other.

The two of them walked to the main door, all of us watching them lovingly. Then, the video cameraman we had hired, as he stepped backwards to shoot them from the front as they emerged from the church, stumbled in a hole in the pavement. But he regained his balance and continued filming as if nothing had happened. We chuckled, but he performed professionally and finished the whole tape. He even included the unfocused segment of his fall, and for Shohei and Masako, the film was a wonderful memory.

In the evening, we rode in a second limo instead of a taxi. An old light blue limo that someone had reserved and then canceled was sitting in front of the Park 55 Hotel. While we were waiting for a couple of taxis, the limo driver called out, "Hey! You want to ride in the limo? I'm free for a couple of hours. I won't charge you a lot." Since it made sense to use a limo instead of two taxis, we hopped in. Twice in one day, we rode in a limo, which none of us had ever done! This one wasn't as fancy as the black one, but it comfortably carried us all together to Pier 33, where our reserved cruise boat was docked.

When we arrived at the port on the Embarcadero, the manager of the cruise line was already there, greeting the passengers. She had given us a special price, as I was a travel agent, but she went further and arranged a special treat for my brother. A waiter brought us a slice of cake for everyone, and there were jaunty polka musicians.

On the boat, we all enjoyed an exquisite dinner and live music. As it grew dark, the band played slow dance music and Shohei, Masako, Thomas and I danced on the foredeck. It was cool and breezy at night on the bay, but we couldn't pass up the chance to dance and enjoy the San Francisco Bay night view: a million lights on the hills outlined the city. Masako's parents and my parents contentedly chatted together as newly-acquainted relatives. The balmy weather pleased everyone, especially the freshly wedded couple, and the day ended more romantically than Masako and Shohei could ever have expected.

On their departure day, I drove up to Park 55 to send them off to the airport. I hailed two taxis for them. When they took off, tears welled up in my eyes and I stood in a daze for a while in front of the hotel. As I drove home on Highway 101, rain began to fall.

Summer passed quickly and autumn arrived. An opportunity came up for us to go to Japan. Thomas and I hadn't been to Tokyo for six years, and were anxious to go back to see all the changes. We landed at Narita International Airport in the late afternoon on the 28th of September, 1990. Narita Airport was packed with tourists. My oldest brother, Kenji, and my parents were waiting at customs. It was great seeing my brother. He hadn't changed a bit. Thomas thanked him for coming to the airport during his busy working hours.

When Kenji's car entered the city, I felt the highway suddenly narrow. An odd feeling went through my body. *I didn't remember the road was this narrow!* When big trucks passed our car, I almost felt an attack of claustrophobia coming on. *No space between cars!* I had to remind myself, this is Tokyo and it has always been this way.

Alongside the road, a great number of architecturally sophisticated buildings and bridges that I didn't recognize dotted the city skyline. While driving in the evening traffic, Kenji explained about newly-built unique landmarks such as hotels near Disneyland, a Port Tower, and many more enormous danchi (public housing operated by government). I was awestruck that within my six-year absence, the city had transformed itself so radically. After over two hours, we finally reached my parents' home.

At my parents' home, we had a little episode. Thomas and I couldn't enter the house. My parents' Yorkshire terrier, Gilbert, barked furiously at us, jumping up and down, and I believed this creature would bite us at any minute if we forcibly tried to get in the house. My mom scolded him and tried to grab him, but the little dog eluded her and came back at us again. It was ridiculous to think this tiny dog could harm us, but, according to my mom, there was a serious claim against Gilbert because he had bitten a neighbor and the victim had to go to a doctor, so I couldn't take it lightly. In fact, I was afraid of this annoying dog, but once I gave him biscuits handed to me by my brother, the vicious dog became a cute puppy. I saw a sign at the entrance door, "Caution—Ferocious Dog!" Finally, we entered my parents' house. I had always thought their house was big, but everything looked smaller than I had remembered. Once my eyes adjusted, the muddle in my perception strangely went away.

Tokyo can be a stimulating and exciting place if you don't mind crowds and pollution. People who love adventure would likely find Tokyo fascinating; the city blends the old and the new in a seamless manner. You see old temples and shrines mixed in with modern buildings. And the nice thing is that you can go practically anywhere you want without having to drive on a complicated system of roads. Japan has an efficient public transportation network, especially within the metropolitan areas, and the transportation is always punctual.

On our second day in Tokyo, Thomas and I snaked our way through very narrow roads to "Ohanajaya," the closest station to my parents' home. It was a fifteen-minute walk. When we arrived at the station, we noticed the ticket area had changed, and a new system for purchasing tickets presented a puzzle. The ticket vending machines were bigger than they had been before, with complicated systems. Above those machines, there used to be a small, simple railroad map, but now the map—three times larger—was spread out, showing all the railways and subway lines in many different colors. It was cumbersome to figure out how to read the intricate map and determine how much to pay for a ticket. I felt awkward, bending my head backward with my mouth half-opened, standing in the middle of the oncoming stream of passengers rushing to catch their trains. I was embarrassed to be taking so long to buy our tickets.

Then what? There weren't any ticketmasters to punch the tickets anymore; instead, automated machines were arrayed around the station. You had to go through an automated ticketing gate. We stopped and watched other people doing it. I inserted the ticket in a slot at the turnstile, then grabbed the ticket at the other end. Thomas followed me. Changes were all over the place, and I was disoriented in the places I used to know well. I had a kind of sinking feeling. It was truly a culture shock.

There were more challenges. Toilets! When I used a toilet in a department store, the toilet wasn't a squat toilet any more. It had been upgraded to a very modern toilet that took some time to understand. There were many buttons: one for shower, one for bidet, and one for sound (to cover unwanted noise), and an adjustable knob for temperature control for the water and toilet seat. While using it, my finger slipped and hit the bidet button. A jet of water got fired at my tenderness. My leaned back was straightened up with the shock.

The speed with which changes had happened was astonishing. I felt like "Urashimataro" (the fisher lad in the Japanese fairy tale). That story goes like this: One day, a boy named Urashimataro was walking on the beach. He saw some ruffians bullying a turtle. Urashimataro helped the turtle. The turtle thanked him and gave him a ride on its back, diving into the deep sea. They arrived at the gate of Ryugujo, an underwater castle, and everyone treated Urashimataro very nicely. Otohime, a prince, gave him a mysterious box telling him the box would protect him from harm, but it was never to be opened. But after he returned to his home, Urashimataro opened the box. He became an old man in an instant. Although Urashimataro had thought he had only been gone for a short time, he discovered 300 years had passed since the day he left for the bottom of the sea.

I thought to myself, *I was only away for six years, but it feels like I was away for decades.*

Besides Tokyo, we visited the city of Kamakura, surrounded by mountains and near the Pacific Ocean. Only a couple hours from Tokyo, it is quite dissimilar, a beautiful city with many old shrines and temples scattered throughout. Thomas loved Kamakura and during his three years of residency in Japan, we often took day excursions to the area and hiked around. Thomas enjoyed less touristy places. One day while hiking, we came across a small nameless shrine standing in a grove of trees. We took our shoes off, sat on the top of the wooden steps, crossed our legs and meditated. On this trip, we tried to re-visit this shrine but we couldn't find it.

In the second week, the very next day after a medium-sized typhoon had passed Tokyo, we took off to Kyoto for a three-day, two-night trip. The weather was clear and sunny after the storm. We took a bullet train (Shinkansen) that only took us a little over two hours for the distance of 500 km (310 miles). Kyoto was an imperial capital of Japan for almost a thousand years—from the eighth to the seventeenth centuries. It was spared the firebombing of World War II. The preserved Buddhist temples and Shinto shrines, as well as palaces, gardens, and architecture give us a window into ancient Japan. Kyoto is a popular destination for school excursions to see our history with our own eyes, so I had been there, but it was the first visit for Thomas. To my great delight, seeing him enjoying the beauty of the historic monuments of ancient Kyoto, I felt proud about being Japanese. The next day we left Japan.

After we came back to the U.S., I became lethargic. Perhaps the jet lag and parting from my family sapped the energy I needed to take on my daily life. I soon left Trans Pacific Travel because I got tired of all the numerous transfers involved in my commute—driving to the train station, getting on the train, getting off the train, dashing to the bus station not to miss the bus, and then trotting for fifteen minutes to be in the office by 8:00 a.m. This time I resolved to find a job near my home. I called the same agency I had used for the previous job. In a few days, they found me employment located within a ten-minute drive of my house. I was amazed how quickly they found a position so close by.

The company was a distributor of Macintosh software, with only two employees. The owners were a Japanese lady, Yoko, and her American husband, Adam. Ron, a Filipino man in his late twenties, and I were the only employees. Ron was in charge of shipping, and I was in charge of correspondence with Japanese buyers.

On the typical, not-so-busy days, Ron and I were the only two in the office. While the owners were absent, we chatted for hours. Ron had lived in the U.S. since he was a child and had served in the U.S. military. I listened to his tales of poverty in the Philippines and how strict military life was. But mostly he talked about funny military stories. Although he thought they were humorous, many of them didn't sound funny to me, for instance, *never draw fire, it irritates everyone around you.* He also tried to teach me phrases like, "Take a chill pill!", "What's shak'n", or "You've got BO." My husband didn't appreciate him teaching me slang. I didn't mind it, though, and I was in fact thrilled about learning some. His chitchat not only made the day shorter but also produced a feeling of equality I hadn't had with English speakers other than my husband. I truly enjoyed conversations with Ron, who had a caring nature, a positive attitude, and aspirations.

I had worked for the company a little over one year, when one day in early October, Yoko asked me to go to Japan with her to meet our clients in Tokyo. *How could I miss that great opportunity?* I said, "Yes!" on the spot. I told Thomas that evening that I was going to Tokyo. He was surprised, but happy for me to get a chance like that.

Yoko and I flew to Tokyo for a week-long trip to acquaint ourselves with our Japanese clients; for Japanese, it is more important to know the people they are dealing with than to know about the business itself. We stayed at the Hilton Hotel in Shinjuku, located in the center of Tokyo, from Monday through Thursday afternoon. From Thursday afternoon till Sunday, I could spend time with my family. The first night staying at the hotel, I couldn't sleep. So I sat by the window and looked down on the night view of Tokyo from the 32nd floor. The constellations were obscured by pollution, but the millions of city lights illuminated the Tokyo night. It was fun watching the cars zipping through the "valley" between tall buildings, making a stream of red tail lights.

I suddenly remembered there were some miniature whiskies in a tiny refrigerator in my room. I hesitated, but "what the heck," I opened a Johnnie Walker and drank it. After a short time, I reached for Jack Daniel's, hoping Yoko and Adam wouldn't find out. Of course they did. Adam mentioned it on the first morning after coming back from the Tokyo trip, saying "Kumiko-san, I didn't know you liked whisky." I looked down at my desk to hide my blushing face.

Meeting with Japanese businessmen was psychologically strenuous because they don't joke like Americans, and I had to use "respectful language" which is an honorific way of speaking. Behaving and speaking like a Japanese didn't come easily after being away from Japan for seven years. A subtle sensitivity was required when dealing with our Japanese clients—be passive, listen to them by nodding my head lightly, and be humble. Our customers respected us because we were living in the U.S. Many postwar children watched American TV programs such as *Lassie, Leave it to Beaver, I Dream of Jennie* and many other popular films, which portrayed America and Americans as a great country and people. For this reason, I believe many Japanese had a romanticized image of America and were drawn to visit America. I had been one of them.

We visited our five primary customers in Tokyo. Yoko had seen our clients before, but this was my first time. All of them to whom I had corresponded said, "Kumiko-san, it's good to see you in person." It was good for me to see their faces. Some of my impressions I had from their emails didn't match, especially that of one person whose written communication style was harsh and demanding. I had never enjoyed communicating with him. However, when I met him, I was surprised to find he was cordial and warm with me. We felt good about our meetings as we have reinforced our working relationships with our customers. Once I was released from work, I jumped on a train and went to my parents' home. It was such a short stay that I spent all my time with my family and didn't explore Tokyo.

When I returned, Thomas was waiting for me at the San Francisco airport. He had taken a day off for me. I was very glad to be home. A short business trip to Tokyo was tolerable, but I remembered the old days when I used to work at Japanese companies in Japan where male employees dominated in the high positions and I often served tea for them. After having lived in the U.S. for a long time, I found Japanese societal constraints on women unbearable. For this reason, I couldn't imagine myself living in Japan, even though I missed my family very much.

For five years, Thomas had been intensely programming a software toolkit for creating Macintosh applications, using all his spare time to realize our dream of becoming rich someday. During our evening walks, cats in our arms, Thomas talked, on and on, about how powerful his program could be. His talk went into great details, but I had only a shallow understanding. He didn't seem to care about that, and talked as if he were convincing himself that he would one day become a success as a software programmer. I was a good listener and didn't show any sign of doubt about his ability to succeed. In fact, I believed he would become a recognized person in this computer field one day. The faith written on my face must have encouraged him to talk more. I envied his passion for his work.

When his software application came close to being released, he asked me to help in starting up his business. Being together all day didn't seem like a good idea, especially in a small apartment; I was concerned it might affect our relationship. But we couldn't afford to hire anyone to help us. So I left my job. It wasn't hard to quit that company, but I missed Ron. I missed our aimless conversations that made me giggle.

We started our business in June, 1992. Our business began as a small production. Thomas took orders and answered technical calls from the customers. I did bookkeeping, shipping, copying diskettes, and chores. Mostly, I spent many hours making demo diskettes to promote our product at convention centers. I remember myself in a navy blue suit, standing with a genial smile trying to distribute demo diskettes in San Francisco's Moscone Convention Center. I randomly approached attendees and called out, "Excuse me sir! This is a new product called OOPC—Macintosh memory management..."

Attendees looked at me curiously, then asked, "What do you have?" People reacted as though they were curious about the demo diskettes in my hand, yet afraid of talking to someone whose demeanor was very foreign. The moment I got their attention, my heart started racing. I swallowed my fear and tried to explain the product with my very limited knowledge. They stared vacantly and listened patiently. Their eyes expressed an obvious bafflement, but didn't ask any questions. At the end of my spiel, they politely thanked me. Some even gave me a tiny bow. Once they parted from me, though, their heads dropped down immediately to read the flyer I had given them.

Our product was very expensive—costing over five hundred dollars—and was targeted to software programmers, so the market was limited. The business only lasted a year and a half. Closing the business felt disastrous to Thomas. His dream was obliterated. Furthermore, the income we received from the business was now completely exhausted. He became an inactive, spiritless person. He sat at the same spot on the couch reading all day. I had never seen him like this before. He was heavy-hearted, dealing with his defeat, and I didn't know how to galvanize him into action. It felt painful to watch him.

Of course, he knew he had to support us. For a full month he was like a zombie, but his spirit finally returned. He started looking for a job. Without investing much time, he found a job that involved some traveling to teach a workshop on how to create a search engine, similar to what we know today as *Google*. At that time, this search engine technology was in its infancy.

I too found a job, at a semiconductor company in San Jose, as a secretary for a Japanese vice president. Working in a quiet research and development department in a first-rate, newly-built office made me proud. But working for my boss, Mr. Yoneda, was quite a mental challenge. Soon after I started, he asked me to help make a budget proposal. So I opened up Microsoft Excel and used different chart types, like bar and line graphs, and even a pie with three dimensions. To the best of my knowledge, the proposal was done nicely. But he didn't like it.

He said, "Kumiko-san, you don't have any artistic sense."

After gathering my composure, I challenged him saying, "Since I don't have any artistic sense, I shouldn't be doing this kind of work, Yoneda-san."

He went back into his office and stayed there for fifteen minutes or so, then came back to me.

"Kumiko-san, I'm sorry. On second thought, you have some artistic sense. Would you please finish it?" he said.

I said politely, "If you think I am capable of doing it, I will continue."

He looked at me with his smile askew. I smiled back faintly, thinking how cantankerous he was. Mr. Yoneda wasn't popular among the engineers, but they respected and were awed by him at the same time. All the other engineers were kindhearted and very supportive, so the job was tolerable.

When spring arrived, we received a letter from my eleven-year-old niece, Aki, saying that she didn't want to live with her mom any longer. Although I knew her mom wasn't treating her well, and I worried about her, I had never thought about having her come to live with us. But I showed the letter to Thomas anyway.

Thomas said without giving the idea much thought at all, "Let's do it."

"Oh! We don't have room for her," I protested.

"Why don't we find a rental house?" he said.

Although I didn't think taking Aki in was a good solution, his idea of moving into a rental house didn't sound bad. We were on a tight budget, but since he was enthusiastic about the idea, we started looking. We didn't tell Aki, as I wanted to wait and see if the arrangement was indeed feasible. A few weeks later, we found a cute, three-bedroom house. The kitchen, dining room and living room facing the street side were all connected, and I loved the rich acacia red color of the cherry-wood floors. In the yard, a spreading pear tree and two leafy plum trees were about to bloom. We liked the house, and the cats were excited by all the activity on both sides: cars and pedestrians on the street, and delightful visitors—squirrels, crows, doves, finches, and butterflies—in the backyard.

Barely a month had passed since we moved into the rental house, when Thomas broached a new idea. It was dinnertime and I had started eating, yet he hadn't even touched the food.

"I want to start painting," he said abruptly.

"Painting what?"

"I want to become a professional oil painter," he said, smiling, with a sparkle in his eyes.

For a moment I was flustered, but his genuine smile, which I had not seen much of since he had lost his dream, convinced me he was seriously motivated. Most people wouldn't think about taking up painting for a living unless they had a strong background. He was different. He dived into the ocean not knowing how cold the water was, and learned through trial and error. I was just glad I hadn't told Aki she could live with us. Obviously it wouldn't be feasible.

He left his company. A truly self-taught person, when he created something, he wanted to control all the aspects of its creation, just the way he had built his computer. So this time, as well, he made his own oil medium. I can easily bring to my mind the sight of him rolling a baby food jar filled with the medium on the wooden floor so it would become colorless and transparent. The cats liked to chase the rolling baby food jar around the floor. He purchased good tools for painting, and the tools and pigments weren't at all cheap. The quality of brushes and oil paints greatly affects the quality of the painting, so I knew he couldn't cut corners on those things, but his new vocation was by no means inexpensive.

Thomas learned quickly, and soon his paintings became decent. But he realized it would take a long time for his oil painting to bring in any income, so he decided to find a real job again. He knew when to quit, and never went beyond unrealistic expectations. His quick actions often amazed me. He soon found a job in west Bellevue, Washington. I was relieved when he got the job, because we were running out of savings.

Thomas left two weeks before I could. I had to stay in order to give two-weeks' notice at my company. During those two weeks, I had to take care of the yard, and that wasn't my forte. I guess I must have disliked it so much that I cut the orange wire cord of the electric lawn mower. Not even realizing for a while that the mower had not been making the motor noise anymore, I kept pushing it in an absentminded way. When I finally realized it was quiet, the rest of the cord was left behind me.

In my last week at the company, my boss invited me to a sushi restaurant after work. Once seated, he asked, pointing his finger at the menu, "Do you like uni (sea urchin)? How about anago (saltwater eel), tobi (roe) and toro (oily tuna) to begin?" These are pricy sushi, but he seemed to enjoy ordering. This sushi was so fresh and tasty, I couldn't put my chopsticks down. After having several cups of sake, Yoneda-san seemed relaxed and showed a cheery face not seen at work. Is that the power of sake?

"I'm sorry I didn't treat you nicer," he said. He took another sip of sake, then continued shyly. "I couldn't sleep that night after meeting you at work."

Then why didn't you treat me nicely? I thought. But I smiled back awkwardly, evading the topic. As I watched him eating, I pitied him.

Disliked by everyone in the department, it puzzled me why he didn't change his attitude. *Well, I should be glad that at least he admitted his behavior towards me has been impudent. After all, I'm leaving. I will just enjoy eating the good sushi.*

Most of our packing had been done before Thomas left, and I finished up the rest. He flew back on the weekend prior to the move. On that Monday morning, the moving truck showed up around the time we had arranged, and most things went smoothly. But in the last moments of cleaning up the garage, I did a stupid thing. I yanked a dirty rug pinned down by a large rectangular mirror. The mirror, left by the previous tenants, fell onto the concrete floor and shattered into pieces.

"Oh my God!" I muttered and covered my mouth.

The loud sound brought Thomas rushing into the garage.

"Holy moley," he shouted.

One thing I hadn't liked about this house was that there were mirrors everywhere and they weren't small. I had never felt entirely comfortable, especially with the large one in our bedroom. When I was living with my parents, I saw my mom covering "Kyodai" (a mirrored vanity) with a cloth cover every night before she went to bed. My mom mentioned when I was young that a mirror would take all the energy from the body while sleeping. Most Japanese are superstitious, and I was too. I felt like it was an ill omen to see the mirror shattered, but I couldn't afford to allow my mind to get emotional, as we had to keep going with the moving. Thomas sensed my feelings and he felt uneasy too.

After we signed the paper handed to us by the mover, we were ready to take off from the house. The cats, Thomas, and I got in our '87 Civic and left the house in which we had lived for only for a few months.

The time we lived at this house was so short, it felt like a transient dream. Once again, we were to start our new life in a different state.

It was hard for the loaded Honda to climb the high mountains of the Cascades. Thomas tended to step on the gas with a heavy foot, and all the while, I was nervously wondering if the car would tolerate that kind of harsh treatment. It finally gave out on us.

We had to take the car to an auto shop and leave it until the next day, with the two cats inside. We found a motel nearby for the night, but, worrying about them, I couldn't sleep well. The next morning when we went to the auto shop, the repair was still underway and the car was up high on the car lift. I saw Mickey in the car climbing up and down, showing his agitation, but I was relieved he was alive and not sick. Rosie was nowhere in sight. Waiting for the mechanic to finish the work, we took a walk around the area. There were no commercial shops except a general store and a small run-down church. The weather on that July day in Medford, Oregon was warm and dry and in the seventies. By the time we returned to the shop, the car was ready, and we resumed our journey to Seattle.

As we entered Washington, an old friend's words flashed in my mind. Kumiko-san, the kindest lady I had met in Tullahoma Tennessee, had moved to Edmond, Washington. She had told me on the phone that the suicide rate in Washington had at some point in time been the highest in the country, and she had warned me not to get depressed by the drizzly rain. But Washington in early July was green and picturesque.

VIII

Seattle, Washington
Communication Breakdown

We stayed at a hotel that Thomas's company had booked for us until the rental house was ready. The owners were renting their four bedroom house out for three years while they were in France. After a week's stay at the hotel, we headed out to our new home in Belleview.

When our car neared the house, pointing his finger, Thomas said, "That's the one."

"Gee, look... lots of roses!" I cried out.

Masses of multicolored red, pink, yellow, and white roses in full bloom covered the front yard and drew my attention. The brick house with bay windows looked prettier with those abundant roses. Although the house wasn't ours, the mere thought we could live in such an attractive house excited me a lot. Moreover, the house interior was idyllic. The kitchen was in the center of the house, and the rooms had large windows. Through the windows, I could see one tall cedar tree in the center of the backyard on an oblong-shaped bed encircled by a white picket fence. Loads of perennial flowers colorfully blanketed the area inside the fence. I was overjoyed.

In early September, my parents accepted our invitation to come visit. I wanted to show them our charming house and Seattle, a coastal seaport city, with surrounding lakes and forests, and a stunning view of Mt. Rainer. The prominent tourist spots like the Space Needle, Pike Place Market, and Ballard Locks would surely interest my parents, I thought. Another of Seattle's lures was its easy access to many beautiful islands.

One early afternoon, Thomas took my parents and me on a thirty-five minute ferry ride from downtown Seattle to Bainbridge Island for dinner. But the most adventurous part of my plan was to take my parents to Vancouver, Canada.

Canada was only a three-hour drive from Seattle. I had never been there and knew only a little about the country, but I thought it shouldn't be a difficult trip. Although Canada is a stone's throw from Seattle, it is a foreign country. I knew I needed to pay attention to the little differences. As soon as we crossed the border, I remembered I had to exchange currency. It was almost five o'clock though, and we had to dash into a bank just before it closed. My parents were a tad perturbed, as I had rushed them.

Just outside the city, we found a small hotel. When I looked at the room rates, I thought they were slightly high until I realized Canadian dollars were worth a little less than U.S. dollars. I had been feeling edgy, but after I had exchanged the money and reserved a room, I felt calmer and suddenly hungry. We took off for dinner. We should have gone to a restaurant near our hotel, but we went to downtown Vancouver city center—a mistake.

I was about to park my car to find a restaurant when Dad exclaimed, "What are those white tents by the waterfront that look like colossal sailing boats?"

"That's Canada Place," I replied. A gigantic building, which reminded me of the Opera House in Sydney, had caught my dad's attention. He wanted to peek at the building, so we did. Again, I didn't think about the time. As we stepped out on the deck, a pleasant breeze was blowing in from the sea, and the stunningly beautiful sunset cast a warm glow over the mountains across the harbor. We snapped many pictures.

We found a restaurant nearby that had a view of Vancouver Harbor. My dad ordered a rare beef steak and my mom and I had Mahi Mahi. I couldn't believe Dad could eat the barely cooked meat. When he stabbed it with his fork, blood speckled his platter, but he relished every bite.

By the time we finished dinner, the sky had completely darkened. The night view was impressive, but I worried about getting back to the hotel, as it was a long drive and I wasn't sure of the way. I had a map of Canada, but it didn't do much good. Driving at night made everything harder. Needing to buy gas hugely complicated the situation. Since it was almost eleven o'clock, many gas stations were already closed. I felt tension building up as I drove blindly. I finally found a small gas station, but it didn't look very safe. Slowly pulling my car up to the gas pump, I turned the engine off and waited for a minute, not knowing what to do next. I decided to go inside. As I entered, an old East Indian man saw my car parked in front of the gas pump and asked if I needed gas. I nodded yes. He quietly filled the tank.

I left the gas station, but had no clue how to get back on the highway. My head started pounding. I was a little nauseous and scared driving in a dark, desolate area. It took me a while to get on the highway, but once I did, I realized I was heading the wrong way, toward the Vancouver International Airport. Returning back to go the right direction, I slowed way down and leaned forward on the steering wheel so as not to miss the right exit; since that point, all the way to the hotel, my posture stayed in the same position—slanted forward. When I finally saw the neon sign of our hotel in the distance, I sat back in relief. It was past midnight. My parents, who had been so silent that I had almost forgotten about them, said in unison, "We are so glad you made it."

The next day, we only went to Stanley Park, and stopped by Eaton's Department Store for lunch. We were there to find a restaurant, but when we were on the food floor, we saw not only a few restaurants but also a food section where they sold wine, cheese, bread, and all sorts of other delicatessen items. My parents browsed slowly, scrutinizing the choices. Mom bought maple-leaf cookies. Dad bought a bottle of wine, just because the salesperson recommended it.

When I bought Canadian smoked wild salmon for Thomas, an idea hit me.

"Dad . . . Mom . . . why don't we have a picnic on the way home instead of eating here?"

Dad and Mom looked at each other, then nodded their heads lightly.

"Where are we going?" Dad asked.

"I don't know . . . some nice place on the way home," I said. Then I suggested, "Why don't you guys buy food for lunch?"

We added a loaf of French bread, some sliced Swiss cheese and ham, and a couple pounds of specialty salad. Then, we headed home. After I had driven for an hour, my dad spotted a small picnic park that had a view of a golf course. We laid out the bottle of red wine and all the food we had bought.

"Such a nice golf course!" my dad said, opening the wine with his newly purchased Swiss Army knife.

I felt gratified and relaxed eating fresh food under the cool shade of a spreading oak tree, knowing that my parents had enjoyed their trip to

Canada. As we packed up the food, my dad started to put the wine back in the sack.

"Dad! You can't bring the bottle of wine back to the U.S! Especially an opened one. Sorry, I didn't think of the customs when you bought it," I said.

"I didn't even drink a full cup," he protested, clearly disappointed.

So, reluctantly, I hid the remaining wine in the back corner of the trunk. I was nervous when we reached customs, but luckily the officer didn't even check the trunk. He let us go through with a smile.

The calendar turned to October. As my parents returned to Japan after spending a whole month, the weather suddenly changed. Even when days started out sunny and clear, they soon turned dark and cloudy. At times, a shaft of rain in the distance told me to run, but at other times, heavy raindrops landed on my face without any warning. Soon the brighter colors of nature faded away, and the earth became leaden and gloomy. It wasn't like October in California, where the sky was suffused with sunlight and it stayed nice all day.

I had hoped the weather would not affect my mood much, but in fact it did. I told myself, *I'm gonna find a job, before I get seriously depressed.* Job opportunities for me were much fewer than in California, but I had some good leads. One of Thomas's friends who worked at Microsoft helped me get my foot in the door there. After a telephone interview, I was invited for personal interviews.

The weather on the interview day wasn't bad for October—at least it didn't rain—but it had already gotten noticeably colder. I was to meet three interviewers on one day, but at different sites. A minibus running around the Microsoft campus would take me to the places I needed to be. The interviews were set for the afternoon, but first I needed to go to personnel for some procedures. The personnel supervisor, a very business-like young lady, gave me some instructions, and then handed me a free lunch ticket.

The interviews went nicely; as a matter of fact, at one point I believed I would get the software localization position (this work is to create technical illustrations for manuals in which the text can easily be changed to a non-English language.) But this hope was dashed by the third interviewer who asked me, "Why don't you have a college degree?"

In my head, I said, *I do have an associate degree. I know it would be better to have a four-year degree, but I didn't have a chance to stay in one place long enough to finish one.*

That was my head talking. What I said was, "Well . . . I don't have a four-year degree, but I'm very capable and can learn pretty quickly."

She didn't respond to my answer and instead stared at my resume in amazement, and then said, "So, why did you move so many places?"

I quickly answered, "Yes, indeed I have moved to many different places, but this time we plan to stay in Washington. Actually we are going to buy a house soon."

Of course my replies didn't satisfy her, and I could see the subtle change in her behavior.

Her smiles became forced, and she soon ended our interview. I knew I wouldn't get the job.

Once I was alone in my car, driving toward home, the anger surged up. "Why can't I have a college degree? Why can't I stay in one place? Why can't he keep his job?" I shouted out loud, squeezing the steering wheel hard. Suddenly, I heard a popping sound. Big hailstones started hitting the windshield as if they wanted to kill my feelings.

From the time the weather changed in the winter, we had bad luck. I remember the worst day: we went to the Washington Zoo, but for some reason we didn't enter. Maybe the zoo wasn't open, or we changed our minds, but whatever the reason, we didn't go in. We were upset over something. I don't recall the cause of the argument. Perhaps the argument was just signs of our misery. We were both unhappy in Seattle. I wasn't happy because I was unemployed. Thomas himself was struggling in his oil painting. Perhaps he wasn't doing well at his work. In any case, his rebukes of me steadily increased. I was uncomfortable being in the car because he deliberately showed his anger in his way of driving. I became more and more agitated watching the brake lights in front of us, turning on and off on the traffic-jammed highway. He suddenly slammed on the brake, but it was too late and he hit the car in front of us. The accident wasn't as bad as it looked, but the sound was deafening because of the deployment of the airbags. The pieces of glass that shattered over the front seats cut the skin on our arms. His frantic behavior changed its course and he became sympathetic. The accident was relatively minor, but clearly Seattle's melancholy weather was getting on our nerves.

We stopped taking walks, and in general, went out less. Thomas spent a lot of time painting. I saw his struggles in painting as well as in programming; however, painting absorbed his emotions. He didn't talk much, and he didn't need to explain things to me, as his painting wasn't abstract. Once he started painting I wasn't to interrupt him until he finished his session. But strangely, even when he could have spared some time to do something fun with me, he didn't. We didn't play our favorite games—Monopoly, Scrabble, SimCity, or Mahjong. He seemed to retire into himself and I became mute. My life was blunt and aimless—no job, no kids— and the cats weren't really playmates.

Feeling lonely and empty, I kept looking for a job. In February, I finally found an opportunity to become an international flight attendant. In less than a week, I needed to fly to Minneapolis, Minnesota for the six-week training. The employment contract was for me to be stationed in Detroit for the first year. I wasn't sure about being away from Thomas for one year, but flying to Japan was particularly appealing. Thomas couldn't say "no" to me, but I could tell from his sad eyes how unhappy he was. A few days after this job news, Thomas lost his job. Our situation worsened. Even if he didn't have any prospective job, the premise was we would move somewhere else. We needed to pack up our belongings. For a few days before flying, I stayed up very late to finish packing.

On the day of my flight to Minneapolis, I was tired, feeling the strain in all my muscles. It was sad to part from Thomas, but not knowing our future made me uneasy. Another reason for my fatigue, I thought, was that I had been taking a blood tonic to pass the medical exam for becoming a flight attendant. But I seriously doubted the tonic had sapped my energy. Six years before when I was in Texas, I had tried to do the same thing with a different airline, but failed because my blood cell counts were too low. I didn't fail this time. Carrying a load of concerns, I flew to Minnesota.

February in Minneapolis was cold and dry. After taking a bus from the Minneapolis airport, I followed the company's directions to a huge apartment complex. So cold was the air that it gave me earaches. While heading to the apartment office, I saw many candidates drifting in the same direction, rolling their heavy suitcases. Four o'clock was our meeting time, and when I entered the large conference room it was already filled with many attractive people. After the orientation, we were assigned to our rooms. My roommate was a young, petite Chinese lady whose round face was charming when she smiled.

Our living conditions were reasonable. A large grocery store was about a twenty-minute walk away, and the metro buses ran frequently;

nothing would inconvenience us during the six weeks. The instructors and trainees were all friendly, but being away from Thomas and worrying about our future, I was constantly distressed. I was losing weight, perhaps falling below the minimum weight requirement. I lost my appetite, and I noticed myself becoming physically weaker. I had a hard time opening the emergency doors of the aircraft. I remember I heard people shouting at me, "Kumiko push hard . . . hard!"

In the fourth week, all the measurements for making our uniforms were taken, and by the fifth week, our uniforms were ready to pick up. But then I failed one of the last tests a week prior to graduation. I became severely ill from drinking water with old ice cubes that had not been replaced for months. The water smelled bad, but I emptied the glass in a gulp. I believed that my roommate, who was constantly drinking ice water, had changed the ice frequently, but she said she had only been replacing one tray. I woke up in the middle of the night vomiting, and had diarrhea throughout the night, but had to take the test the next morning. Dehydration almost paralyzed my internal organs, brain and body. I took the test, but I couldn't even finish; I needed to run to a restroom. I could have retaken it, but I was too weak to focus, or even to walk.

It was a total disaster not to be able to complete the program, and I returned to Seattle to an empty nest. When I stepped inside, the house looked hollow and deserted, which made me feel even sadder. Thomas had gone to Oregon. The cats were gone, too. I cannot recall what happened immediately after that deserted feeling hit me. All I remember now is that Thomas took me to Victoria to console me. He even booked a suite at the Fairmont Empress Hotel. After coming back from Canada, we left Seattle to move to Oregon.

IX

Portland Oregon
New Turn in My life

At the end of April, we moved to Portland, Oregon. The short three-hour drive to Portland from Redmond didn't impact me. In fact, I felt like we were taking a daytrip. The scenery along Interstate 5 was no different than what I had seen coming north a year before. But one image that had printed itself in my mind during our move from San Francisco to Seattle brought on an odd feeling this time when we drove past it. It was an old railroad bridge on a hillside along I-5. Which state it was in I couldn't determine, but when I saw it again while moving back south, it gave me a strange feeling, like I was moving backward, a notable moment of confusion. When we arrived in Portland, it was late afternoon. My first impression was that the downtown looked clean and neatly designed. This not-so-big city provided me some sort of comfort. I couldn't know what kind of future it would bring to me; even so, the energy I felt at that moment was pleasant.

We stayed at the Mark Spencer Hotel in downtown Portland for a little over a week, until we found our new home. Thomas had already started working at a software company in Northwest Portland, and I was alone in the hotel room with two cats. I was glad Mickey and Rosie could see pedestrians and cars passing by from our fifth-floor room; I thought that would entertain them. Looking at their furry backs, I wondered what was in those little minds. Cats are place-oriented and moving can be quite traumatic for them. Maybe they had gotten used to it.

During that week of hotel life, I spent most of my time roaming around downtown. Pioneer Courthouse Square, located in the heart of downtown, was within easy access of the hotel. The majority of the time, I enjoyed lounging over coffee at the Café in the Nordstrom department store that stood across the street from the Square. The Café had comfortable chairs and sofas and it didn't generally get crowded with shoppers on weekdays. Even better, they served American coffee with free refills, so I could drink as many cups as I wanted and sit restfully on a sofa for a long time, undisturbed.

I had a "Kodak moment" taking in the view from the café located on the third floor; it burnt into my memory. Under a dark leaden sky, the old county courthouse and shops around the Square looked gloomy in contrast with the cozy amber lights inside. My mind was addled, but I didn't entertain worrying thoughts. I just tried, unsuccessfully, to imagine my future. I guess my mind was as cloudy as the sky.

Thomas and I looked for our new home. As always, he listened to me regardless of our realtor's strong recommendations. I have no memory of arguing over this matter. The agent was concerned that the condo we decided to rent could be leased for only two years or less. I didn't worry because two years was too far away to think about, as our lives had been so unsettled.

The small but clean two-story condo with a petite front yard and tiny closed-in concrete backyard was just perfect for us; the location was most suitable, and the milieu, I thought, would influence us positively, hemmed in as the condominiums were by the Willamette River and the West Hills. I thought the circumstances would set our new life in Portland off to a nice start.

Our neighborhood was favorable for walking. There was a long walking trail along the Willamette River to Willamette Park. It was quite scenic, and Thomas and I delighted in sauntering along the river after dinner. The cats, too, loved our neighborhood. To most people, carrying cats around in one's arms might seem absurd, but for reasons of cleanliness and to keep them free from fleas that they might pick up from the ground, we had kept up this custom since they were eight weeks old. We didn't take them on our usual walking path, just for a few blocks around our neighborhood. We liked holding our cats, and the cats seemed to be luxuriating in our arms. Our neighbors smiled when they passed us; who knows what they thought about us carrying cats whose noses were sticking upward, ears up, eyes wide open, glancing at all the objects they encountered, observing everything serenely from our arms.

Since I didn't look for a job immediately, Thomas encouraged me to start painting in oils. His earnest wish was to see me happy, despite the fact that he was the one who was creating all the perplexities in my life. At any rate, oil painting, which I had always wanted to try but never had, intrigued me. He bought me a steel easel, allowed me to use his painting supplies, and showed me some basic steps in applying layers of paint. I had always liked watercolor painting in my school days, from elementary through high school. Oil painting is fixable and not like watercolor, so I liked the practicality, but it was time consuming. Mixing colors to create realistic hues was a trial-and-error process but a fun challenge. The hardest part for me was applying more light in order to make contrasts.

I worked on three paintings. The first one was a simple mountain with a moon in twilight. The second was a landscape, with a Japanese persimmon tree in the foreground and an old barn somewhere in the middle ground, encompassed by a field of rice paddies. The third was a young lady in a cream colored, tea-length ballerina dress made of yellow satin, with a half-slip crinoline. The first one was a practice painting, for me to understand and feel the texture of the oil and pigments; I pretty much followed Thomas's guidance. In the second one, I put my emotions into the painting, as the landscape itself brought me nostalgic feelings of a Japanese autumn country scene. I liked it the best. For the third, I measured the parts of the body, trying to understand anatomical balance, and painted with as much accuracy as I could at my level of understanding. I must have gotten some talent from my dad who was an artisan, for I received compliments and the painting was used in a calendar at my workplace later. My oil painting ended after only about a month, when Thomas asked for my help on his company project. *So much for that!* Perhaps he sensed the agitation and guilt I felt when I wasn't working.

It was toward the end of July, while taking our evening walk, when Thomas made his request.

"Are you interested in creating fonts? At work, we need someone to create Arial fonts. I think you can do it," he asked.

"Hmm . . . I don't think I can do it. I don't have that knowledge." I said.

"Hey! It's not that difficult. Come to my office. Peter will show you. He is a programmer and he needs the work. He is a sweet guy," he said, as if the job was as easy as painting a wall.

The project was to create Arial fonts for the Macintosh by converting the PC version. For someone who had neither knowledge nor interest in creating fonts, it was a lot to be entrusted with. Nonetheless, Thomas eagerly pushed me. I hated it because he always measured things using his own yardstick. I had never met anyone that self-confident.

Thomas was all self-discipline. He had been a self-taught learner since childhood. Once his aunt Dona told me that he was a solitary child. He had a study room in her house where he examined insects he had collected. She told me sweetly, "Thomas didn't come for dinner, no matter how many times I called him. The stubborn kid stayed there till late evening." His love of learning remained and his openhearted curiosity and passion for knowledge amused him. But what he didn't understand was that others didn't necessarily share his enthusiasm, and he couldn't compel them to have the same passion or expectations for perfection.

I hated when he pushed me to do something I didn't feel comfortable doing, but I hated to say, "I really can't," when faced with a challenge. Since I never clearly said, "No!" to him, he installed a font editing software, Fontographer. He said, "You can take your time. Why don't you try?" But soon I learned they were expecting me to complete the whole set of fonts, 8, 10, 12 and the standard symbols, within two months.

The work was extremely tiring and it was an eye-aching job. Creating fonts requires that all the characters, numbers, and symbols have a precise height, width, and space so that they look well-proportioned on the printed page. In addition, the style of the fonts has to be consistent across all the characters, numbers, and symbols. Checking those spaces and constantly clicking the mouse button made my right arm numb. Also, looking at the screen so intensely without blinking for a long time caused a strobe sensation in both of my eyes. It took a while to get rid of this spasm. But finally, as I was expected to do, I finished this project and received two thousand dollars. Total.

I realized I would be better off if I had a job, but before committing to one, I wanted to visit my family. Once I started a job, taking a long vacation would not be easy. I hadn't been to Tokyo for three years.

September was a good time to visit Japan. Air tickets were less expensive and moreover I would enjoy *kouyou* (autumn leaves). The Japanese admire *kouyou* just as they admire cherry blossoms in spring.

One night over dinner, I blurted out, "I want to go to Japan."

Thomas didn't answer right away. He spent several minutes pushing fish bones to the side of his plate with his chopstick. I stared at him. When he raised his head, he said "Okay." The next day I bought my ticket, and departed in the middle of September for a three-week trip.

I was stunned by how much Tokyo had changed again in three short years. I found the city too hectic, the Japanese girls too fashionable and superficial. On one occasion, my youngest niece, who was nine years old at the time, stopped me when we were going out.

She criticized me saying, "Auntie Kumi, Japanese people don't dress like that. Your black pants are faded and look worn out. Your white shirt also looks a little worn out."

"Wait! I look decent. But why do I have to be bothered by you about what I wear!"

"Then I don't want to walk with you," she responded with a disgusted look.

"Fine, then don't walk with me," I said.

She puzzled for a while, then requested, with a better attitude, "Please, change clothes and look nice for me."

Another time, my older niece, Aki, told me that my makeup was a bit old-woman looking because my eyebrows were not lined nicely; she thinned them, but while plucking, she mentioned that my bra was sagging and wobbled to and fro and didn't give a slim appearance. *My word* I thought, but my sister-in-law, Masako, agreed with Aki, who was just fourteen at that time.

Focusing on how I looked took extra energy. I didn't want to spend money or time on such vanities, but I did try to look nice while I was in Japan. I guess I had become too practical and placed less value on those things. In my childhood, my mind was culturally programmed to be a follower, to not stand out, but the longer I lived in the U.S., the more I felt I didn't want to worry about how others saw me. I didn't want to look like everyone else.

Two weeks had passed since I had left for Tokyo when Thomas decided to join me. His decision was a total surprise. He called me back a half-hour after I had spoken to him.

"Your tone of voice didn't sound good on the phone," he said. "I was worried about you. Are you all right?"

"Yes, I'm fine. I just miss you."

"Me too . . . I decided to come over to join you. I'll be getting my ticket Monday, first thing in the morning," he added.

"How about your work?" I asked.

"I'm gonna take a week off," he said, as if he was taking a day off.

I started wondering what had really made him worry. I had said, "I'm missing you a lot." *Did I sound so sad?*

Surprised by his quick decision, frankly I didn't know how to respond, though I didn't think his decision was rational, considering our finances. I didn't try to change his mind. While pondering these thoughts, I recalled what he had said when I returned from the flight attendant training. He said, "I cried when you were in Minneapolis." *Well . . . it will be fun to travel with him.* Suddenly, I missed him more than I had a few minutes before, and forgot about my worries.

Thomas appeared at Narita Airport in high spirits. My plans changed because of his surprise visit. I spent less time with my family and more time going out with Thomas. As my parents urged us to go out, we went to Nikko for a one-night trip. It is a historical site in a region of mountains, gorges, and lakes, where many famous shrines and old temples are found.

In Nikko, we visited one of the most famous shrines, Tosho-gu, which was dedicated to Minamoto-no-Yoritomo, Toyotomi Hideyoshi and Tokugawa Iyeyasu as "gods of samurai (warriors)." The path to the shrine was lined with old stone lanterns engraved with names. Encircled by cedar trees, planted in around 1600, the shrine compound was austere. There were a number of open-air stalls on both sides of the path as part of the fall festival. White smoke drifted from a booth in the distance, carrying the sweet aroma of grilled squid with teriyaki sauce. Thomas shut his eyes and tried to take in the sweet smell. I threw a glance at him.

We looked at each other, and said in unison, "Let's get one."

We bought two. Holding the squid on a skewer, he looked happy. Sometimes he seemed more Japanese than me.

When we reached the *Yomeimon* gate of the Toshogu shrine (built between 1617 – 1636), the awe-inspiring wood carvings covering the building magnetized our attention. Human figures with colorful painted-on kimono were carved across the lintel of the gate, and through the telephoto lens we could see the details of the carving. Thomas took many pictures of those men. He loved temples and shrines. I was glad he appreciated the good points of Japan.

Returning from the Tokyo trip in the middle of October, I promptly looked for a job using a temporary employment agency. They quickly found me a part-time position as an assistant administrator with a microelectronics company. I was enjoying working, when six months later, a rumor of a mass layoff spread through the company, and I became concerned about my position. *Here we go.* Just before the Portland Rose Festival in June, I was called to the general manager's office. Mr. Izumi's expression was grave.

He first asked me to have a seat, and then looked at me apologetically.

"I'm sorry that we need to let you go. But we will call you back when we hire in the future," he said, and then deeply bowed his head as if I were his superior officer. This wasn't a normal scene you would see in Japan. I was astounded.

Bowing in Japan is customary, but how we bow is complicated. There are two variables to the bowing: how deep you bow and how long you bow. The informal bow is bowing down about fifteen degrees with the hands at the sides. This bow is used for casual occasions for all ranks. The formal bow is typically used in business. It is twice as deep with palms faced down on the knees or on the sides and held for a few seconds. There are additional bows performed based on the situation. But formality is important and acknowledging the hierarchy is even more so. Typically the person of the lower rank begins to bow first, bows deep, and rises only after the person of the higher rank is upright. In this situation, Mr. Izumi being the highest rank in the plant bowed to me, the lowest rank. Quite honestly I didn't know how to respond, so I stood up, hands on the knees, and did a forty-five degree bend for fifteen seconds.

In March, nine months after being laid off, I was rehired as a translator at the same company. I was thrilled, but nervous, as I had to take three days of training to learn the names of the chemicals and hazardous materials, and then pass a test on them. I sweated the necessity of passing tests. In the class, I met Yasuko. We bonded instantly. In all those years living in the U.S., I had never found a friend to whom I could relate and with whom I could enjoy close companionship, until I met her. I liked her. She was in her mid-thirties at that time. Her long black hair had some gray already, which made her look a little older than her age, but she was sincere and naturally attractive. Her thoughts were often deep and rational, which I liked about her. We had lunch and breaks together. We even talked after work. I had forgotten how good it was to have a close friend. Our friendship doubled my joys and I felt good about myself.

The work was stimulating. Interpreting requires guts and spontaneity, along with skill in the language, not to mention there must be good chemistry between workers and interpreters. I found it interesting to see myself acting differently when I was translating. Being quick enough on my feet to work with those engineers, who had time constraints for all their projects, wasn't my normal behavior. I often heard my inner voice asking me how I could possibly act like that. I frankly amazed myself, but doing interpreting automatically reset my mind and attitude. I had to be beyond all sense of fear of making mistakes.

One incident I still remember was when a highly-positioned engineer who had just arrived a few days before got upset with my way of doing interpreting. He was concerned about the efficacy of my communication.

"Can't you change the tone of your voice? We are not happy about those contract workers. You should let them know how unhappy I am about their work," he said loudly.

Wakarimashita (understood), I said firmly.

Raising my voice a little higher, I continued working. In a half minute or so, he abruptly stopped me again.

"Look! Can't you talk like I do? Do this the same way I do when I talk to them."

The rising tension in the room silenced everyone. There were about ten workers in the room—half contractors and half engineers. I barely managed to finish the meeting.

My work was demanding and sometimes rattled me.

In the spring of 1997, the owners of our condo returned home as planned. Two years had flown by very fast, and we needed to find a new home. Luckily, moving was easy for us this time, as we found a condo to rent only a few blocks away. For the whole third week of April, every night after dinner, Thomas and I lugged boxes to the new place. The following Sunday was the last day we had to finish up our moving. The temperature reached eighty degrees by early afternoon, and the breeze was refreshing. From a window on the second floor of the new house, I could see Thomas busily pulling a hand truck piled high with boxes. *Wow, he's been working hard*, I thought. For a while, I watched him toiling with the heavy boxes, but soon I started feeling a little bit of a squeeze in my chest. I disliked myself for not being able to help as much as I wanted to, but I needed to prepare for a three-hour safety protocol interpretation that I was expected to do on Monday.

Maybe I should help him more, I thought for a second. But soon another thought erased that idea: *But why? Why do I always have to be inconvenienced? I really want to prepare for this work. I need time, plenty of time,* I grumbled to myself. I knew that this time he had done nothing wrong; from the beginning we had agreed on the two-year rental contract. I buried my face in my hands and paced in a circle by the window, thinking about all the moving we had done in the fifteen years of our marriage. I finally sat down at my desk and stared at the notebook covered with scribbled words—words that I had to translate—*particles per cubic meter, clean room environment, carbon dioxide.* I couldn't concentrate. Thomas didn't complain, and he carried most of our remaining stuff into our new house alone.

Thomas was happy for me that I had found work I really liked. He even seemed all right with my doing extra work for the company. But when I began going to work every Saturday, he finally expressed his complaint.

One night over dinner he brought up the subject. "Does Yasuko work every weekend? Who else works on weekends?"

"Does that bother you?" I asked.

"We don't spend much time together lately," he said.

"I know, but this job . . . I really want to take this job seriously," I said, but immediately I felt angry. I continued fretfully, "I want to pursue some profession. You know, I have *never* been able to hold any job because of our always moving!"

I dropped my eyes. When I raised my head, I saw the startled look on his face.

"I'm very sorry you've had a hard time living with me." He shifted his eyes away as if he was looking for words. We ate in silence for some time.

"You know, Kumiko, your birthday is coming soon," he finally said. Then, a few seconds later, he added, "You'll like my gift for your birthday."

He secretively started shopping around a few weeks before my birthday, May 25th.

The day before my birthday, Thomas took me to "our" sushi restaurant, Sushi Land, where the plates with sushi were rotated in a circle by a conveyer belt. We sat at the counter. While eating, Thomas abruptly asked a funny question to an old couple sitting next to him.

"How long have you been together?" he asked.

"Well . . . almost twenty-five years," the wife answered.

"Wow . . . a long time. It's very admirable," he said.

Thomas seemed to be very impressed. *What was that about?* I thought, but I didn't question and only wondered. After dinner, he stopped by Zupan's market to buy me a carrot cake and a sunflower bouquet.

The next morning, when we were about to eat breakfast, he placed a small box wrapped in silver paper in front of me.

"Happy Birthday!" he said.

"Ummm, what is it?" I asked, my eyes shining, though I knew what it was from the size of the box.

"Open it," he said, raising his chin up with a grin.

"Oh, my God! It's beautiful!" I smiled and said, slipping the sparkling emerald and diamond ring onto my finger on top of the wedding band, then thanked him with a deeply sincere look.

"Glad you like it." He gave me a big smile.

But, strangely, his happy expression began to disappear as the day went on. Around four o'clock, he took me to a restaurant. He had always reserved a nice restaurant for my birthday dinner, but he hadn't made a reservation this time. I was puzzled, especially because four o'clock was too early for dinner. Because it was too early, the nice restaurants weren't open yet, so we picked one that was open, which wasn't special at all. Another surprise was Thomas didn't order dinner for himself. He didn't even order a drink. He just watched me eat. It was most peculiar behavior for him, and bothered me a great deal, but I didn't know what to think of it. He appeared emotionally distant, and seemed disengaged from the moment. I didn't know if I was happy or not any longer.

X

Turbulence

I started feeling a sense of disconnection from Thomas after my birthday. I couldn't tell what was making me feel like that. The strange feeling welling up inside me must have made me become more alert. One evening soon after my birthday, he went to our bedroom. He bent slightly to reach his drawer under the bed. Standing in the hallway, I caught his intense eyes as he glanced over his shoulder, and I detected something odd in his look—it was very subtle, but noticeable enough to make me feel like I needed to find out why he had acted like that: his treasure drawer also stored condoms.

The next morning I woke up about a half-hour earlier than the usual time. I first glanced at him to see if he was asleep, then slipped off the bed, and tiptoed into our office. As I was strongly driven to follow my urge, I looked around his computer desk. I soon laid my eyes on his black Tumi briefcase with lots of organizer pockets that was placed under his desk. I hastily unzipped those pockets, searching for something—I didn't even know what I was looking for. "Bingo!" I was amazed at my keen instinct. I found a love letter from a lady, gushing over how smart and gorgeous he was, and blah, blah, blah. The ultimate words, *You are finally mine*, made me black with anger.

I didn't know what to think, but I ran into the bedroom. In a shaky voice I demanded, "What is this letter?"

Thomas responded in a calm voice, "Go to work! I'll explain when you get home."

My body was shaking and became suddenly heavy. Walking out of the house was tremendously hard, and felt exactly like I was leaving my heart behind. I didn't want to leave the house until I got some answers. The train of thoughts unleashed by the letter nauseated me and unfamiliar feelings rushed in. At the office, it was strange how my brain was totally engaged with the work, but my emotions were mixed up and disordered. When my free times of lunch, break, and bathroom breaks came, the thoughts of his affair assailed me; I sobbed in the bathroom.

Thomas came home about the same time I did, and we went to a restaurant, Papa Haydn's. He didn't get emotional and, as a matter of fact, he seemed very much disconnected. I keenly observed his behaviors. His eyes weren't really looking at me, and he showed clear signs of discomfort when I asked questions about what was happening between us and what I was facing.

Out of despair I said, "If this was just an affair, I am okay with that, but you have to stop doing what you are doing." I continued, "You know, I can forget and forgive you."

There was a silent moment, and then he finally spoke. "We'll be fine. Don't worry." And then he cast a quick glance down onto the dining table.

"Are you sure? Can I believe in you?" I questioned. He didn't say a word, but lightly nodded.

I believed we would be all right, but things started quickly changing, and the distance between us widened. His girlfriend called every day. *What a witch!* Every day I sensed differences in him, and his kindness and our togetherness diminished. My intuition and awareness became very acute, and my senses were on alert twenty-four hours a day. I couldn't sleep nights for the sickening thoughts that ran through my mind.

On a Friday, three weeks after the revelation of his affair, when I came home, Thomas wasn't home yet. Suddenly, I was agitated and felt driven to look for any evidence pertaining to his affair. I started roaming around, thinking, *What am I looking for? I don't know.* I looked around the house, bright with sunlight shining through the skylights. I felt like a thief whose mind was on finding valuable things while the owner was absent. *I need to find something concrete, to understand what he is up to, or to beat him at the game he is playing.*

To begin, I approached the tall, oak cabinet that stood in our living room downstairs. Opening the heavy middle drawer, I glanced through the files that Thomas had organized by categories. They were tightly packed, and what I was doing suddenly seemed almost ridiculous. But any second thoughts flew away when I saw a brown, spick-and-span envelope slightly sticking out. *What is that?* I yanked it out from the cabinet. At first, I couldn't comprehend the bunch of official papers, but I composed myself with a deep breath and focused on the letters on the pages. The pages had numbers to the left side of each line—with which I was unfamiliar—but I saw the words, *Petitioner: Thomas,* and *Respondent: Kumiko,* on the first page, then, further down, words explaining that the marriage was irreconcilable.

Irreconcilable! My eyes fell on this word. *How was it possible that he could say our relationship was irreconcilable? I didn't even know our relationship was bad.* Then I realized that this was a divorce petition. My body started trembling; I could see my right hand shaking. I lost my mind. I felt the whole world become silent for the moment. But soon I came back to my senses. I had scarcely managed to tear up the decree when Thomas arrived home. He was furious, and told me how expensive it would be to reissue those papers. I was dumbfounded that he was already proceeding to end our relationship. At this point, I realized it was futile to try to persuade him not to leave me.

The war began between us. On Saturday, I couldn't think of anything but his girlfriend. *Who is his woman?* I badly wanted to know who his girlfriend was. I was baffled all day. Later in the evening, a thought came into my mind: *Maybe that saleslady who worked at the jewelry shop in the department store!* Thomas had taken me there to resize my ring.

I remembered what the saleslady had said while measuring my finger. She snapped, "You guys go somewhere else after this? Don't be around here," looking directly into Thomas's eyes. Because of the way she looked at him, I had felt weird. Why did she have to be bothered about where we were? I thought this could be a hint that she might be the one.

The next day, I waited for Thomas to leave the house. Around noon, he finally put down his oil painting brush and went upstairs. He dressed up neatly, and left the house. Ten minutes or so after he had left, I pulled my car from the garage. I drove down to the mall. After parking at the west side of the mall, I scuttled inside the building, snaking my way through the crowd of shoppers and keeping an eye out for Thomas.

I entered the department store and stopped a few aisles away from the jewelry counters. Much to my consternation, I saw them, standing across the jewelry showcase from each other, talking like lovers do. Resting her arms on the showcase, she leaned over flirtatiously, exposing her cleavage from her low-cut blouse. *Sinister bitch! She stole my husband!* I watched them until I felt sick, then left there in despair, and quickened my pace to my car. Once inside, I shut my eyes for a while, and rested my head on the steering wheel. *Damn it! How did this happen?* Exasperating and nauseating thoughts circled in my head, and I realized I needed to be tough to get through this mess. I floored the gas pedal and drove away.

Soon after I had discovered his girlfriend, I rummaged through Thomas's desk, hoping to find her home telephone number. In his notebook, I found the number. Thomas parenthesized her jewelry shop name and its' number next to her name and her home number. I waited till a Sunday afternoon to call her house when she would be at the department store, so as to talk to her husband. Her husband answered.

As I heard a male voice, I said angrily, "Your wife and my husband are having an affair. Your wife stole my husband."

His gruff voice reached my ear after a moment of silence.

"Who are you? What the hell are you talking about?" he shouted.

I abruptly hung up the phone. I believed that would cause some big friction in their marriage.

Thomas frantically convinced me not to have my own attorney, saying things like how profligate it was to have another attorney. (Ironically, he later paid the attorney fees for his girlfriend, who was married and had a son, to go through her divorce.) He kept saying that he still loved me. It was incomprehensible to me that a person could love two people at the same time. What an insolent, injudicious, egotistic and cruel thing to say to a person whose mind was totally deranged. Such nonsensical statements tore my heart to ribbons.

He was willing to give me the money we had in our savings, but in the beginning he was unwilling to pay alimony. *Communication breakdown!* His mind was pretty much on his girlfriend, who constantly called and disturbed our situation. *Could she already have been his fiancée?* I doubted it, although his concern was all for her; whatever he allowed for me was just the minimum obligation to the person with whom he had spent fifteen years.

Nights were awful. Sleeping with an iceberg was torture. Food couldn't go through my gullet; the valve seemed closed to anything except liquids. Surprisingly though, my head was clear and functional. My boss in the translation department, Eiko, showed me tremendous empathy and tried to support me in many ways—offering her house for me to stay in during this time of turmoil, thinking of my safety, taking me to a cafeteria to console me, and giving me some liberty to do what I needed. She gave me full support, although she was well known to be rigorous and somewhat threatening to most of the engineers in the plant.

Every day I shrank more. The object in the bathroom mirror showed how I had lost weight terribly. My chest bones stuck out like a skeleton. Food wasn't on my mind. There were countless things I needed to mull over to prepare for the divorce. But the biggest disturbances were the constant calls from his girlfriend. She grated on my nerves.

One day, soon after I discovered his affair, Thomas told me the story of how the affair had started. He said, "She discounted five-hundred dollars on your ring. Quite honestly, I didn't know what to do about it. So I joked about taking her to lunch, and she took it seriously."

I curtly asked, "What did you guys talk about?" trying to elicit some clues that might explain to me what was going on between them.

"She said she had some issues with her husband," he answered bluntly.

Indeed his girlfriend was evil. She started keeping her dress in my closet before I had even gotten out of the house. My heart was wrenched by the force of two people's ill treatment. My life went into a dark age. Thomas's parents were one-hundred percent on my side, and tried to convince me to have my own attorney at their expense, an offer which I kindly refused. Fighting was not my nature. Perhaps, it might have been the non-confrontational character of Japanese, who abhor lawsuits. Along with this propensity, I didn't want to make Thomas my enemy, since I was alone in this country, so I avoided litigation. However, I needed to make an adequate settlement to start my life without a partner. Although I didn't hire an attorney, I did ask for consultation to go over the tentative divorce decree.

As I drove to the attorney's office to make my four o'clock appointment, Route I-84 was already crowded with early commuters, but traffic still flowed as fast as usual. My mind was half-occupied with thoughts of this consultation and half-focused on not causing any accidents. Driving in downtown was not my *forte*, and finding the right address and a parking spot took some nerve, actually a lot, but I arrived at the office on time in a state of adrenaline rush.

When I opened the office door, I saw a lady typing at the front desk. After asking my name, she told me to wait in the attorney's office, pointing her finger straight at a little secluded room. In the small, dimly-lit room, the attorney's mahogany desk and a tall bookcase of law books stood gravely. When I sat down at the heavy desk, I felt the weight of the matter which I was about to discuss.

As the attorney entered the room, she turned on the lights. Without any warm-up conversation, she started on her work. Perhaps she didn't want to charge me unnecessarily, by taking time to sympathize with my situation. In a businesslike manner, she answered all the questions I could think of for this first visit, and agreed to read the final divorce decree, in order to determine if it was in my best interest.

It was past five o'clock when I left the office. The sidewalk was a shadowy valley between towering buildings and brightly lit shop windows. No bright thoughts flowed into my mind; all were dismal and sad. Tears rolled down my cheeks. *This winter will be a lot colder than any other winter I can remember.* The slightly chill winds felt like fall.

I needed to move out of the house. I had difficulty in finding a place that would be safe and comfortable, and of course, inexpensive. On weekends, I drove for many miles to look at apartments and communal houses listed in the newspaper. When I saw the filthy or sunless places, bleak thoughts of the future daunted me. It was scary, for in fact I had never in my whole life lived by myself.

One Sunday afternoon, I hit on the idea of getting rid of extra clothes. *I don't need them. I don't need the memories. I can't carry them all with me anyway.* Yanking them from their hangers, I piled dresses, coats, and suits on the floor, tossed them onto the back seat of the Honda, and drove off to find a commercial dumpster. I saw a big one behind a strip mall. I grabbed as many clothes as I could at one time and threw them into the dumpster. It took three trips from my car to the dumpster to unload them. Surprisingly, my attachment to those clothes wasn't great, yet the action itself made me sad for a while. I took a deep breath, and slowly let it out. When I slipped into my car, I felt lighter.

A recent acquaintance, Katherine, who herself had gone through a divorce, had mercy on me and offered me a dormer room in her house for three-hundred dollars. I decided to take it, although her casual arrangements—nothing was put in writing—worried me a little. My belongings were few: my computer, two desks, two mahogany end-tables given to me by my Dad, a floor lamp, pots and pans, some dishes. I had agreed in the divorce decree that Thomas could have all our furniture and other things and I kept money instead, thinking about going back to school. I minimized the things I needed in order to lighten my load. In that way, I thought it would be easier to move.

On a Saturday morning in mid-August, I moved out of our house. Moving didn't take much time, except for my heavy, wide computer desk, which Thomas had a hard time getting up the very narrow staircase of Katherine's house. My dormer room was large enough to give me plenty of breathing space, even with my furniture adding to her bed and dressers, which were there for me to use. The only inconvenience was the tiny amount of food storage space Katherine had set aside for me, as her food filled up the refrigerator and cupboard.

Cooking was difficult. I minimized my use of the kitchen, and nibbled lots of junk food in my room. I acted as meek as a lamb and didn't use the living room much, just stayed in my room. My brand-new habit was listening to soft rock music on the radio and I let the music play faintly all the time.

Katherine showed some sympathy for my situation, and tried to alleviate my pain by telling me the story of her divorce. She was a quite attractive lady in her early forties, and it was terrible that her husband had gotten into an affair with her best friend.

One evening, soon after I moved into Katherine's house, she invited me for drinks on the patio. Her garden was filled with all sorts of brightly hued flowers: dahlias, petunias, hydrangeas, sunflowers and many more, which added charm to the old blue Victorian-style house. Katherine had just splashed the flowers, so the water droplets beading up on their petals, along with the evening summer breeze, made the surrounding air fresh. Although the sun was still strong, the patio umbrella made a shady retreat. Setting two glasses of iced lemonade on the table, she started the conversation.

"How are you doing?" she asked.

"Oh . . . okay."

"You know, when I separated from my husband, I couldn't stay home. I needed to go somewhere far away from the house, so I took a long journey for a few months," she said, reaching for her lemonade on the table.

"Ummm, is that right?" I murmured.

"It took three years to recover, and I cried buckets of tears," she said, as if that would be my doom too.

For a while, I was lost in her conversation. I thought buckets of tears would be a lot of crying.

Even in the midst of turmoil, Thomas and I were still talking to each other. He called me often. One late night soon after I had moved out of our house, he came to my new place and asked me to get in his car. In less than ten minutes, we were arguing. But even though we were so testy with each other, we frequently met. Katherine didn't like me meeting with Thomas. She often rejected his call and once drove him away when he had come over to see me. One evening, he came to the gate of Katherine's house to leave a tiny yellow post-it on the concrete staircase at the front entry. I spotted it when I came home from work. He invited me to dinner. It was crazy to meet him or even talk to him, but I couldn't reject him. I still loved him.

Katherine could be kind in some ways, but cold in others. A few weeks after that conversation, she told me to move out for two weeks because her friend was going to visit her. *She can't toss me out like that!* I thought. But what could I do? My best friend Yasuko had already gone back to Tokyo with her husband. I thought maybe I could ask my boss, Eiko, but that seemed like a bad idea since I was going to be leaving the company soon. I didn't have anyone to ask if I could stay in their home for two damn weeks.

A hotel? An inexpensive hotel might be a way, I thought. I calculated all the expenditures including meals for fourteen days. I punched the rough numbers into my calculator, but the sum was too high. A few days before I had to be out, I happened to see Thomas coming home from work. I reluctantly told Thomas I needed to find a place to stay for two weeks. He suggested I stay at his place. Although I had imagined his girlfriend would call him every night, I thought I could handle the situation for those weeks. I badly wanted to save money as I had already requested my transcripts from all the schools I had attended in order to enroll in Portland State University.

Of course, it wasn't easy. My feelings of attachment to the cats, Mickey and Rosy, and furniture we used to share, were real. The feeling of emptiness, not being able to own his heart that once had been mine, and having to act distant were unbearable. In the daytime, I was at work, so I wasn't tormented by familiar objects, but the nights were difficult, as Thomas and his new love talked every night on the phone. I often wondered how she was dealing with her husband, especially since I had called her house and told him of their affair.

After an abject two weeks, I returned to Katharine's house. It was an uneasy situation, especially as Katherine had treated me like a pawn in a chess game. She didn't even refund the money for two weeks. What I really didn't like about her was she even tried to control my personal affairs. She didn't want Thomas to call the house, which was understandable, but it wasn't her place to intervene.

I realized I needed a better environment and one further away from Thomas. I decided to find a place where I could be comfortable and feel free to cook. Before starting the 1997 fall quarter at Portland State, I found a new place, a communal house located on the east side of Portland. I felt good being away from the Johns Landing area. The new environment didn't trigger depressing thoughts.

Nonetheless, I had lots of unsettling dreams—all dark, disorienting, and chaotic. But one particular dream vividly imprinted its image in my head. In the dream, I was in a foreign country. Outside was utter darkness, but I quickly recognized that there were a number of stalls lined up like those in shopping arcades often seen in third world countries—places I had been to such as Amman and Cairo.

Naked light bulbs hung from each shop's ceiling, lighting up the foreign products. People bustled about, all black shadowy figures, and I was standing like an onlooker. I took this dream as a good sign simply because I saw some lights.

Every night, a series of images created by the fearful sensations in my mind emerged in my dreams, as if I were wriggling out of my miserable situation. I held intense jealousy towards Thomas and his woman and my subconscious desires and hopes mingled with fear for my future. Dream images haunted me without mercy. I tried to understand their meanings. In one strong dream, Thomas was growing a bunch of sunflowers in a dark barn. I said in my dream, "Wow, they are pretty!" But the second thought ensued, "How could sunflowers possibly survive in the dark?" I nonsensically reasoned that their relationship would not grow, and that soothed my ego.

XI

Back to School

My despondency and humiliation from the divorce made me realize how important it was to have the academic background I had always been earnestly seeking. "God mingles something of the balm of mercy, even in vials of the most corrosive woe." Charlotte Bronte's words in *Shirley* were my salvation from this devastating divorce which had ended fifteen years of marriage. Engrossing myself in schooling indeed nourished my soul. I, therefore, focused intensely on studying, but let my feelings come out when I wasn't studying, so that I could cry to my heart's content. This was my way of coping with divorce, but since some students I met at school, and also Thomas's parents, had been strongly recommending I have some sort of counseling, I finally decided to take their advice.

One day after school, I visited the PSU counseling service center. A young lady with an oriental look appeared in the room. Her tactless manner—perfunctory simile and focus on filling out the questioner in front of her instead of on me—led me to think she could be an intern. I had heard some counselors were students. I speculated, how could this pretty young lady—as a matter of fact, very attractive lady, with a sparkling diamond on her ring finger, obviously enjoying the best and happiest time of her life—possibly understand about the dissolution of my fifteen-year marriage?

When she asked exactly the same questions in the second session that she had asked in the first, I was discouraged from going back. The questions were not helping me. I was asked about why I didn't feel anger; she strongly believed I should feel ire. She urged me to release feelings of anger from my system in order to heal. I didn't feel anger, only sadness, profound sadness.

The method of healing she had learned was to release the anger. But my method, if I had one, was to avoid getting into those negative emotions, and I truly didn't want to feel hatred, resentment, or hostility toward Thomas. My counselor offered to prescribe Prozac or Paxil. I was dumbfounded that she so quickly urged me to take such strong medications. In any case, I didn't need them. I was the type of person who didn't take any pills unless a doctor strongly ordered me to.

Japanese say this word— *shikataganai*—which means "It cannot be helped," in order to maintain dignity in the face of an unavoidable tragedy or injustice, particularly when the circumstances are beyond their control. Japanese people tend not to blame, but to succumb, as many Japanese think blame won't do much good. This culturally-instilled mentality led me to think positively in order to live harmoniously. I badly wanted to accomplish something that could make me proud of myself, because my self-esteem was piteously low. Crying was actually helping me and cuddling my soul, like soft rain helps crops to grow.

There were other programs to support students at the university, and one of them was a mentor program for women returning to school. The school provided me a mentor, Alison, with whom I became good friends. She was, indeed, a great support in helping me to reestablish my life. On the first day I met Alison, we strolled on the school campus.

She said briskly, "You are my protégée. I mean I am your mentor, and I want you to feel comfortable talking to me. About the school system or anything..."

There was a pause. Alison then asked me gently, "Why did you come to this school?"

"Aaah... I am getting a divorce. I thought I needed an education," I answered.

"I'm sorry to hear that. Tell me if there is anything I can do for you," she said, turning her head to look into my face.

Leading a lonely life, I was greatly appreciative of her kind words. Not only did she show me compassion, but she also gave me the opportunity to become her friend.

Another good support was my friendly academic adviser. Her reliable information helped me select which classes to take. She had an affable personality, which charmed many students and a good knowledge of teachers and their classes. She strongly recommended I take only a few classes the first quarter to find out how much I could handle. Although I could start my junior year as an English major since my Japan credits were all accepted, I took a one-hundred level course, "Introduction to English Fiction," and a three-hundred level "Japanese Literature" class.

On the first day of my English Fiction class, I was apprehensive. I sat in the second row from the platform in the center of the class. Dr. Mariels was perhaps in his early fifties, a clean cut, tall, slightly bony man. He sat taciturnly at his desk, looking at us with wide eyes through his black-framed spectacles. His stern look was a bit intimidating.

Dr. Mariels always glanced at us unhurriedly from left to right and back again from right to left a few times before starting his class, to see who was there and who was not. He didn't take attendance. He always gave us reading assignments from the textbook and we reviewed the contents as a group, getting his philosophical input along with our classmates' viewpoints.

On the third day of class, he gave us a quiz with ten questions about symbolism, and I flunked. When I received my test back at the end of the class, my dream of going to school was blown away. *It's over! This is it! I cannot go to school!* The shock that my score was so low made me almost faint. I shivered with despair for a moment until an idea hit me. Pushing my resisting body from the desk to stand up, I brushed off my pride, and then rushed into Dr. Mariels' office to beg him to let me retake the test.

Dr. Mariels looked slightly bewildered, but noticing my desperate look, he spoke softly with compassion, "If you want to do that, then answer the same questions you missed and bring the test back to my office before ten tomorrow."

I responded, "Thank you very much. I will bring the answers back to you by tomorrow before ten." I bowed deeply.

He slowly bobbed his head a few times.

I did the best I could, trying to grab the last ray of hope. I returned to his office the next morning and handed the paper to him with an appreciative expression. He gave me a score of nine out of ten. After that, I strived to understand how to study with the help of my mentor, Alison.

School disciplined me with the order of its system—deadlines for assignments, requirements, and group projects, but it perfectly suited my new single life. Being busy was good for me, otherwise, I would have been too lonesome. Studying was a good diversion from dejection. Coping with divorce the first year, my mind operated in either an ON or

OFF mode. If I was not "ON", engaged with study, I was automatically in the mournful "OFF" mode. When I wasn't studying, I thought about happy times spent with Thomas. All selectively recalled memories jumped into my mind, and then all sorts of ill thoughts against his girlfriend ensued. I don't remember how many times I wished they were unhappy and prayed that Thomas would come back to me.

In the months after our divorce, I frequently questioned myself. Could I have saved our marriage? What could I have done better? Crying became a habit. Sometimes I didn't know if my tears or my thoughts set my mood. At times I didn't even know why I was crying, but I wailed to the point where my body couldn't lift its own weight, and I crashed onto the floor and gasped with rage.

My life changed completely. Without much cooking and cleaning to do, I had ample time. Having total control of my time and my money allowed me a great deal of freedom and at the same time cultivated independent thinking. Diligence, endurance, and frugality became virtues. My philosophy of life was to be alert, for whatever was ordained to happen would need to be coped with by prudent action. Carelessness became the most disagreeable word, because it was costly.

My communal house didn't provide me what the Japanese call a "sweet home," so I spent many hours in my second home, the PSU library. On the third floor, against the west window overlooking the soccer field, I sat at a desk that I called my favorite spot. The desk wasn't usually occupied, and its surroundings were quiet and deserted. I not only felt secure sitting in this, *my spot*, but also became attached to it. I could eat my lunch at this desk cautiously, and took a catnap when I felt like I needed one.

I flung myself into my studies in the library and minimized staying at my new home. My shoebox-size room had a single bed provided by the house owner, along with my only furniture, two desks. There was a tiny walk-in closet in which all my other belongings were stored with no space to spare. I didn't mind this Spartan lifestyle.

As a single woman, I had to manage all of my affairs alone, so I used my money wisely. I could have had a bit more luxurious living situation, but instead I chose to invest the money in my education. To me, my choice of living in this house made a lot of sense—it was convenient to school and to a grocery store. Also, the living conditions were comfortable enough for a student. I was fortunate to have a Japanese housemate, which was beneficial and less stressful than sharing with other foreigners for several reasons. Once in a while, my housemate and I shared Japanese food, but more importantly, having common ground on things such as hygiene habits (not wearing shoes inside the house), and manners (being sensitive to others), provided me some peace of mind.

As my sense of autonomy gradually increased, I realized that getting out of my marriage wasn't as horrible as I had envisioned. In fact, a liberty of consciousness slowly grew in me, brought out my adroitness, and started showing up in many ways. One day I realized the finish on my car needed some touch-up. So I went to a Honda dealer to buy the matched paint. Then, while touching up the spots, I saw the paint on the windshield wipers was peeling, so I fixed that too.

Much later on, while I was driving, I saw smoke coming from under the hood. I immediately parked my car on the side of the road. I smelled burning oil. The leaked oil covered the engine. I didn't take the car to an auto repair shop because I heard the service charge would be over three-hundred dollars. Through much testing, I finally found the problem. It was the oil cap that was not sealing tightly. I only paid twenty-five dollars to get a new cap. Those little car repairs, which I had never even thought of doing by myself before, buoyed my confidence.

Three seasons had passed since my divorce, and summer was on the way. Brighter days lifted my feelings a little. I reflected on the time I moved into this house. From my desk, every day I watched the maple tree in our neighbor's back yard. The tree brought me the seasonal emotions. Particularly, the first autumn after the divorce was the hardest time of my life. Seeing this old maple tree swing with the strong winds, the leaves parting from its branches, dancing and swirling into the atmosphere like confetti, made me sorrowful despite the vivid colors, bright yellow and red. If the purpose of life is to experience all sorts of feelings to understand this mundane world, I surely felt one—true pain. If I hadn't had enough compassion before, I developed more, for in going through this plight, I cultivated compassion for all life. I understood that, after all, we humans are vulnerable, things are changeable, and people need kindness.

School life had grown familiar by the fourth term, and life as a whole seemed to be more complete. Bit by bit, my sadness was fading away. My mind became engaged in school activities, and I aspired to finish college as quickly as possible. Boy, I was ambitious! In the first summer term, I took three classes: Internship, Art, and Geology. Without taking any prerequisites, I challenged three-hundred-level Art and Geology classes. Summer classes were intense. I immediately realized how hard it was to follow the Geology class without any previous knowledge. But, amazingly, the six students in that class were a tremendous help. Since I didn't have a basic knowledge of geology, they brought me some essential books. In the field trips, all my classmates were like my teachers, telling me what the names of shrubs, trees, and plants in the wetland were, or what the names of rocks in the basaltic volcanic filed were. With their support, I was able to get through the class, however, the three-hour final was daunting.

The Watercolor class was one of my unforgettable memories. I must have not read the syllabus for the class very well. One afternoon while waiting for the teacher before the class started, a young muscular African-American man, about medium height, entered our classroom and walked casually toward the center of the room. He was very amiable, and with no words, he started disrobing until he was completely nude. I was shocked, for I had never seen or expected to see a naked man in a public place. I nervously fidgeted until our teacher appeared. The teacher finally stepped inside, pronouncing placidly, "Peter, here, is our sketch-model. Our afternoon class will be doing a quick sketch." It was indeed quick, maybe ten or so minutes for each pose, his arms and legs moved into so many different positions. I tried to force my attention to moving my hand on the paper, but my mind stubbornly locked onto his lustrous muscles. It was an unnerving time, but now that I look back on it, I can laugh about my naive reaction.

The two-week internship held at Mt. Hood Kiwanis Camp taught me a life principle. We all need to be in tune with others for the sake of self-cultivation and self-realization. Working as a counselor for children with disabilities, I witnessed how hard their lives were. In this two-week program, each week we were assigned a different autistic child. The first week I worked with Jan, a seventeen-year-old girl, and the second week with Edward, a fourteen-year-old boy. Both had mild autism with minor communication disorders. They were able to compose only simple sentences. Their longer sentences were not understandable.

Toward the end of the second week, we had to produce a skit as a group. In our group, Edward came up with an idea for the skit. Using a character modeled on Cookie Monster from the *Sesame Street* TV program, he sketched out the part of the monster. He drew it in great detail with lots of numbers and dimensions. He was very good at numbers, which reminded me of the character in the movie *Rain Man*. I kind of understood Edward's scribbles, but the teacher didn't choose his idea because of his inability to communicate. He became sullen. I felt helpless.

Edward impressed me. When we did a project in which the kids could make anything they wanted to, using any of the materials in the art room, Edward made a doll-size cowboy. He used wood sticks, scraps of fabrics and leather, ribbons, buttons, beads, crayons, paints, and all sorts of tools.

"Edward, what are you making?" I asked from the other side of the workbench.

"A cowboy!" he said, and then raised his head, holding up his work to show me.

"My goodness! It looks like a real cowboy, Edward!" I said, walking around the table to sit next to him. "Who taught you?"

"No one . . . I watched TV," he answered shyly.

"But look at your work! Gee, I'm very impressed!" I said, patting his shoulder.

His eyes shone.

I continued asking curiously, "How do you know those details?"

"I can remember if I see it once," he said, looking down at the cowboy.

Astounded by his work, I wondered, *How could he possibly remember those details?* The leather was precisely cut and shaped for the cowboy hat, vest, and pants that were glued onto the well-proportioned body made of fabric and wooden sticks. The cowboy's bushy eyebrows and mustache were drawn in black ink and his boots were shaped just like the ones I had seen in Westerns on television.

He whispered, "I'm gonna give it to my brother."

"How nice, Edward!" I said softly.

At this point, I just thought he was a very gifted boy. But when his mother came to the camp on the last day, she told me that his younger brother was deaf, and Edward always took care of him. I was moved.

I realized there are many people who are tormented by these incurable disorders, yet they live with these issues and struggle every day. I felt like I had glimpsed another world and learned something precious that I would have never known if I hadn't gone to this camp. I will always treasure the time I spent with Jan and Edward.

I worked during school vacations, accepting any kind of part-time job available at the time—retail sales at department stores and at the Duty Free Shop in the Portland airport, and waitressing at restaurants.

One job I will never forget was a brief stint at a family-style restaurant. My word! That was the worst job I had ever had.

The restaurant was only fifteen minutes away from my home, but being a prep cook, I needed to get up by 3:30 in the morning to be at work by 4:15. In my half-awake state, my head didn't fully function, but my hands moved quickly through the repetitive motions. I chopped and diced vegetables, and cut and sliced fruits for many hours, standing in front of a deep steel sink. There were three other people working the same shift doing the same thing. We needed to keep the salad bar bins filled: a hectic job. Once the restaurant was open, we needed to keep an eye on the salad bar. People who were sloppy caused us a lot of work.

On one occasion, my manager screamed at me, saying, "Kumiko! Do. Not. Waste!"

Startled, I peered into the bottom of the large square mayonnaise jar I was holding. There was a tiny bit of mayonnaise remaining. I snatched up a scraper spatula with a long handle, but she scolded me again.

"Use a tiny one!" she said, glaring at me.

"Yes," I said, in a firm voice.

Whew! Don't get upset. This is a temporary job. I clenched my teeth hard. Running back and forth to refill the bar made me weary indeed, but worrying about whether or not I had completely scraped out the contents from containers stressed me out.

Besides doing part-time jobs, I began an export business with my second-oldest brother, Shohei, in Tokyo. Soon after I had moved to the communal house, my brother called me. "Would it be possible for you to buy air-freshening products from a company in your country, and ship them to me?" he asked. As I heard his inquiry, I thought, *Oh no! Not now . . . I just got divorced.* But he said, "I'll pay you." I wasn't up for helping to start a business, but reconsidered because any income would be helpful.

First, I checked out the company he had in mind online. The very next day I called and asked about the possibility of buying and shipping their products to Japan. I learned it would be possible. The same week, I met with an expert in international trade law to find out how I could set up the business. After making sure I wouldn't get into any trouble helping my brother, I called the company back to buy their products. It was a nerve-racking experience negotiating a good price with the company. The order wasn't small. It weighed more than half a ton all together. The company told me I needed to create an order form with a letterhead and find a shipping company. Besides the difficulty in learning this new enterprise, my lack of strong speaking and writing skills was a big challenge. Once the business was established, it went pretty smoothly. But there was always risk. For instance, one time, the shipper called me to check on some damaged products. Right away, I hurried to the shipping company near the airport. It luckily only needed repacking, but it rattled me nonetheless.

When at last I graduated after the winter term of 1999, I felt I had obtained a license to feel equal to Americans. My new resume with a four-year college degree looked and sounded better than it had with a two-year associate degree in English, taken in Japan. With that, I thought, I would surely be able to get a good job with an American company. Immediately, I launched my job search, checking in newspapers, on the Internet, with employment agencies, friends, social networks, companies, and the PSU Career Center. I sent out over fifty resumes. I got leads, but nothing panned out. I wondered why I wasn't having any luck. Then one day, I read a large-print ad for a job fair to be held at a convention center in downtown Portland. *A big job fair! I might have a chance!*

The cavernous convention center was filled with numerous booths and hundreds of applicants shopped around. All kinds of corporations were recruiting their future employees from showy booths with conspicuous company logos. I was nervous, but I approached some company representatives. Unfortunately, they didn't show great enthusiasm for me, as they were looking for specific skills, which I apparently lacked. After an hour of rejections, I stopped trying and stood in a little open space and watched other candidates as they eagerly talked with representatives. Watching the frenetic scene, I remembered how competitive the work world was. *Aha . . . aha . . . too corporate, too large, too political!* While I stood there in a daze, a lady dressed like a businessperson bumped into my shoulder, hard. She didn't apologize. Perhaps she didn't even realize she had jostled me as she dashed toward a booth. The dog-eat-dog work world suddenly didn't seem so appealing. I felt like fleeing back to the security of school. I went home with mixed feelings about what to do next. Maybe I should go back to school!

It occurred to me that the desire for high educational achievement that had been cultivated in me during my school days must have been simmering in my subconscious; perhaps it had sabotaged me in finding a job. I realized I wasn't ready for a career.

Once the idea of going to graduate school became stuck in my mind, I met with the head of the Linguistics' department to ask about the possibility of getting into their graduate program.

She looked straight into my eyes and bluntly said, "It would be a waste of your money." I sat like a stone, not even blinking. She continued, saying, "Schools wouldn't hire someone with an accent when they could hire a native speaker."

After a few seconds of silence, I finally said, "You are right. I understand." She was being honest. I stepped out of her office, and stood numbly in the middle of the hallway.

After some consideration, I concluded it might be rewarding to become a divorce mediator. This time I decided not to ask for advice, but went ahead and applied to the Conflict Resolution program in the Philosophy Department.

A month later, when I received a sort of rejection letter, I felt as if I had been kicked in the head. But after rereading it several times—I guess my mind calmed down some—I noticed a suggestion that if I could prove my ability to meet their expectations after taking a few graduate classes, they would reconsider. I regained my enthusiasm and started taking graduate classes during the summer term of 1999.

XII

Online Date

At the beginning of fall term, a feeling of emptiness hit me. While I was an undergraduate, I never thought of having a boyfriend, nor wanted to have any relationship. My self-esteem must have improved by virtue of having finished college. I began to feel more open about having a relationship again. I remembered how much richer life had been with Thomas. *Well then, why not find someone who can fill my empty heart?*

No kids, no pets, no debts, no obstacles . . . I didn't need to worry about those issues that often get in the way when you have a boyfriend. The only thing that worried me a little was that I lived in such a tiny shoebox of a room. I wasn't sure what men would think about that. Then again, I assured myself that if my living in a tiny room would bother a man, then he wouldn't be the right person for me. I forced myself to think that way. I wasn't going to be with someone who thought the outside of me was more important than the inside. Nonetheless, I tried to hide my circumstances as long as I could. Of course, I would reveal everything before committing to a serious relationship.

Thanks to advanced technology, there were many new ways of finding a mate. The first thing I tried was "Local Telephone Dateline." It was easy. I set up my own voice mailbox with a brief message introducing myself. An interested man could call my mailbox and listen to the message. If he liked what he heard, he could leave his number for me to contact. Many people wouldn't favor this approach, but I was desperate. I actually met good people. Without doubt it is important to be careful in meeting strangers, but I somehow had a "latent power" of discerning good or bad people by their tone of voice. This could have been because for years I had been practicing understanding people from their voices more than their words, due to the language barrier. It's like the way animals sense bad people or good people by their appearance or the way people look at them. Of course, I cannot say it always worked, but my intuition was keen.

Remarkably, all the men I met were gentlemen, and I never felt threatened. I met them in safe places like Starbucks, a shopping mall, or a family restaurant. The drawback of the telephone dating service was that I didn't learn much about the men before I met them, so I soon switched from the telephone dating service to an online service—yes, that famous one, Match.com—so I would be able to select the people whom I would like to meet.

> I wrote my profile like this:
>
> 46 year-old female, Oriental, 5'4", 97 pounds, living in Southeast Portland, Oregon, seeking 40 to 50 year-old male for a long-term relationship. I have been divorced for two years and am thinking that I should find someone. Age doesn't matter so much, but it does matter to have someone who has the willingness to make efforts to build a solid connection. Intangibles, such as love, esteem, attention, respect, and caring are hard to find. Mutual efforts are required to keep a good relationship. I prefer a man who is honest, sincere, and trustworthy. E-mail is a different approach to finding a friend. I can learn more about a person's inner qualities. It is better to

know the true value of the person. I am honest and lenient. I have a positive self-concept. I enjoy reading, hiking, talking, and visiting art museums. I like art, computers, and theater. I used to travel a lot when I was young, so I have seen some foreign countries. I think that I have a wide range of vision. I have no children. If this entices you, please send me a message. Waiting to hear from you.

This was my profile, with no picture attached because I wanted to do this in a covert way. The responses were amazing and I was shocked at the power of online dating services. Eight people responded within a week or so. The first person was a Tri-Met bus driver (no photo and not much personal information.) The second was from Hawaii (too far away.) After that, I don't recall the order of respondents, but there was a man from Los Angeles who was a commercial scriptwriter (too glamorous,) a writer from Portland who had a couple of books in bookstores (too slow to respond,) and a sixty-year-old retired anesthesiologist (a little too old.) The three remaining people were an owner of a software company and two attorneys.

There were vast differences in the information people provided about themselves. Although I knew it was hard to decipher such things, I looked for someone who showed sincerity in their emails. I actually got a feel for what these three were like. But one person swiftly responded each time with a lengthy letter. This was one of the attorneys. His emails were always full of interesting tidbits about his personal life and his plans. His openness piqued my interest and I connected to him on a mental level before getting to know the other people.

After exchanging many e-mails, I finally met Frederick at Starbucks. The Starbucks at Pioneer Square was crowded that day and vibrant with the energy of morning coffee drinkers. The shop was brightly lit, but not enough to see people's faces clearly at a distance. I sat a little away from the center of the room, looking towards the entrance, waiting anxiously for the "6'1" slender man" who was supposed to appear at any time. He had said he would be wearing a blue shirt and black pants or something similar. About five minutes past our meeting time, a guy in a black coat rushed into the shop looking like someone who was looking for someone. He didn't exactly fit the image I had in my mind, but, since he was the only guy in the room who seemed to be looking for someone, I tried to catch his eye. He looked around in a strange way, then approached the counter and ordered coffee. After grabbing his coffee, he turned around, glanced around the whole room again, and then pushed out the door. I was mortified and didn't know what to do. I thought I should leave, but I wasn't a hundred-percent sure that man was the one I was waiting for, although I believed he was. Just as I was thinking about leaving, another man hurried in and immediately approached me, smiling. I let out a big sigh of relief.

Frederick sat down at my table, but then suggested we move to a small round table by the window where we would have a little privacy. He initiated our conversation. It was a strange sensation to be evaluating each other, searching for a mutual sense of attraction while we were smiling and pretending to be focused on our conversation. We weren't total strangers, by virtue of having written emails for a long time, and having made some connection already. It was like taking a driver's license test: you have passed the written part, but now you need to take that actual behind-the-wheel test. I wasn't a talker, but he was. I let him talk. I studied his face while he went on and on. I realized he resembled my dad and this thought eased my nerves. After an hour of conversation, he looked at his watch, and asked me to take a walk along the waterfront.

It was the end of September. The sky was a deep blue that made the clouds whiter by contrast, and the air was fresh and crisp. I kept up with his pace while we chatted, and walked toward the waterfront. He spoke with the same passion he'd shown in his writing, and showed no sign of difficulty finding subjects he wanted to share with me. With a mission of evaluating and understanding this person, I discreetly observed him. His sincere and amiable manner pleased me, even though he talked so much.

We reached the South Waterfront and sauntered along the banks of the Willamette River. Walking in high heels on the skinny path of inlaid stepping stones wasn't comfortable, but being careful not to step in between the stones, I managed to balance my concentration between walking and listening. However, when we got to the turnaround point, he said something I couldn't comprehend, and I momentarily lost the balance I was keeping.

Looking into my eyes, he abruptly said, "I am dating a couple of women."

I halted and breathed in deeply while my brain vainly searched for something unfathomable. Then I took a few steps. "Well . . . ," I began, but no words followed so I waited for him to say something. He had said this as if it were not such an unusual thing, but obviously he read in my face that I wasn't happy about it. So he said that he wasn't engaged to anyone else at that time and continued, "What can I do with you?" I thought, "My word!" This line offended me very much. It sounded conceited, as if he thought I already belonged to him! I hadn't even decided whether or not I was going to date him in the future. I wasn't sure how to understand his confession. Although I understood honest was good, I lost a significant amount of my interest in him.

After his confession, our conversation became dull. He remembered all of a sudden that he was supposed to go to the courthouse to listen to a trial he was interested in, so he walked me to the bus stop to send me off to school, as I had an afternoon class.

When we got to the bus stop, he asked me suddenly, "Do you like salmon?"

I told him I did.

"How about salmon, broccoli, and rice? Does that sound good to you?" he asked.

It took a few seconds to realize he was inviting me for dinner. I was amazed. He had already been thinking about the dinner menu. He wasn't at all shy about leading the way. I wasn't sure it was a good idea to go to his house on the grounds that I didn't think I should even be involved with someone who was already dating someone else. My inner voice said *No!* Somehow, though, perhaps because of his charming smile, I couldn't cut him off abruptly, and say, "Sorry I cannot meet you again." I surprised myself by agreeing, because it wasn't my way.

The day of our dinner date, Saturday, was another of those beautiful early autumn days. Looking out the classroom windows, I daydreamed through most of my eight-hour mediation class, imagining all sorts of scenarios, both good and bad. The three o'clock break came—the time to call him, as he had asked me to confirm our date, and to get the directions to his house. The voice coming through the phone was cheerful, but slightly softer this time. He said he had played tennis and cleaned the house and told me what he was going to do till the time we met. After our conversation, my mind began going over the directions he had given. *Well, so . . . I need to take US- 26 toward Beaverton, and get off at the exit for Cornell Rd, then . . . it must be crowded around five o'clock, even on Saturday.* I lost focus on the rest of the lecture. The class dismissed at five. I went to a restroom to fix my makeup and changed my clothes to a more feminine look—from pants to a skirt— and took off from school in haste.

Frederick's directions were pretty good until I got into the apartment complex. Then I got confused. Somehow I went to the wrong house, but the person in the house let me use her cell phone to call him. I felt awful making such a mistake, but when I saw him he was smiling and welcomed me. His kind gestures took away some of my nervousness.

As I stepped in the house, I immediately noticed there was very little furniture, and I remembered he had written in one email that he had recently split-up with his live-in girlfriend. The few pieces of furniture didn't indicate much about his taste, but the house was clean and things were neatly organized, which gave me a positive impression. In any case, the grilled salmon smelled delicious and I began to relax a little.

The heavy dining table with lion's-paw legs was set with a bottle of white wine, two wine glasses on black tablemats, and two tall skinny candles. He soon carried in a large salmon fillet on a serving platter, and then placed it at the center of the dining table. He lit the candles. Nobody had treated me like this. I thought this could be the epitome of a romantic dinner to captivate a woman's heart. But after dinner, when he suggested that I sit on the couch, my heart started racing. I was aware of what might happen, but I believed I could handle it. I braced myself for his move. I tentatively sat down at the end of the couch to give myself some comfortable space, but he sat next to me. Staring at my eyes, he asked, "How do you spend your leisure time?" I faltered in my reply because I was nervous about what his next move might be.

Soon he squeezed closer. "Can I kiss you?" he whispered. I stared at him for a long minute before finally whispering, "Yes." I followed my heart and not my head. I believed the reason for Thomas's affair was that I had never been a good sexual partner, because I didn't even know how to kiss, and never realized how important that was to him. I had been determined that if I had another chance to kiss someone, I should do it as if I really meant it, so this time I did.

The kiss charmed Frederick more than I wanted to on what was only our second date. I had never kissed anyone that way before. Frankly, it wasn't because I had any passion for him at the time—it was too soon to have that sort of feeling, especially for someone like me, whose head and heart coordinate with each other very well. But I simply believed that one of the reasons Thomas left me was I was too passive. That thought must have made me kiss Frederick in a totally different way than I had ever done: it was like the way you see people kiss in movies. My kiss was light and soft but by no means passive. It was a mistake, and I shouldn't have done it the way I did. He was ignited and he became pushier, pleading with me to stay.

"I won't do anything you don't want me to do, I promise you," said Frederick, his eyes twice as big as before.

"It's very late, and I need to go home," I said, standing up and reaching for my purse.

He tried very hard to convince me to stay, but my head was strong enough to say "No." I liked him already, but was unwilling to go further and I needed to take a deep breath. I hurried to the door, but as I grabbed the knob, I turned back to catch his eye to say, "Good night."

My little heart was pounding when I slipped behind the wheel of my car, not a bad feeling though, like in Diamond Rio's song, *Beautiful Mess*:

I can't think straight…

I can't concentrate…

it's not your style…

I smile…

What a beautiful mess I made.

Ahh … Ahh …

I stepped on the gas in a daze, and then glanced at the clock on the dashboard—already past midnight. I was intoxicated with the still lingering sensation, and the tail lights on the highway ahead of me were fuzzy.

The next morning, I woke up with the disturbing recollection that he had said he was dating other ladies. *Nooo, I can't handle that!* This thought bothered me. In fact, it bothered me enough to call him to say I couldn't see him again. I pushed his number with mixed feelings.

The voice that came through the phone was sweet, as if we had made love the night before.

He asked me softly, "How are you doing this morning?"

I became momentarily lost for words, but regained and firmed up my voice because I was delivering bad news. He heard me out, listening to me without interrupting. It was strange that he didn't give me a definitive response, but we ended our conversation nonetheless. I wasn't sure if he understood or not. I was more confused than before, and didn't know what to think of him after this conversation. My inner voice told me, *He didn't sound like he was upset, but he wasn't happy either. But if this isn't working, then it isn't meant to be.* I wasn't going to give up my convictions, for it wasn't a good idea to fall in love with a person whose mind was on someone else, right? I wasn't going to fail in a relationship again. No way! I kept saying this to myself like a mantra until the phone rang an hour later. It was Frederick.

He abruptly announced, "I decided to stop dating other women. I talked to my daughter after I talked to you. She said, 'I should stick with the person I think can make me happy.'"

He paused, waiting for me to say something. I still kept quiet.

He said decisively, "So I'm letting you know this. As a matter of fact, I am going to call the others after I finish our conversation to tell them I have found someone."

The little victory made me feel *gooood*, and instantaneously, his words captured my heart.

Words are magic, aren't they? I already felt a tiny bit of love for him in the conversation. Why do we fall in love? Is it predestined and my act was simply a reflex? I remembered the words that Thomas had spoken at the end of our relationship, as we walked in the park.

"You know, Kumiko, a person *can* love two people at the same time," he said to me, while my heart was totally sunken. "I still love you."

"No way! You cannot. Loving two people at the same time is impossible!"

I didn't understand about love then, but I thought I was beginning to understand what he had meant.

Frederick and I started dating. We met only on weekends, as I had to go to school. I was concerned that our dating might sabotage my studying, but unexpectedly I found I could focus on my studying even while managing our dating time. Dating was actually refreshing and rewarding, in that I could take breaks from studying. It had the effect of softening my brain muscles with dreamy thoughts.

Frederick's easygoing and down-to-earth personality helped me loosen my uptight disposition. He seemed to be able to cope with issues without making too much fuss. His tone was almost always positive whether he was offering encouragement or constructive criticism, or making a request or suggestion. Most definitely, his charm was intended to please his loved ones. For instance, he often fixed food like a devoted mom who cuts an apple into the shape of a rabbit, or makes a pancake into a face of Mickey or Minnie Mouse.

Frederick's view of life was, I thought, commendable. On several occasions, he said, "I like to practice law, but I wouldn't mind working at a McDonald's Restaurant. I could still be happy." However, once in a while, in a firm and decisive lecturing tone, which I hated, he threw into my furrowed face, "You should think how blessed you are. You know there are so many people in this world who aren't blessed like you." At times, I thought it wasn't worthwhile to complain, as I only got lectured. After all, he was a lawyer; when it came to an argument he was technically better, despite my good axiomatic arguments, so eventually, my complaints tapered off. All in all though, we were still new to each other and dating was hot and voluptuous.

On Thanksgiving Day, he invited me for the feast. As I entered his house, the aroma of roasting turkey that filled his apartment welcomed me. The rooms were brightly lit and looked especially warm and cozy, as outside it was dark and pouring rain. The TV was on for the NFL game.

Frederick bustled around, arranging plates of turkey, bowls of salad, and glasses of champagne. Finally, all the food was spread on the table. He cut a slice of turkey for me. His first try at cooking turkey was, I thought, a fantastic success; it was deliciously browned.

We watched the football game while relishing the food. Frederick was a football fanatic. I was only mildly interested in football, but surprisingly, we both liked the Miami Dolphins. I was a Dolphins' fan simply because I had lived in Florida and Thomas had cheered for them while we watched the games together.

While watching the game, I thought about how there were some similarities between Frederick and Thomas. They were both from Florida, and had even attended the same University in Georgia, though Frederick had been in the Theology graduate program and Thomas did his undergraduate major in economics. They were about the same height, both slender, and had almost identical voices when they sang. Frederick had two brothers and Thomas had one; both were the youngest in their families. A girl from Tokyo falling in love with two people with so much in common seemed almost magically coincidental.

The year 2000 was approaching. Since being accepted to graduate school, I was happy about my life and less concerned about world matters. People were worried that the change of century would cause some sort of "Millennial Bug." Not understanding much about the year 2000 problem, known as Y2K, I didn't think too much about it. Having little money in my bank account, I didn't worry about the computer system crashing, although I was a little concerned that I might lose my schoolwork on my computer. Frederick had gone to his brother's house in Melbourne, Florida to cheer in the New Year with his family. I thought about the pleasant December weather, recalling the time when Thomas and I had lived in Melbourne. I wished I were there, but I was pretty contented being alone, as I considered our relationship to be solid and still sizzling. I counted down the last few minutes of 1999, so I could give Frederick a call to say, "Happy New Year!"

"Happy New Year!" he said heartwarmingly, then continued, saying "I just came out of the swimming pool. Right now I'm in the Jacuzzi sipping wine with my brother."

"You must be having too much fun. Don't you feel guilty having all that fun by yourself?" I joked.

Picturing his brother's house with envy, I sipped at my boxed wine in my pint-size room. *He's a doctor, so I imagine his house must be pretty nice. That sort of luxury, I will never experience in this life. Maybe in the next! My life has been eventful, but I haven't had the best of luck. Ummm . . . luck . . .* while thinking of my fortune, I thought of Frederick's.

He didn't seem he had much luck either from the bits and pieces I had heard about him on different occasions. He told me he had many ups and downs in his convoluted second marriage. Because of his wife's capricious desires, he was forced to close down his successful business. "Sometimes a spouse can drive you crazy," he once told me. These events were far enough in the past, they didn't stir my emotions. But his recent break-up had happened just six months ago, right before their planned wedding day, so I was apprehensive that he might have too much emotional baggage. I assumed his recent failed relationship might have changed the direction of his life like mine had done to me.

He had become a full-time attorney, opening his own practice in his flat. I remember his small complaint. "I don't mind working in a small office, but I feel embarrassed when I need to ask my clients to move their chair so I can open my cabinet to get their files." I adored his down-to-earth attitude, and I was comfortable with him. By nature, he was funny and laid back. For instance, one day his car got stuck in the snow somewhere on the way to Mt. Hood. We should have given up the idea of driving up the mountain because the snow situation was iffy, I thought, but, no, he took the risk.

"What did I tell you?" I said.

"Don't worry. Relax!" he said getting out of the car.

"We'd better hurry up, otherwise we'll be stuck in the middle of the mountain road till tomorrow morning. It's already getting dark," I said, feeling agitated.

"Don't worry! Someone will come," he said, as he tried to get the car out of the snow.

Fifteen minutes later a car descended. The driver helped us. Another car stopped and helped us too, but we could only make the tires waggle a little in the snowdrift. Luckily, the third person, who had a shovel, succeeded in getting the car out on the right track.

I said, "You are living at the edge," to which he responded, "You are damn right," and he laughed. He didn't get irritated easily like Thomas did. He enjoyed life spontaneously, which was fascinating to me.

One warm afternoon in March, Frederick called and said he was coming to my house to take me somewhere. I was excited about his spur-of-the-moment proposal, but at the same time I was mortified by the idea he would see my tiny room. In the six months I had known him, he had never seen my shared house.

While waiting for him, I timidly watched through the living room window blinds, thinking about how awful it would be if he saw my room. When I heard the knock, I took a quick deep breath to swallow my pride, then slowly exhaled before answering the door. As I opened the door, I saw him smiling. He immediately said, "Get in the car! We are going to Angels' Rest in the Columbia Gorge." He didn't enter the house. I jumped in his car.

I didn't know exactly where Angels' Rest was, but whatever he had planned, I was happy to be carried away.

"Kumiko, I brought my picnic backpack," he said with high spirits, as a matter of fact, very high spirits.

"Nice!" I replied.

The familiar sight of the Columbia River Gorge brought back old memories of the good times I had shared with Thomas. Although my spirits were high, my emotions were mixed for a while. We came to the trail entrance after what seemed like a short drive, and slipped out of the car. With the pack on his back, Frederick led me to the trail with gusto. I followed him first, but I soon outpaced him. Our relationship was still really new, so my behavior was a bit pretentious. I wanted to impress him and not disappoint him, so I hiked the trail at a fast pace, putting myself in high gear.

He, by contrast, ambled along, enjoying the view, and periodically singing out "No pain no gain . . ."

I didn't respond to him each time, but chuckled at his words. The pitchy smell of the fir needles and clean forest air were invigorating. Thomas had loved the woods, so we had hiked a lot, although when we hiked we challenged our physical limits. With Frederick, hiking was relaxing and hassle-free. Walking along the trail with this brand new boyfriend, I felt ecstatic.

When we came to the open space on the top of the mountain, the view was stunning with the clear blue sky and the warm spring sun just above us. Deep down at the bottom of the gorge, the spectacular Columbia River snaked around the land. Frederick found a secluded spot for us that had a little privacy so we could have a rest. We sat on a big flat rock. He opened his burgundy-colored picnic backpack and started pulling things out—place settings and napkins, wine glasses, a wine opener, and a cutting board. He had brought pepper jack cheese, apples, nuts mixed with raisins, and crackers. He squeezed everything between us and then, lastly, grabbed the red wine, taking it out from the bag with a charming smile, as if he were a little conqueror over my heart. I thought this gesture itself was romantic.

In such an enchanting setting, somehow anything he said was agreeable. I felt truly happy. The happiness I had been deprived of for a long time suddenly returned and it reminded me I could feel intense joy. But one thing I didn't think about was that there was no restroom and we both needed to use one badly. We weren't yet comfortable enough with each other to do our business in the woods, so we descended the mountain at top speed. I ran, trying not to show my tensed-up face to him, and he followed. We both hurried down to the parking lot where the restrooms were. Emergency over, we slid in the car and cruised back through the Columbia Gorge in the twilight. Gazing at the orange sunset sky with silver clouds, I thought I had had such a lovely day. I felt a little closer to him.

Sometime in April, though, he informed me rather apologetically that he had to offer his apartment for an indefinite period to his old girlfriend, who had decided to move to Oregon. I thought letting his old girlfriend live in his place was too bold for me, as our relationship was still new, only six months old, and I did not yet fully know him. Of course, I didn't favor the idea at all, but the decision had already been made and I had no power to change his mind. It was weird that he was so defensive about supporting his old girlfriend. He tossed out all the reasons he could come up with.

"Mary is a funny person and a bit crazy. I mean she isn't literally crazy. Well, to be quite honest, I don't know how to describe her," he said, scratching his head.

"Why can't you?" I asked.

"Anyway you will see what I mean once you meet her. You might like her because she's good at entertaining," he said, as if there was a possibility I might become her friend.

"How long will she stay at your place?" I asked brusquely.

"I don't know," he said. "Her brother and I were friends when I was in junior high school, and her mom used to invite me for dinner."

He tried to convince me that helping her out was the right thing to do as a good friend. So, I decided not to worry about her, but frankly it puzzled me how he had depicted this woman who was his girlfriend for a short time many, many years ago. The word "crazy" troubled me.

One evening after my mediation class, I met Frederick and his old girlfriend, Mary, at the Pioneer Square Starbucks' coffee shop in downtown Portland. They were on the way to his house from the Portland Airport. It was around 8:30 in the evening and there were quite a number of people in the coffee shop. I approached their table and stood just behind Frederick, trying not to cut into their conversation abruptly. Mary looked at me first, and as soon as he realized I was standing there, he immediately stood up and introduced me. "Kumiko, this is Mary." She had long curly blond hair, nice features, and under the dim lights, she appeared to be fairly attractive. Her demeanor was confident, and, as Frederick had suggested earlier, she indeed had some ways to charm people when she held a conversation. She even looked coquettish. When I gathered all my impressions of her in my mind, I felt a sudden premonition that she might be bad news for me.

On Saturday afternoon, a few days after I had met Mary at the Starbucks', I went to Frederick's apartment. Mary was there, using the computer in his office. When I greeted her, I noticed her skin was dry, and she looked older in the daylight. In the early spring, the air was still chilly and she was in a bright pink sweater and blue jeans. She looked casual and relaxed. But when night fell, she changed to a sexy nightgown and drifted around the house like she owned it. The worst part was that she walked across the carpeted-floor like a sneaky cat so she could hear our private conversations, and sometimes startled us. Mary's insensitive actions toward me could be construed as harassment, so I tried to keep some distance between us, but she approached me with her schemes.

One early Saturday evening, she asked me to take her to the Fred Meyer store to buy a pair of shoes. Mary used Frederick's car often, although he took her just about everywhere she needed to go. But since she asked me, I felt obliged to take her. Mary circled to view the displayed shoes a couple of times, then said, "I don't see what I like." She suggested having coffee at a nearby café. I wasn't up for it, but I assumed she had a craving for a cigarette with coffee.

We bought coffees and sat down at a table outside. Mary lit her cigarette before sipping her coffee, and then initiated small talk. About ten minutes or so later, she switched to the main subject she had on her mind and shifted our conversation as if she were tacking a boat. At one point, she turned her face slightly to the side so as not to blow the smoke into my face while looking into my eyes intensely. That sly and condescending look on her face disgusted me.

"You know, Kumiko, you think you are seriously dating him, but he's not serious! He's never kept any relationship for a long time, and you will be history soon," she said, puffing her cigarette.

"Umm . . ." I said, but determined not to reply because I thought my response would only prolong our conversation.

She watched my reactions carefully, but as I apparently didn't respond the way she had expected, she continued needling.

"You're not his type. I don't understand why he's dating you. If you don't want to be hurt deeply, you'd better leave him right away," she said in a grating voice.

When I still didn't show the irritation that she wanted to detect, she finally got into details. I couldn't tolerate this any longer.

"I would like to go home. This is my business, and not yours," I firmly said.

She wanted to linger, but I insisted I needed to go back.

When we returned to Frederick's house, my anger exploded. I asked him to go into his bedroom right away.

As I shut the door, I bombarded him. "Mary is not only crazy but she's also cruel! I can't believe what she told me. She wants to destroy our relationship. She said all kinds of bad things about you."

"I told you she's crazy. Just don't believe what she tells you," he said nonchalantly.

"I'm very serious. I want you to tell her not to bother me anymore," I said in an accusatory tone.

It was unbelievable that he didn't grasp how badly I was hurt. He didn't protect me. Seven months of dating was not long enough to understand him. I seriously thought about leaving. Still my inner voice said "stay", so I did, but her malicious words settled in my head like sediment in a bad wine.

Mary's pestering continued. Frederick kept telling me he was only offering his place to let her get established. His lame solution was to keep me out of her sight. Our weekend dates were outside activities, playing tennis or discovering fun places. He injected loads of excitement, so our dates were entertaining, but I truly wished he'd command Mary to stop harassing me.

One Saturday night, Frederick took me to a brewpub called the Grand Lodge, situated in the small town of Forest Grove. This lodge was particularly amusing because of the fascinating decor. On the floors, there were mosaic tile designs and on the walls, paintings of bizarre human caricatures in vivid primary colors. Painted sun faces and elves smiled down from a pipe that hung from the ceiling. I was struck by the fairytale atmosphere. After Frederick gave me a tour, we went into the restaurant and settled into a booth. The reddish tiffany-pendant light radiated a warm and cozy ambiance and created an intimate mood. He gazed at me while holding my hands. With so much attention, I thought he was going to propose. He didn't, but I began to wonder if Frederick could be *the one*.

Our relationship was moving forward despite Mary's malicious intrusions. I ignored her and focused on other important things, school mainly, because I was finding graduate school challenging. Well . . . I had thought the same thing when I was an undergraduate, come to think of it. There were many questions that tested our memory skills, and my memory wasn't as strong as that of the younger students. In any case, in my graduate classes, we did lots of research and I enjoyed doing that part of class. Then I was assigned by our teacher to do a survey. The word "survey" caused a panicked adrenaline rush. Interviewing professional people made me uneasy.

After much distress, an idea leapt into my mind. *E-mail! That's the answer.* After a week of brainstorming, I finally formulated twenty survey questions. My survey was to find out if attorneys or counselors mediated conflicts differently than mediators who had no special background except mediation training. Surprisingly, I received a response from all the fifteen professionals to whom I sent the survey. They gave serious consideration to my questions.

The first attorney to respond wrote:

"Divorce mediation, far beyond all other types of mediation, is unique amongst the others because it wavers between counseling and the law. To explain, couples need a person to "hear" them, sometimes for the first time in their lives, far more in divorce mediation than in other types of mediation. I feel this happens because we are mediating the dissolution of one of the most important relationships and experiences they may ever have. Additionally, the courts have made dissolving a marriage highly statutory and as such one must be aware of the law in order to successfully mediate a divorce."

My survey went far better than I had expected, and this successful experience increased my confidence in dealing with the public.

Mary finally found a job and left the house after staying there for three months. What a relief! My school and personal life began to mesh together nicely. Frederick and I became more intimate—intimate enough that he asked me to live with him. He had been suggesting that I nestle into his house soon after we met, but I needed to be alone for the first demanding year of my graduate program. Around September, when Frederick's new house was about to be completed, he asked me again to move in, as I had finished taking all the classes. I started considering his proposal because in the second year, I would only need to complete my practicum and write a thesis paper.

Dating him for a year, I had learned how trustworthy and reliable Frederick was, and it seemed we had made a good connection. Nonetheless, I was still not sure living together would be a good idea, as our future plans weren't well defined. Even so, I hoped things would go well and eventually we would tie the knot. With this hope, I decided to move into his new house, although it took three months to come to that decision. My thinking was unclear on a few things: first, I didn't know how to explain to my parents about cohabitation with my boyfriend; second, I believed living with a man without marrying wouldn't be a wise idea; and last of all, I was concerned about how I would manage my study time. So I proclaimed loudly and clearly that I wasn't planning to be a roommate forever, and Frederick seemed to understand. I was being truly honest about who I was and I expected him to do the same. Frederick had already shown me how sincere he could be so, I thought, we just needed to work on building the foundation for our future.

XIII

Moving to His House

On moving day in early December, Frederick came to my house in a big shiny borrowed pick-up truck. The large truck occupied all the space in the driveway. As it was already evening, he immediately set out to load my furniture onto the truck. He zipped back and forth between the house and the truck, and cleaned out my room in no time.

"Are you ready?" he asked.

"Yeah, I guess so," I said, and then looked around the room to make sure I hadn't left anything, and confirmed, "I'm ready."

"Then, hop in the truck!"

That was a bit hard to do, as the body was jacked up so high, but once I had climbed inside, I found the soft leather seat comfortable and the view quite amusing from the different height.

Gravely, I asked Frederick, "Do you think we'll be okay?"

His voice was deep and soft. "Don't worry. It's gonna be fine."

We drove out Highway 26 to the new house in Hillsboro. Misty rain started sprinkling and the view was hazy. *I hope I'll be okay*, I prayed. Although I was happy, feeling almost as if we were already married, I was apprehensive about the changes I was going to face.

As we carried my belongings into his house, I smelled the newness everywhere. My desk faced the bay window in the breakfast nook—my study room. His house wasn't entirely completed, and the floors were unfinished except for in the bedrooms, which were already carpeted. Frederick was installing the hardwood floors by himself, having learned how to do it at Home Depot. The only place that had to be immediately finished was the first floor, as that floor was used as his law office. Therefore, there would be a few difficulties in this living situation. Nonetheless, the prospect of living in a new house was uplifting.

Soon after I had moved in, though, I realized his house wasn't *my* home. It was an awkward feeling to be surrounded by everything that was his—the house, the furniture, and even the two cats (his buddies). Moreover, I lost my freedom and privacy. I had to spend more time with his daughter and his friends. All of this required a good deal of mental adjustment.

I decided I needed to change my thinking so as not to feel like a hermit crab. Although I paid rent—the same amount I had been paying at the previous house, plus the cost of food, telephone calls to my parents, and other personal incidentals—I started feeling I had become dependent. Of course, I didn't show my feelings outwardly, but deep in my heart, I neither felt comfortable nor equal to him anymore.

Time became so precious. Cleaning house took four hours every Saturday, and shopping for furniture for his new office ate into my time as well. Socializing with his family members consumed many hours, and I weighed how deeply I should become connected to them emotionally. He also expected me to spend time with his friends, however, I needed to make sure to allocate time to my studies, for it would be a total disaster to fail in both my relationship with him and in my academic goals.

My six-month graduate internship began at the courthouse in Hillsboro in January. I worked under a supervisor who coordinated for the Center for Victims' Services. After advocate training, I started helping people who were applying for restraining orders. My work was to help petitioners fill out over ten pages of detailed questions before submitting them to the court for hearings. Sitting next to the extremely agitated clients, the advocates wrote down all the incidents and conditions they had suffered. The stories of abuse made my blood curdle.

On my first day at work, I helped a lady fill out a questioner. She was clearly so agitated that she was somewhat incoherent. Covering her bruised face, she barely managed to answer the questions. Her swollen eye and cuts at the corner of her lips terrified me, but there were even worse cases than this one. Later in my practicum, one of my co-workers told me of a lady who came to the restraining-order with only one hand, due to her husband's torture. Luckily, I had been off that day. Advocates had to listen to many stories of cruelty.

Working in the restraining-order room transported me into a dysfunctional world, and attending the trials and hearings opened my eyes to the cruelty, vulnerability, and imperfection of human behavior.

The courthouse environment was intense. One day I was walking down a skinny hallway heading toward the café, when all of a sudden, a rhythmical metal sound streamed into my ears. I turned around and saw ten people in orange uniforms, all of them chained together, shackled at their ankles, hands cuffed. I must have slowed down, because the inmates soon passed me. It was a peculiar feeling to be so close to them.

Such scenes, I believed, only appeared on television shows like *NYPD Blue*.

During my practicum, an unexpected, but nice surprise occurred. A judge and a probation officer from Japan came to our courthouse to assess the American restraining-order system. My supportive supervisor asked me to assist them so they could understand the U.S. legal system as it pertained to restraining orders. *Good gracious, what a great opportunity!* I thought.

I had never even met any type of attorney when I lived in Japan. In fact, I had never heard anyone—my family, my neighbors, or my friends—say they were involved in legal disputes. Even when my brother and his first wife divorced, neither one of them had an attorney. In Japan, a very high percentage of divorces are obtained through mutual agreement, and the details of the divorces are usually worked out by counselors instead of a judge in a courtroom. Divorce is usually ugly, so I thought it would be difficult for the separating couples to make a mutual agreement just by using a counselor, especially when children were involved.

I was shocked when I heard that in Japan only one parent is allowed to maintain custody after a divorce, and it is not unusual for the parent without custody to have no contact with their children. That felt awful to me. I imagine it is horrifying for Japanese couples to divorce when the couples are still in their child-rearing years.

In Japan, there is a common trend, *kateinai rikon*, which means, "in-house divorce"; the couples live in the same household, but have almost zero communication and no sexual relations.

My old friend in Japan told me, "You may not know that in Japan *kateinai rikon* is growing in acceptance."

"Gee . . . that's intolerable. How can they live like that?" I asked her.

"I know. I have a friend who has that arrangement. Her husband comes home late, and leaves for work early in the morning. On weekends, he leaves the stereo at high volume all day. She has no clue what her husband is doing all day," she said in disgust.

"Oh my God! I wouldn't be able to stand it. Why don't they divorce?"

"She'll divorce her husband when he reaches his retirement."

"Wait! But there are many years to live like that."

"Don't worry. My friend is enjoying her life. She takes English language lessons and a dancing class. She can occupy her mind."

That's crazy, I thought. Pondering the situation more, I assumed a couple's unhappy marriage might be caused by the demands some Japanese companies make on their employees. These companies expect their employees to spend their time strengthening ties with clients and colleagues by socializing—going out for drinks after work or playing golf on weekends. Meanwhile at home, the wives do all the household work and childrearing. Couples who haven't had much time to develop their relationship tend to fall into dysfunction. I imagine when their children leave the nest, many of the wives feel really empty and alone.

To meet such a highly-placed person as a judge from a supreme court was a great honor and privilege. It occurred to me that I was in a unique position, for I had lived in both countries, which had given me a great opportunity to see the issues that the judge and the probation officer were addressing. We sat at one of the round tables in the restraining-order room and talked nearly an hour.

The judge's placid face and soft voice made it easier for me to talk to him. He folded his arms in front of his chest, and started to speak. "We need to take big measures such as increasing police presence, preparing shelters, providing counselors, and so on. If something happens to the people, they don't get immediate help."

"Yes, indeed, that is the problem in Japan," the probation officer said flatly.

"I can see the problem," I said politely, nodding.

As I listened, I thought about a conversation I had had with another intern. She did her research in Portland, where there is a sizable Japanese population. She mentioned there were very few Japanese abuse cases reported. However, contrary to her research, my church friend told me there are some abused Japanese women who run to the church to escape from their husbands or boyfriends. I suspect Japanese women in general are reluctant to report abuse. I, of course, fathomed the importance of the introduction of restraining orders in Japan because some cases involved situations of extreme danger. I further believed it was important to educate Japanese to be more proactive and not to tolerate abuse. I really enjoyed the conversation with those highly-positioned Japanese officials. The following day, the judge and probation officer left on the next leg of their journey to do the same research in different states.

Sometime in April, Frederick's daughter, Ellen, moved in. Only one season had passed since I had moved into Frederick's house. I thought it was too soon to have such a big change. But within a month, Ellen's boyfriend, Noah, joined her. Shortly after he moved in, she announced she was pregnant. Ellen and Noah married in June. Within six months, things had dramatically changed. I felt like I had been sucked into a whirlpool.

A remarkably sweet daddy to his daughter, Frederick treated Ellen like a princess. I rarely saw Ellen cook. More often, Noah did the cooking. On Saturdays, Noah mopped all the floors, took care of the yard, and vacuumed their room. Frederick and I swept the floors and cleaned our room and the third bathroom. Ellen merely dusted the surface of the refrigerator, stove and kitchen counter. During the week, Noah worked at his part-time job while Ellen took some college courses. Frederick supported them financially. He always focused on her needs and desires. His lack of attention to me burned me to the depths of my soul and resentment smoldered there. I needed to re-evaluate my place.

My frustration created skirmishes between us. Subsequent events were like termites, causing serious structural damage to our relationship. The situation felt oppressive and stressful. I tried to hide my concerns, but they grew as time went by. I wanted to express them in a diplomatic way, but I didn't have such skills, so we often fought. Frederick had more power and influence since it was his house, plus he was encircled by allies. I wished I were back in the serenity of my old room in my previous house.

I struggled with the circumstances in which I was entangled. Striving to fit in with his extended family, I was on an emotional rollercoaster. The dynamics were too complicated, as I had lived with only one person, Thomas, for fifteen years.

Not wanting to leave him, I stayed, resolving to cope with the unpredictable, disorderly environment.

Summer was too short for me and we soon entered a new season with a new arrival. In September, Ellen's baby, Kevin, was born. The household became super busy with an infant around, but Kevin was adorable. He seemed to love me instinctively and enjoyed being carried on my back, where he slept like a doll, listening to the Japanese lullabies I sang. As soon as I put him down on the bed, he would wake and cry. With no experience holding a baby, I worried that perhaps he wasn't comfortable in my bony arms; nonetheless, he appeared to be perfectly all right when I held him. He seemed to sense he was safe in my arms. I dearly loved him. Even so, having a newborn baby in the house was demanding.

Three seasons had passed since Frederick's kids had moved in. I noticed we all seemed to have adapted to our living conditions somewhat. I felt a bit more at ease with his family, and that feeling must have affected Frederick because our relationship improved. Frederick became emotionally closer to me. One morning in December, he surprised me by presenting the idea of going on a trip to Seaside to spend the night of New Year's Eve. This was a surprise indeed, for he always wanted to celebrate any special day with his daughter.

We left home that evening without a hotel reservation. All the hotels along the ocean were totally booked, but we finally found a small hotel inland. The hotel looked dated, but the room was clean and good-sized. We lit the dozen candles we had brought. The candles and the blue glow from the TV cast flickering shadows on the walls. When the New Year arrived, the fireworks on the TV screen brightened our room and the glittering lights and cheers from the TV excited me. We popped the champagne and kissed, saying "Happy New Year!", then we made love.

After we celebrated the arrival of 2002, we took off to the beach. Strollers were out here and there, loitering around under the starlight on the clear, crisp night, their voices loud with the joy of welcoming the New Year. I caught their jubilant vibes, and that added to my joy. My mind bubbled with thoughts, particularly two big ones—I wanted to graduate from school and to get married this year. As we walked along on the beach, he said, "This will be a nice year for us." I believed he was insinuating that we would marry within the year. Many happy thoughts ensued. Under the brilliant starlight, the whitecaps danced as if they could sense my joyous feelings.

Every so often, Frederick took care of Kevin. The six-month-old baby had become more mobile and slept less than he had a few months ago. Frederick wouldn't just put the baby carrier on the floor while he worked in his office, he had to pick the baby up to feed and cradle him in his arms.

Busy as he was, he made every effort to find time just for us—arranging a coffee time with me, taking me away to the beach once in a while, or exploring new restaurants. Perhaps he also wanted to get away from the house to have quiet and relaxing hours. For me, Frederick's car was my retreat, and it didn't matter a whole lot where we went as long as I was away from the house.

In late February, Frederick took me to Crater Lake for an overnight trip, which was a soul diversion. The lake was awesome, but eerie. The deep sapphire water almost stole my spirit and I felt weak in my knees. With the sky covered by wintery gray clouds, the caldera took on a sinister appearance. The lake resembled silver-black velvet. Maybe it was from this spookiness that I felt an ominous presentiment. A worrying thought crossed mind. *I hope Frederick's kids won't play with my computer.*

When we arrived at home, I opened my computer. *Everything looks good*, I thought. Since my mind was in a playful mood, I tried to open my favorite game "Majan"—the only game I'd kept on my computer for years for my entertainment. But the Majan icon wasn't on the screen. This puzzled me. In searching frantically, I kept thinking *the program couldn't have disappeared on its own*. Finally I concluded. *Umm . . . who touched my computer?*

"Frederick, my computer game, 'Majan' is gone. Somebody must have used my computer," I said.

"I don't know. Maybe the computer did it by itself," he said, as if it were no business of his.

"No! No way! That's ridiculous!" Application software won't wipe itself out," I argued furiously.

"Well, it happens sometimes," he retorted.

"Are you kidding me? Can you ask your kids?"

He convinced me I had somehow caused this to happen or the computer somehow did it by itself. I realized that, after all, he was a father, and he was doing his job to protect his family. I was unhappy my favorite game vanished, but the worst part was that I became paranoid about losing my thesis. Consequently, I had to take the extra time to make back-up copies every time I worked on it.

Around April, Ellen and Noah found a cute house in northwest Portland. They became independent. It was good for them to establish their own nest. Of course, Frederick was always available to them, but I thought it was good for Noah to feel he was the head of their home. Our household became peaceful. Quiet. Things went smoothly and I thought I finally could focus on my thesis.

But my thinking seemed to be paralyzed. I became more and more frustrated and overwhelmed as the days passed, and the thesis defense deadline grew closer and with it, the pressure increased. I only had a month to finish. At one point, I became frustrated with one of my thesis committee members, a professor who knew the methodologies well and was supposed to provide me the writing structures. She was too busy to meet with me. When I finally had a chance to meet with her, her advice was vague. The pressure finally reached a point where I needed to contact the Chair of the Philosophy Department to ask if there were any chance of replacing that professor. Professor Gould invited me to his office and dealt with my issue as if it were his own. I was astonished, and thought it was quite remarkable that he immediately called my advisor, Barbara, and asked her to find a good replacement. Barbara called him back with the name of my new committee person. The whole arrangement was made within thirty minutes.

I found my new committee member, Professor William Greenfield, to be tremendously helpful. In a speedy manner, he asked me to bring my thesis paper to his office. He was going out of town and said he would read my paper on the airplane. By our next meeting, he was already able to tell me exactly what I needed to do and how to do it. He provided me precise instructions, and that was an incredible help.

Meanwhile, I also met with Barbara to go through the details of my paper. She advised me it needed numerous changes and some rethinking. Barbara had always been a huge help and had given me the support I needed. I still remember the line she used to say when I wrote things in my thesis without having supporting facts: "Kumiko, that might be a little bit of a stretch." She never criticized, but encouraged me with kind-heartedness, which I appreciated from the bottom of my heart.

With all the help I received, I felt prepared for my thesis defense on May 10th, 2002. In the conference room (one of the plushest at the university) there were four professors and fifteen audience members. My nerves were strained as I stood at the podium, thinking about what sort of questions would be thrown at me. Before starting my presentation, I had taken a shot of Pepto-Bismol, not wanting to have any stomach disturbance, as I had been developing an ulcer. I told myself, *Calm down, it's gonna be okay.* I proceeded with my speech, remembering Frederick's words, "Talk slowly and clearly so every word you say will be understood by the audience." I thought my presentation went well, and I was able to answer all the questions. Then I heard Robert saying, "Great job!" and a burst of applause resonated in the conference room. I felt I had gained a decisive victory. In a trance, I skipped down Park Avenue from campus to the Pioneer Square MAX Station to catch my train. Just before boarding the train, I called Frederick. "Congratulations!" he said, "I'm happy for you. We have to cerebrate." His delighted words made me even happier.

Finally, my big day arrived. I slipped into the graduate gown and then placed the green hood over my head to drape around my shoulders and over the back of my gown. Frederick had been waiting for me, and when I was ready, he grabbed his Nikon and slung it over his shoulder. "Let's go," he said gaily. When we stepped outside, it was cloudy. But in the distance, I saw a shaft of sunlight piercing the clouds and illuminating the area—an auspicious sign to me.

When we arrived at the Portland Memorial Coliseum, there were already huge crowds. Frederick and I were soon separated, as I had to get inside with my group. Once our group of students marched inside the hall, I immediately scanned the crowd for Frederick. Two years ago, I had stood in this coliseum alone. This time, I felt ever so happy, and the joy could even make me believe that all the stubborn knots of tension in my neck, shoulders, and along my back would be massaged away by rapture. As I heard the marching music "Pomp and Circumstance," a sudden tingling sensation welled up inside me and triggered tears. Finally my name was announced, and I proceeded to the Dean. He said, "Congratulations!" I bowed and smiled with a new-found confidence.

All my schooling was done. *Phew . . . I don't need to read hard books or worry about deadlines anymore!* A sweet eruption of a deep, soft giggle rose often with no reason for a few weeks. Since Thomas and I had divorced, four years had passed. In those four years, I had been plodding along, determined to complete my undergraduate and graduate school. Now it was time to look for a job, I thought, but first I needed a few weeks of a mental break.

One early morning, a few days after my graduation, Frederick abruptly presented his idea.

"How about going on a camping trip for two weeks?" he blurted.

"Hmm?" I was in that half-waking-up stage.

"How about traveling to Olympic National Park, the San Juan Islands, and maybe Victoria?"

"Camp what?" I asked.

He repeated himself.

As soon as I understood his words, I became wide-awake and curious about those places he had named. Camping didn't sound good, but going to islands intrigued me. I tried to think where the heck those places were. I only knew Victoria, Canada.

"And let's stay at a nice hotel somewhere in Vancouver for the last day of the trip," he added.

"That sounds good," I shouted, then rolled over on my side to give him a quick kiss.

"Why don't you do some research?" he asked.

"Yes, I will," I said excitedly, and then quickly slipped out of the bed.

Right after we finished breakfast, I went up to my office nook and typed the names of the island into a "Google" search.

First I searched "Olympic National Park." A stunning image came up of a sunset over the Pacific Ocean with its rugged coastline. Next I typed, "San Juan Islands." In the archipelago, there were six islands. I checked out Orcas, San Juan, and Lopez. All looked breathtakingly beautiful. Now I understood what they looked like, and was much more excited about going on a trip that not only had spectacular scenery, but also offered numerous attractions. That was all the more reason to explore this alluring archipelago.

I gathered all the information so Frederick could make the final decisions. Meanwhile, I busily prepared stuff to bring on the camping trip. I imagined what it would be like living outside for two weeks. *Umm . . . I will need a lot of clothes and food*, I reasoned. Obviously I wasn't a camper—camping gear didn't come to my mind first.

We needed to make plans for the fourteen-day trip, but we decided the plans wouldn't be fixed and could be changed by any impulsive ideas which, as it would turn out, popped up a lot. Even so, I made a long list of possible things to do. On the list, there were all sorts of things—recreation facilities, tourist activities, and attractions—I jammed it with all the things I thought we would enjoy. There were so many choices to make. When we put our heads together, ideas flew around.

"Let's do some biking," Frederick suggested.

"Rent a bike? That would be fun," I agreed. "You know, Olympic National Park has good accommodations—hot spring pools, fishing places, and hiking trails." I showed him some website printouts I had already made.

"Hot springs! I like that," he said, nodding.

We needed to determine where we wanted to stay in Olympic National Park and Victoria, and on Orcas Island and San Juan Island, but we didn't reserve any campsites: we would take our chances finding good ones.

Monday, a week after my graduation, we were ready to set off to the Olympic National Park. Soon after breakfast, Frederick started loading the boxes of food, the clothes, tent, sleeping bags, airbed, outdoor oven, chairs, and other things into his Chrysler Concorde. He called it "Fat Daddy." All the prepared camping provisions and equipment were squeezed into the car, leaving only the front seats empty. Fat Daddy looked really heavy. If someone had seen our car, they might have thought we were moving.

Before shifting the car into drive, Frederick said, "Let's begin our vacation by toasting with coffee. Now that we are officially on vacation, you can do anything you want." I liked hearing the word *vacation*—because I hadn't had a vacation for years. Our moods were soaring high like a kite in the sky. We were free from our duties. Fat Daddy ran swiftly up the interstate highway to Seattle.

Once we arrived in Seattle, we stopped by the Pike Place Market and had lunch at a restaurant on a pier. The day was hot and bright with a little breeze. I sat on a chair facing Puget Sound, waiting for Frederick to bring our lunch. The sun was at its highest point. Things looked so lovely. Boats dotted the bay, and seagulls glided effortlessly. At that moment, I felt like my soul had been plucked up and was gliding with those seagulls. I wore a wide-brimmed white hat, a cobalt blue short-sleeved shirt, and khaki pants; I looked summery. Frederick came back with our lunch, and sat down, remarking how pretty I was. Soon our stomachs were filled with fish and chips and beer. The food energized us for heading out to the first destination.

We camped that first night in the Olympic National Forest. The June air was cool and fresh. The long journey ahead of me inspired me to unwind and enjoy myself, so I mentally pushed the "play" button. We chose a flat and smooth spot to put up Frederick's small tent, orienting the front side for a good view. Actually, as we were deep in the woods, it didn't make much difference which way we faced, nevertheless, we took care with our setup. The forest was tranquil because the camping season had not yet started. We were lucky to enjoy nature with few human noises.

We covered the picnic table with a tablecloth, and then hiked down to the Sol Duc Hot Springs Resort, carrying our swimsuits and towels. After rambling down the hill for fifteen minutes or so, we found the pools. Frederick said, "See you outside at the pool," and walked away into the men's changing room. I hurriedly entered the women's changing room, and put on my newly-bought, light-green bikini. I felt a little self-conscious about wearing a bikini, as I hadn't worn one since high school.

We met inside the fenced hot spring pool area. When I stood at the poolside, I felt the cool breeze on my skin. There were four pools, and I stepped inside the smallest one, which no one was using. Frederick jumped in and sat next to me. Sitting in the hot mineral water, I felt totally relaxed as all my muscle aches evaporated with the rising steam.

Once we were back at the campsite, Frederick started making kindling to build a fire. When the fire started crackling, I realized there weren't any other campers around us. The deep woods were deathly quiet. He placed a grill over the fire for the salmon and I used a small stove grill to make rice. When the sky had darkened, the campfire became our focal point. Frederick poured me a glass of red wine. Just the two of us eating by the cracking fire, we laughed out loud in our rambling conversation. We stayed up for hours before we zipped open the small tent and turned in for the night. Finally, we squeezed into the sleeping bag. In his arms, I watched the last flickering of the flames project onto the tent.

We left the national park around ten the next morning, and drove to Port Townsend to catch our ferryboat to the next destination, Orcas Island. By the time we got to the port, the lines had already formed, and they looked quite long. Nonetheless, pretty soon we were guided to drive onto the large ferryboat. Once our car was situated in a tight parking spot, we excitedly ran up the stairs to the deck where we could look back at Port Townsend and watch as it gradually disappeared over the horizon. A few hours later, a strip of gray started to appear in the distance. As we approached the island, I heard the ferryboat's loud horn. Soon the engine revved in reverse, and the boat shuddered. The water started to boil along the sides of the boat, and then I heard the announcement that we had arrived at Orcas Island. From a distance, the island didn't appear to be developed, but I liked the desolated look: it reminded me somewhat of the Japanese islands I had visited when I was a child.

Orcas Island was having a big festival and crowds of islanders filled the town. It seemed everyone was out participating in the free-spirited procession. They were costumed and masked, and they paraded about in the highest of spirits. The radiant scene under a transparent blue sky appeared to be blessed by the sun god. We followed the loosely-organized procession and took many pictures.

Suddenly, Frederick said, "Go under, between the stilts. I'll take your picture. Hurry up!"

"No! I can't do that," I protested.

"Just go," he said, and pushed me.

I ran and quickly stooped under the crotch of a long-legged performer. His face was colorfully painted like the sun—lemon yellow, burnt orange, flake white.

"Smile!" Frederick shouted.

I grinned into the camera. I felt like a kid, and this silly feeling rejuvenated me. My spirit was totally overtaken by this droll summer solstice parade.

Our first day on the island ended merrily, but the next morning something unfortunate happened. We were about ready to make our breakfast when Frederick complained that something was wrong with his ear and asked me to check it for him.

"Something's buzzing in my ear. Do you have a bobby pin?" asked Frederick.

"What's in there?" I asked nonchalantly.

"I don't know, but I hear a buzzing sound. It must be a tiny bug. Can you see it? I need to get it out of my ear. It might be a spider," said Frederick, very agitated.

"I don't see anything."

I looked into his left ear, but I couldn't see any objects in there. I wondered how serious his problem actually was, but it was apparently very serious for him. With a panicked face, he said, "I need to go to a doctor right now!" I was surprised at his behavior. He had always kept perfect composure when dealing with his problems, his daughter's and mine as well.

Unfortunately, it was Saturday, and that inconvenienced us a great deal in finding a doctor. First we needed to drive a couple miles down the hill from our campground to the town to look for a pay phone and phone book. When we entered the downtown, I soon spotted a payphone booth. He called a listing that was printed in bold type: Orcas Medical Center. The voice that came over the phone was recorded, but said that the clinic was open 10:00 a.m. to 2:00 p.m., so we headed there as quickly as we could.

As we entered the clinic, the hall was dim, the only light coming in from the windows. There were no other patients. We wandered around until, finally, his name was called. We entered an examining room and the doctor, a tall woman in her late thirties, introduced herself and asked Frederick to explain his problem.

"Let's take a look at your ear," the doctor said.

She washed her hands, and then stuck an otoscope in his ear. After moving it around at different angles, she said, "Yeah . . . I see a tiny bug."

Hearing that, Frederick finally relaxed enough to even be able to joke about it. "Would you evict the uninvited tenant?"

The doctor smiled and said, "Let's try." She poured some liquid into his ear to float the bug out.

I was staring at his ear, but I didn't see the bug, and the doctor didn't see it either. But the bug, whatever it was, seemed to have come out.

"Thank God!" I thought.

Our next destination was Friday Harbor, the main commercial center of the San Juan Islands. Our ferry docked in the harbor about lunch time. When we drove off the ferry, my eyes immediately fell on the restaurants that faced the port. In the distance, I could see the white smoke of fish cooking. Once on the street, we could see people eating on the restaurants' decks. The smell of the fish and the sound of laughter drew us in. We picked the restaurant that had the best view of the port and then happily crunched crispy fish and chips and drank cold black beer.

Friday Harbor had a pristine beauty although the island was highly commercialized for tourism. There were many attractions on the island, but we enjoyed checking out the anchored cabin cruisers and sailing yachts, then peeking into the stores and galleries, trying a few gourmet restaurants, and picnicking in parks. We spent two days driving around Sun Juan Island, returning to our campsite in the evenings. I enjoyed camping in the beginning, but as time went by, the novelty wore off and I was ready to go on to the city of Victoria, British Columbia.

Victoria was in its vivacious early summer mode. The English-style city was energized by the crowds of tourists. It presented a totally different image than it had when Thomas and I had visited in the cold early spring five years ago. The summer events and balmy weather enlivened the whole city. In front of the Fairmont Empress Hotel lay a small placid harbor packed with sailboats. Along the marina walkway, a lively art fair attracted crowds of tourists from all over the world. Those colorful sights presented a merrier and prettier impression than I remembered from my last visit.

Frederick and I snaked through the closely-arranged booths, stopping here and there to browse oil paintings, hand-painted etched vases, and beaded jewelry. Many items were made by First Nations' people. At one shop, I lingered for a while to examine the jewelry which a Haida artist had made. Perhaps my eyes fixed on that piece of jewelry sent a message to Frederick. He said in my ear, "If you like one of those, I can get it for you. Find the one you like," he urged.

I grinned broadly at him. He helped me pick out a blue-beaded gemstone bracelet.

The next day, we went to the Fairmont Empress Hotel. When I entered the hotel, the lobby evoked old memories, for Thomas and I had stayed at this hotel. But the flash of memory quickly vanished. Frederick suggested we have the royal afternoon tea, but the high price stunned us when we looked at the menu, so instead we went to a teahouse in downtown and had an Assam tea with a petite cake. The deep burgundy-red tea and pungent flavor reminded me of the tea I had many times relished at the Terrace in the Harrods department store when I was in London for six months in 1979.

On the last night of camping, we cooked a salmon over the campfire and opened a bottle of Shiraz from the San Juan Island's grocery store. Frederick used up all the remaining firewood. We sat in front of the fire and stayed up for a long time talking about our childhoods. The stars were faint and there were only a few.

The next morning it was totally overcast and the day didn't look promising. Taking out the tent stakes, Frederick asked, "Can you help me roll up the tent?" When he took the last stake out, the tent collapsed in a sad heap. *The camping is over*, I realized. I felt a tad blue that the vacation was coming to an end. We packed up all the camping equipment and left.

To set out for Vancouver, we needed to take a ferry. The weather in Vancouver was unexpectedly better, much warmer. It was already past one o'clock when we docked, so we did a quick sightseeing tour before locating a tourist information center to find a nice hotel. We reserved a hotel in Richmond, twenty minutes away from downtown Vancouver.

The building was inlaid with dark glass and resembled the United Nations' building, though it was much smaller. *Such a cold-looking appearance it has!* In contrast, the interior was warmer and far more inviting and its ambiance was pleasing for the end of our long trip. Since we had an hour to kill till our special-occasion dinner, we explored the small marina near the hotel to stroll along the river causeway. The hour quickly passed by and we had to go back to our room to dress up for dinner.

The restaurant in downtown Vancouver was in a twenty-three-story building. In the elevator on our way to the highest floor, Frederick's eyes rested on me as if he were appraising an antique, and then he said, "You look like a movie star." My tight black dress and black high heels might have had the special effect of creating a sensual image in his eyes. I actually had never worn such a skimpy dress in front of him, or anyone for that matter. His comment made me feel like I was walking on air. We sat at a table by a large picture window with a view of the city lights. He ordered a glass of wine, and I ordered a cocktail. The view, the food, the cocktail, and our conversation cast a love spell.

I felt content with him and I thought, *how far we have come!*

In the morning we soaked in the Jacuzzi one more time and then we left the hotel. "No hurry going home, five hours of driving. If we leave Vancouver after lunch, we'll be home by dinner," said Frederick. The weather being gorgeous, we decided to visit the botanical garden. Being bathed with sunlight, the cedar-maze was shiny and refreshing. After spending a couple hours at the garden, we set off for the U.S. Canadian border around one o'clock.

As we approached the border, I noticed all the lines were dreadfully long. The cars crept along inch by inch, despite the fact that many customs' agents were on duty. After two hours, around four o'clock, we came to one of the agents. We had made sure nothing would be suspicious to the agent's eyes, so I was relaxed. After putting the gearshift in park, Frederick handed our driver's licenses to the officer. The officer scanned them in a fraction of second, and he immediately cast his eyes onto me. My face stiffened.

"Can I see your passport?" he demanded.

"I don't have it," I said, wondering why he was asking me that question.

Pointing his index finger straight at a building on the other side of the road, the agent ordered us to park our car next to the customs' office for further inspection. We had no choice but to obey. Frederick drove up to the customs' office with a serious look. I felt resentful and desperate.

I said to Frederick, "You know, I have been to Canada four times before without carrying my passport. Why do I need it now? Why could I come into Canada, but not leave?" He didn't respond, so I started talking to myself in almost inaudible Japanese, "Such crap; it's like a cockroach trap." At that moment, I thought of the cockroach trap in my parents' kitchen. The trap was made of thin cardboard in the shape of a little green house with a red roof that had a sign over the door saying, "Hotel." The inside of the house was covered with sticky glue to entrap cockroaches. "Can check in, but cannot checkout!" I suddenly raised my voice loud enough that Frederick had to respond to me this time.

He looked at me with a perplexed expression, and then finally said, "You will be fine."

We got out of our car and entered the customs' office, which was crowded with people who apparently needed to be investigated. We walked toward one of the windows at the office counter, and waited in line behind a few unfortunate travelers who were foreigners like me.

When our turn came, an officer asked me the same question, "Can I see your passport?"

"I don't have it," I said to the officer,

"Then, are you carrying your alien card?" he asked.

I said, "No" in a faint voice.

"The security has gotten very tight since 9/11," declared the officer.

Frederick questioned the officer with a lawyer's attitude as to how I could get out of Canada, but he was respectful.

The officer turned his face toward Frederick and then spoke to him in a tone that had softened significantly. "If she doesn't have her passport or alien card, she has to pay the fine." The fine, two-hundred dollars, had to be paid in Canadian dollars, which we didn't have. The banks were already closed, so there wasn't any way to get me out till the next day. *We were detained between two countries!* Frederick and I had to camp out again. This detention totally destroyed our trip. Putting up our tent one more time near the border, my mood darkened.

I said to Frederick cynically, "You know, life is not meant to be too much fun." Then I murmured, "Oh well, I thought I prepared very well for this camping trip. Then again, life is unpredictable. Right, Frederick?" He smiled at me but didn't comment, so I murmured again, "Such is life." Not having citizenship was inconvenient, but changing my citizenship was fearful for me. I often thought, *What if I become seriously ill and I have no one to rely on? Then how could I survive in the U.S?* My life had been so unstable, and I never felt ready for the big step of changing my nationality. I hoped though, that someday I would become an American.

That would make travel easier. At the airport, customs' officers wouldn't raise their eyebrows and ask lengthy questions about my purpose for coming back to the U.S., or take my fingerprints. Perhaps a citizenship would make me feel more established, compelling me to regard America as my own country.

The next morning, after having retuned from the long vacation I sat at my desk at home. I sighed and sighed. I really disliked job hunting. A hot tea helped ease my mind a bit. I forcibly braced for the challenge and updated my resume. *It will be difficult to find a mediation position without any experience*, I thought, but I began checking the online classified ad sites, newspapers, and other places. No mediation jobs were listed. A week passed. The pressure started building up. I had known it wouldn't be easy to find this kind of job, nevertheless, I hadn't expected these jobs to be so rare. For a few days, I wondered what to do. I was stumped. I had been in this situation many times, and I always hated the experience. But this particular job hunt felt like trying to get a royal flush.

Finally, coming out from my state of shock, I told myself I needed to change my strategy. Just waiting for the ads to show up would be wasting time. I should start making phone calls directly to organizations and law practices. I randomly contacted over fifteen places. I soon learned that the majority of mediation service centers were hiring volunteers to fill their positions. I grouched, *I cannot be a volunteer. I need to make money*. I found it difficult to believe the majority of mediators were not paid. Most mediators who received compensation were lawyers or counselors. Wracking my brain, it occurred to me to look into the Divorce and Conciliation Mediation Service Center at the Washington County Courthouse, where I'd had some exposure to mediation during my practicum. Getting my hopes up, I called to see if there were any opportunities.

The person on the phone was apologetic. "I am sorry, we are currently not looking for any mediators, but I will let you know if any opportunity arises."

I had already known the mediators who worked there had over ten years of experience and would not go anywhere until they retired. Totally discouraged, I realized there wasn't much I could do, so I started looking into other areas of employment.

I sent my resumes to more than thirty companies and waited. After a month without a single response, the waiting became unbearable. I detested just passing the days aimlessly. During those vexing days, a thought flitted through my mind that this might be a good chance to invite my parents to visit. More than a year and a half had passed since I had moved into Frederick's house, and in that time, I had not told my family about him. My parents would have been uncomfortable if they knew I was living with a man outside of marriage. There were some signs I could sense that they might have discovered this already: first, they didn't call, second, they didn't ask many questions but just listened. Last of all, they seemed more concerned about my contentment. When I was living in the previous house, they had called once a week. Because of all this, I had been longing for the day I would be able to introduce them to Frederick. *Now might be a good time!* I thought.

But there was a complication. A few months after Frederick's daughter and her family had moved out, Frederick's friend, Tom, moved into our place so he could deal with some problems. Tom had been staying with us for two months, and we had no clue when he would be ready to leave. I knew my asking my parents to visit wouldn't be good news for either Tom or Frederick, but I presumed that a month's notice would be sufficient time for Tom to look for his own place.

So I dared to ask Frederick, "Would it be all right to ask my parents to come here?"

"Ummmmm . . . what shall we do with Tom?" He groaned for a bit, but then immediately became the caring, sensitive person I knew. "I think it's time. He should start looking for his own place. Invite your parents to come. I want to meet them."

Frederick's permission suggested, I thought, that he was indeed thinking of me seriously. That night, I delightedly dialed my parents. Since my parents had been worrying and wanting to see how I was living, they accepted our invitation.

When we heard my parents' arrival date would be September 1st, Frederick was determined to complete furnishing his new house before then. For a whole month, every weekend was dedicated to furniture shopping. His old furniture, which was still in good condition, was replaced with new, to create a modern look that wasn't to my taste. My preference was the opposite, a traditional warm and cozy look. He liked leather couches, and I liked fabric. He liked glass-topped dining tables and I liked wooden tables, preferably maple. I knew I couldn't strongly inject my opinion, as this was his house, but I hoped the house interior wouldn't look too cold or antiseptic. On his shopping list were two beds, one for us and one for the guest room, a dining table set, a shag rug for the living room, and even geometric paintings and potted plants that would provide a shot of color.

I had a strange feeling when we were shopping for furniture. Buying a dining table and bed is an intimate thing that usually committed couples do, so being just a girlfriend, I didn't know how to behave. Should I act like a future wife and insist on what I wanted? At times, I could believe that one day I would become his wife, but at other times I wasn't sure. Frederick wasn't certain if I would fit into his family circumstances, more precisely if his daughter would accept me as his wife. Early on in our relationship, Frederick had mentioned he had no idea why his ex-girlfriend had called off their wedding, but he later revealed she had some resentment towards his daughter.

In any case, I made sure to let Frederick know clearly what I liked and disliked. He considerately incorporated some of my strong preferences, although he definitely had his own particular taste. Because our preferences in décor choice were hardly close, we spent a significant amount of time checking each and every furniture shop in our vicinity to find pieces we could agree on. Good gracious we were picky!

One day, while we were looking for wall sconces at a lighting shop in Southeast Portland, we sat down at a table to have coffee at the in-store snack bar.

Forking a muffin, he abruptly asked me a funny question. "Do you think you look like your mom? You know, people often say that your parents are a good indicator of what you may become."

I rolled my eyes up to think about what she looked like, but I couldn't find the right words. So I decided to say, "My mom is a nice person," to emphasize her inner beauty, but I wondered why he had asked such a question. Was it a hint that he was thinking about marriage? I began looking for furniture a little more seriously.

My parents arrived in Portland a week after Frederick's friend, Tom, had left. On their arrival day, I was anxious until I saw them, even though their flight was direct and they didn't have to worry about transferring between terminals. I left home early enough to meet their plane at two o'clock, but was caught in traffic for thirty minutes on the highway. Breathless, I entered the airport and ran to find them. A few minutes later I saw them following the crowd of their fellow passengers. My shoulders dropped in relief—they had made it.

My mom, who was seventy-nine years old, wanted to look pretty when she met Frederick and asked me to doll her up, so we stopped by the Fred Meyer near the house. At the coffee stand inside the store I bought a coffee for my dad and tea for my mom. We sat at a table in the corner, and I opened my cosmetic bag to put makeup on her face. Her small face had more wrinkles, and the age spots were more prominent than they had been the last time I saw her. She smiled at me all the time while I applied her makeup. I felt her breath on my hand as I put lipstick on her. Her warm breath induced a mixture of happiness and sadness. I was happy to see my mom, but it was hard to set eyes on her aged face. She suddenly stood up and unfastened her suitcase. She pulled out a case and handed it to me. Opening it, I chuckled. It was a short wavy hairpiece I had bought for her a long time ago. I gently placed it on her thinning hair, securing it with hairpins. She looked a lot younger, and, more importantly, she seemed to be satisfied.

As we walked toward my car, my dad remarked that he admired me for driving the same old car. Scratching my head, I grinned at him. He smiled right back. When we got inside the car, I turned the key, but the engine didn't start. I suddenly remembered I had not turned off the headlights since parking at the Portland Airport. *No!* I thought. *I don't want my parents' first introduction to Frederick to start this way.* My dad and mom waited stoically while I tried to think of what to do. I went back to Fred Meyer and reluctantly dialed Frederick to rescue me. He came in no time. As his car approached, I said, "There he is." My parents got out and stood stiffly in the parking lot. Feeling a little flustered, I introduced them to Frederick. "I am very happy to meet you," Frederick, bowed with reverence.

Reciprocating, my parents vowed in unison.

"We are very honored to be invited," said my dad, then vowed deeply with my mom.

I embraced my parents, then said, "Frederick, let's go home so we can sit and talk."

We tailed Frederick's car.

The next day we had to host Kevin's first birthday. I thought it was too soon to introduce my parents to Frederick's daughter, her family and her husband's family, as they hadn't even had a chance to get to know my boyfriend. In any case, nearly twenty people, including Frederick's and his daughter's friends gathered at our place. As Frederick and I had to do everything for the party, we were both plunged into a whirlwind of work. I could not pay any attention to my parents, who sat in their chairs, smiling, for the entire six hours. Kevin, in contrast, crawled around on the floor, getting everyone's attention. He was in a great mood. He zeroed in on all the new toys, grabbing each toy and putting it to his little mouth. A couple of times Kevin chased me around when I carried the food into the living room. I wanted to pick him up, but l let him play. While Frederick was busy hosting, I stood in the kitchen to keep refilling the party dishes and plates of food. I couldn't sit down until late evening. But despite our exhaustion, we were pleased that the party went well. I felt a sense of connection with Frederick's family members. I hoped my parents liked Frederick's family.

On this visit, I did not take my parents on a long trip. Instead, I drove them around the suburbs, mostly showing them the golf courses. My father didn't ask me to take him to play golf, but was satisfied to just hit balls at a driving range. Six years before, at the age of seventy-six, he had been able to play eighteen holes of golf with his young American counterparts. Six years made a noticeable change in his movement. At the driving range, he took quite a bit of time to tee-up. His swing was slow. His balls dropped way shorter than they used to. In contrast, my mom's vitality was still admirable in spite of her fragility. She walked with quick short steps, but her gait was sturdy. Aging changes in their bones, muscles, and joints stirred my pity, and I felt sad.

On Friday, in the second week of my parents' visit, we came home from our usual short outing around four o'clock. I noticed Frederick's car wasn't in the driveway.

"Where did he go?" I mumbled to myself. About a half-hour later, I heard the front door shut. With a single glance, I perceived something was odd. Then again, he tended to be more animated than most people I had known, so I brushed off my notion about his strange actions and instead worried about what to make for dinner. A moment later, I heard the front door bang again, but he returned quickly.

"Don't come downstairs! Stay upstairs until I call you!" he shouted from the entry, and scooted downstairs into his office.

"Okay!" I shouted back.

Fifteen minutes later, Frederick appeared and asked me to come downstairs. As his face expressed that he had some sort of ulterior motive, I was on alert. Wondering what might be waiting for me, I followed him. He opened the office door and let me go in first. No sooner had I entered his office than I saw tall candles and flowers. Pink carnations, yellow chrysanthemums, and a few white lilies were laid in a row on the coffee table and three tall taper candles were stuck in the flowers. In front of them, a champagne bottle and two tall skinny glasses stood on an oval silver tray as if for some special occasion. All of sudden, I began to grasp Frederick's intentions. The blood rushed to my head and my body stiffened. My thoughts raced to understand his gesture, but I kept them to myself and waited for his next move. He asked me to sit on a cushion he had prepared. *Here it comes!* My heart fluttered. He bent down on one knee and took a small velvet case from his pocket. Then looking straight into my eyes, he opened the case in front of my face. I must have appeared dumbstruck. My gaze immediately fastened upon the brilliant white diamond. I had never received a diamond from anyone before. I don't know how long it was before I raised my head to say, "Yes" to his proposal. When he heard me, his face broke into a big smile, and then he hastened me off to bring my parents downstairs.

"Tell them we're engaged, and bring them downstairs, because I want to tell them something," he said.

So I leaped up the stairs. My parents' anxious expressions instantly transformed into radiant smiles as they saw my excited face and the sparkling ring on my finger that I held up to show them.

"We are engaged!" I said. Not waiting for my parents to respond, I rushed them downstairs.

My parents entered his office, but appeared not to know how to conduct themselves—whether they should sit down or stay standing in order to respond to Frederick. Frederick stepped forward, and in an aside to me, asked me to translate. We made a little circle like a football team in a huddle.

"I promise to send her to Tokyo once a year, and I will be a faithful husband," he said. with an air of profound respect. Then he looked at me.

So I translated to my parents what he had promised.

"Thank you very much. We are very happy for you," they said formally in Japanese, and then made a deep bow in unison.

To hear these promises from his mouth, my parents were very pleased. Their youngest child and the only girl in the family, who was living alone in a foreign country, had found her life partner.

On the night of our engagement, Frederick revealed that he had asked my good friend from my previous job, Yasuko, how to propose marriage in the Japanese tradition. That explained an incident which had puzzled me for the last few months. Yasuko had left the company in September 1997, about the same time I left. She and her husband moved to Japan to help in her mother's business, but every July they came back to the house in Portland and stayed for a month. To throw a big party was their annual custom and they invited me every year. The summer of 2001, I took Frederick to the party. There were more than fifty people there, and the two-story house was jam-packed with Yasuko's and Brian's friends. During the party, Frederick vanished. I looked for him everywhere on Yasko's property, but couldn't find him anywhere. I looked for Yasuko, but she, too, was missing. After I had waited for over an hour, he finally showed up. His quiet disappearance disturbed me, but not wanting to bicker in front of Yasuko's Japanese friends, I let it go. With his revelation that he had received the protocol from Yasuko as to how a man proposed to a girl in Japan, my worry evaporated. I appreciated his effort, but I felt sorry that Yasuko had had to leave her guests for such a long time.

On the following morning, my mom walked into my bathroom when I was putting on my make-up. Seeing me in the mirror, she said, "Frederick-san faintly resembles your dad." I looked at her eyes in the mirror and responded, "Hmmm . . . You think so?" My dad had a chiseled face with deep set eyes and thin lips, which was not typical for Japanese. Although his "western" look might have something to do with it, their facial resemblance was very subtle. I chuckled about her comment, as she was still looking at me as if she wanted me to agree with her, but for some reason I couldn't say I'd had the same thought.

Frederick became more serious about connecting with my parents. In his spare time, he often drove us to the neighborhood golf course. To my joy, my dad looked amused at the driving range, but his smile widened even more when he heard Frederic crying out, "Good shot!"

On weekends, Frederic took us on excursions. One of them was to Skamania Lodge in Stevenson, Washington for dinner. Along the way, we all golfed at a pitch-n-putt course at the McMenamin's Edgefield Pub Course in Troutdale. Having had some wine before playing, we were relaxed. My mom, being a little tipsy, enjoyed playing also. The last weekend of their stay, we did a wine tour in the Yamhill valley. Vineyards on the rolling hills were splendid in September.

All the travel plans Frederick made were thoughtful, and his attentiveness to my elderly parents was notable. He was always a valet boy for my parents so they didn't need to walk unnecessarily. His kindness to my parents made me feel good about our relationship.

The month flew by quickly. My parents left for Tokyo contented. I was relieved their concerns were lessened. Mine too. I was old fashioned. I had felt it was not morally right to live together before marriage. My discomfort had gotten worse when I started attending the Japanese Baptist Church, as they focused on sins. I originally began going to this church to find subjects for my graduate thesis on intercultural marriage between Japanese and Americans. In that church, there were plenty of intercultural couples. I did not intend to join the church, but drawn by the kindness and generous nature of the members, I continued attending. To make friends in church was easy. Many times my church friends tried to induce me to be baptized, but I kept refusing, as I did not have a strong conviction.

In retrospect, I had never contemplated religion much as a young person in Japan. I just respectfully followed the Japanese traditions, as most Japanese do. Today many religions are practiced in Japan, but most people follow a meld of Shintoism and Buddhism. Religion does not play a major role in the everyday life of the average Japanese person. The birth and marriage ceremonies are mostly Shinto, while funerals are Buddhist. Going to a shrine made me feel like a follower of Shinto. My family tradition was to visit the Tsurugaoka Hachimangu Shrine in Kamakura on New Year's Eve. Japanese people do have customs and rituals that are observed on special occasions like birthdays, weddings, funerals and religious holidays. Some of the traditions are fading, but most Japanese continue to follow some rituals.

Frankly, I don't know much about Shintoism and Buddhism. In my shallow understanding, Shinto is the indigenous religion of Japan and Shinto gods are in everything—water, fire, wood, sky . . . even in my desk. If I want to iconize my desk, then the desk can be a god for me. So I have always treated material things with respect. Buddhism focuses on attaining enlightenment to rid oneself of the tenacious idea that everything lasts forever, because all is transitory. The belief is that one should not become attached to things or people. My aunt taught me when I was a child that everything changes and will be reborn or reincarnated into a different form. She said, "Behave well; otherwise you might be coming back in a form which you don't want, such as a fox or raccoon." I was spiritually oriented but not very religious.

Living in the U.S., I started picking up some knowledge of Western religion because people discussed it openly. Churches have various means of evangelizing. Occasionally some pious people knocked at my door, bringing flyers. While surfing TV channels, I saw all kinds of Christian programs and on the radio I heard their sermons and songs. I spotted fanciful churches all over the United States. However, I had generally taken an objective view of the spectrum of religious faiths until I started going to the Japanese Baptist Church. Some of the stories I heard during the services moved me. During one devotional meeting, an old Japanese woman stood at the center of the stage, and told us a story of a hard time she'd experienced:

> *One time, my money ran out, and I wondered how I would survive. The next morning, when I opened my house door I saw a big box piled up high with food: ham, cheese, milk, bread, beans, flour, fruits and more stuff. No indication who left the box. I could guess that was someone from the church. When I squatted down to look at it, tears fell. I still don't know who gave it to me.*

"Amen!" a Japanese woman shouted.

I liked to listen to the encouraging, heartwarming and inspiring stories. While sitting in a pew, I listened, but also observed the believers. I noticed particularly that the Japanese women were very animated. They expressed their faith through their music, swaying their bodies and singing American Christian songs in an earsplitting key. They all looked as if they had halos. Perhaps in their eyes, I was a lost sheep and they felt sorry for me. I did not feel comfortable when, once in a while, they talked about sins, especially because I was living with my boyfriend, but I had determined to open myself up to understand the Christian thinking.

However, when I started attending their Bible study, I realized it wasn't for me. I couldn't see some of the Bible teachings the way my Japanese church friends did. Not being able to grasp some tenets, I felt ill at ease. Since I couldn't force myself to believe something I had reservations about, I began visiting the church less frequently, until finally I completely stopped attending. Although I had only six months of exposure, I was glad I had learned something of what Christianity was about. There are conflicting ideas in my head, and I still have not figured out what I believe.

Nonetheless, I was glad Frederick and I were engaged and that I didn't need to feel uneasy about cohabiting. I was truly content with this almost-ideal man: he was kind, intelligent, charming, very funny, but modest—which I valued the most. I say, "Almost ideal," because there was one significant thing that bothered me. Frederick sometimes carried kindness too far, to my way of thinking. Being with just him was enjoyable, but other people always seemed to be complicating our lives—his daughter, son-in-law and grandson and his old friends. Sharing life with other people who had no connection or sense of loyalty to me was quite challenging; it in fact required an inconceivable amount of mental strength. After three long years, we finally reached the point where we were getting married, so I believed our relationship dynamics would be twisted around and Frederick would think about me first. But *no*. I was too optimistic. One incident totally blew my expectations away. It was as bitter as gall.

A few months after our engagement, we had a big argument. His daughter called when we were about to eat dinner. After waiting for more than thirty minutes, I dared say, "Dinner will get cold." He lowered his eyebrows and pressed his lips hard. His mean look upset me. But as he put the phone down, he came to me and began lecturing. I was insulted. Bravely using this occasion to express my built-up frustration over discordance related to his friends and family, I confronted him.

I started in. "I'm very hungry. You could call her after dinner. She calls every day. Why do you always think of others first? Can you put me in a little higher place than your people?"

"Why do you think you are more important than anyone else? Why do you have to be different?" he said, with contempt in his voice.

His provoking comment disheartened me, but I regained my composure and became as brave as a lion. "Marriage takes strong binding. It should be similar to a pyramid structure. You and I should be at the top, and others come under us."

His dismay at my bold statement must have been monumental because he shouted at me, saying some words that meant something like the Aesop quote, "Be aware lest you lose the substance by grasping at the shadow." Then he warned me concretely: "Love the people who are important to me, otherwise, you will lose me." He slammed our bedroom door and left me alone. I sat on the floor and held my knees in place so I could rest my head on them. I didn't know what to think, but undeniably understood on which side my bread was buttered. Frederick had many people he wanted to keep close. There were inevitably more activities than I was always up for. I understood he needed to be a good father for his daughter's family and wanted to be a reliable friend to his friends, but at times his support was overstretched in my eyes. Sometimes I felt neglected and less important, as he paid great attention towards those people.

What had been lacking in our relationship was that Frederick didn't assure me that I was a significantly important person to him. The situation was easy for Frederick, as my family was all in Tokyo, I had no children, and my few good friends didn't involve themselves in my life like Frederick's did. My attention towards him was much greater than his towards me. Maybe it *was* my huge ego that made me feel competitive with others in his life, but if Frederick had always taken my side perhaps I could have acted differently toward his people and even given him support when he needed it. The biggest issue between us was that he often didn't back me up.

XIV

Déjà vu

Two months had passed since my parents' return and I still had no job. The pressure was boiling up. Sitting on a chair and reviewing my life, I was suddenly aggravated. *Four years of my hard work, time, and money. And still I have no job! Why didn't I get a degree in something more practical!*

The unemployed life had begun to engulf me. Besides my feelings, the balance of my accounts had reached the point when I needed to bring in some income. Christmas was just around the corner. Since our engagement, Frederick had become supportive, but I didn't want to financially rely on him. So, putting aside the notion of finding a "real" job, I applied for a seasonal sales job at the JC Penney at Washington Square Mall during the Christmas season. I often had to work until midnight and Fredrick tried to match his schedule to mine so as to have our time.

Meanwhile, we discussed our wedding day and other logistics. The engagement period was like a trial period, a reality check, and the relationship became volatile because he and I closely scanned our compatibilities. I reflected on this later and realized I was mistaken in thinking I had gained some power and influence over our relationship. In reality, our engagement did not give me any power, but only confused me. I thought I had gained the leverage to ask for what I wanted once in a while. My conundrum was how to secure my place, as Frederick had so many people who were influential aside from the influence of his daughter.

One day in January, I was enraged. I don't recall exactly what the quarrel was about. All I can remember is it was triggered by some minor annoyance. Perhaps I was inconvenienced by his family or friends. Maybe I was in a cross mood. In any case, this time my temper reached its peak. I began packing my clothes. He told me with a serious face, "Kumiko, you have said seven times that you want to get out of our relationship."

I was dumbfounded.

"If you want to leave, leave. But I am not going to take you back," he shouted.

I had acted before I thought and regretted my impulsive behavior soon after he said that. Bursting into tears, I said I was sorry many times and even begged him to take back his words. He forgave me that time; however, a week later, we had another argument that made him decide to end our relationship. He told me to move out of the house.

When I heard this, I felt like my body was being sucked into an abyss. Our relationship had never gotten on the right track: it had always been shaky. It was as if we were trying to build a house on sand. Now it was over! He told me to find someone else for my emotional support, so I had to shield my emotions. He said he'd allow me to stay until I found a place, but he obviously wasn't comfortable being with me anymore.

I asked myself, *What the hell am I doing? Why do I keep screwing up my life?* This wasn't my first experience of losing a man. Alas, I had done it again. The only good thing was I had built up some immunity to heartbreak, although the desolation and necessity of finding a place and a job were a double punch.

Life is such a challenge. It is like an oil painting—layers of colors, no guarantee of success or failure, but fixable to some extent. Inspiration—a burst of sudden creativity—might elevate the painting, but at the same time it might ruin it. Critical acumen makes the work more eye-catching or desirable, but most certainly, skills enhance the work. Life is like that. Life demands lots of skills so as to make our living more successful or enjoyable. My questions in retrospect were in vain, but still, I asked myself out of curiosity if I had had the skills necessary to co-exist with someone like Frederick's daughter. Could I have lived harmoniously with them? *Oh well, it's over anyway*, I thought in despair.

Early the next morning, I got empty boxes and a newspaper from a supermarket. I scanned the classified ads to look for a shared house and circled two low-rent places in the same area. After making appointments, I drove up to see what they looked like. Unsurprisingly, those places weren't satisfactory. One wasn't clean, and the other was in a bad neighborhood. The following Tuesday afternoon, while I was still finishing up packing, a church friend happened to call me. I had to tell her about my leaving the house. "What happened?" she said in a worried way, but she soon seemed to realize it wasn't a good time for me to explain, so she immediately asked what she could do. A few minutes later, she called me back to say, "I have a friend. She might have accommodation for you. I'll give you her phone number."

After we ended our conversation, I dialed the number. The lady invited me right away. She was a tiny Japanese woman whose complexion was dried and darkish. Although her vulgar language shocked me at first, she was gracious and offered me a room in her newly-built townhouse. Her husband was absent due to a restraining order she had obtained. Surprised to hear she had filed for a restraining order, I wondered if the police were involved. In any case, her new townhouse had a modern interior with arched doors and a marble-top island in the spacious kitchen. I liked her house and was tempted to stay there, but the strong odor of her cigarette smoke and my fear of her angry husband made me uneasy, so I politely declined her generous offer, saying, "Thank you very much for your kindness, but I think I want to keep looking for a permanent place."

The living situation in Frederick's house became suffocating. We had cut off our feelings. During the day, I tried to be outside, looking for my new home. Parking my car somewhere along the sidewalk, I often killed hours sitting in the unheated vehicle. Strangely, even on the freezingly cold days, I didn't feel cold. That surprised me, because I was keenly sensitive to cold. My attention must have been diverting, warring for my future.

On the fourth day of looking for a place to live, an ad caught my attention. The house features were printed in large font—WOMEN ONLY! CLEAN, QUIET, SPACIOUS, GOOD LOCATION, CABLE, GUEST ROOM/OFFICE, EXERCISE ROOM. I immediately rang the number. The landlady answered cheerfully, and asked me right away to come over for an interview. I grabbed my purse, and hastened to her rental house.

Once I got there, the landlady showed me all the rooms. This chatty woman in her fifties was friendly, I thought, but when we finally sat down at a table, her demeanor and tone of voice suddenly firmed. She rattled off to me the strict house rules and conditions.

She proclaimed, "Men are allowed in the house only with my permission beforehand, and male guests can't stay overnight. Smoking in the house is prohibited. I prefer a quiet person. That's why my tenants are over thirty. You know, they tend to be quiet." She finally paused and looked straight into my eyes. "Do you listen to music a lot?"

"I don't have any audio equipment of any kind," I answered.

She jumped to the next question. "Do you have a boyfriend?"

She looked at me inquisitively, like I must have a story to tell. So I told her I was getting out of my relationship. Hardly had she flashed a sympathetic expression when she asked about my ability to pay the rent. I said, "No problem."

"I need three referrals," she said.

"I have three names, but only one of the numbers. May I call later?"

"Yes, can you give them to me when you get home? I can't wait long."

I only gave her Frederick's number, and then left. As soon as I arrived home, I received a call from her. Frederick must have said nice things, as she willingly agreed to rent to me. I explained to her I would move into the house on February 1st, after I came back from a trip to Tokyo.

Frederick had already bought me a ticket to Tokyo before our break-up happened, so he convinced me to go. Under the circumstances, I was not up for it. *How can I face my family?* I would have to hide my feelings of desperation and especially my humiliation, and feign cheerfulness. But of course, I did not want to waste the ticket. So I told my parents a few weeks prior to my visit, "Our relationship ended, but since Frederick already bought me a ticket, I am coming to Tokyo."

It didn't surprise me that my parents, who had been anxious about knowing my wedding date, did not even ask me the reason for the breakup, but tried to comfort me. Concealing his emotions, my dad said tenderly, "Well . . . we get to see you again."

I always appreciated my parents' unequivocal support. They never criticized me and showed the most pure thoughtfulness and total respect for my decisions, bad or good. Going home after a second failed relationship, I felt as ashamed as a dog that has gotten the worst of it in a dogfight.

On my departure day, Frederick took me to the Portland Airport to send me off. When his car reached the airport departure ramp, I felt acute tightness in my chest, as if a piece of food had lodged in my windpipe. The whole drive had been awkward, but when I saw the airport, my heartbreak at the separation reached a crescendo. *It's over. Get a grip on yourself, Kumiko!* But the airport had an effect that made the situation worse. Being carried away to a far country was to write *finis* on my relationship. My heart felt even more deeply torn.

Once confined in the airplane, fresh memories seemed suffocating. When night fell, the sky turned the porthole into a mirror that reflected the dim lights above me. My long face in the window looked pathetic. The weight of reality set in. I thought about not coming back to the U.S., but erased the thought quickly, as I knew it would be hard to adjust to living in Japan after being in the U.S. for nineteen years. I had become too independent to fit back into Japanese society. I couldn't follow the roles of Japanese women and live up to the expectations Japanese society places on them. In addition, there would be zero chance of finding a job in Japan at my age. I would only run into a wall, and wouldn't be able to make my own living. Finding a husband would be difficult, too. In fact, I didn't know if Japanese men would want a woman who had been the wife of a foreigner. Then I realized I might not be all right with a Japanese man if he were typical—expecting his wife to clean the house, wash dirty dishes, do the grocery shopping, prepare meals, and serve tea.

My old boyfriend's name popped into my mind. I had dated Mr.

Koike for five years— long before I met Thomas. He had been my co-worker at a travel agency and he often took me out after work. Our relationship was purely platonic. One day he asked me, "Can I be your boyfriend?" Then he said with conviction, "My dad is the head of police station in my hometown, and he is a powerful man. If anything happens to you or your family, you'll be fine. I'll ask my dad to protect you." As sweet as he was, I didn't want to be tied down yet even though he was a gentleman, a bit westernized, and always treated me like a lady.

Many times I had thought about Mr. Koike in the course of my divorce, and reflected on our relationship. His dream was to own a travel agency in the center of Tokyo. He realized his dream, and became a successful businessman in that industry. I liked him very much, but I wasn't in a hurry to get married at that time because of my passion to explore the world. I later traveled to London, Paris, Los Angeles, Hawaii, Cairo, Amman, Bangkok and Taipei.

If I had become his wife, perhaps I would have never needed to work and could have stayed at home, enjoying a reasonably nice life, surrounded by my family and my friends. I might even have had my own children. Although Thomas and I had tried to make a family, it hadn't happened. Most likely I wouldn't have had children with Mr. Koike either. Well then, hmmm . . . what kind of life could I have had? I might have worked for a corporation, but in Japan, when women got older, they were often pressured to leave their companies. Once you left a corporation, it would be extremely difficult to be hired by another. Your only option would be to take a job in the service industry, such as a restaurant, supermarket, or department store, unless you had special or unique skills.

What about education? I would have been less encouraged to go back to school. Since Japanese companies prefer to hire employees straight out of college, most Japanese believe going back to school doesn't make much sense. You rarely see older students in Japanese colleges. In contrast, American schools and companies offer opportunity for older people to develop themselves through continuing education. So, although I felt sad and lonely, I realized it would be better for me to stay in the U.S. to start my life over.

Finally, the airplane touched down in Japan, and I regained control so as not to display my doleful face. Japanese will try to avoid embarrassment and shame to maintain self-respect, and I was no exception. The automated customs' office door had scarcely opened when I saw my dad, mom, my older brother, Shohei, and his wife, Masako, and one young lady I didn't recognize. They were all frantically waving at me—my family, who had never abandoned me, who had supported me in all my endeavors and always worried about me, even though I had left them and gone thousands of miles away.

I embraced my mom, and then thanked everyone for coming to the airport, especially Masako and Shohei, who had taken the day off to meet me. My eyes finally rested on the young lady who had been smiling at me all the time. I whispered in Shohei's ear to ask who the young lady was.

He said, "Aki."

I exclaimed "You are kidding? Aki? Oh my gosh! She grew a lot."

I approached Aki (my older brother Kenji's first child) and said, "You know, I honestly couldn't tell who you were. I had to ask Shohei."

When Aki gave a chortle, I knew it was her. She was nineteen-years old. In four years, her face had matured and her body had grown into a slim but more feminine look with larger breasts than I remembered. Seeing her so grown-up made me feel old, but being cocooned in the presence of my family, I felt blissful and fortunate.

On the nearly two-hour drive to my parent's home, my eyes were busy taking in familiar landmarks and the changes in scenery along the expressway. Modernization, industrialization and regional changes in Japan had been continuing for decades, regardless of Japan's stagnated recession, and every time I had been to Tokyo I had noticed new high-tech bridges, architectural skyscrapers, and modern houses. In seeing those changes, I always felt the lapse of time. While observing everything, I was bombarded with small questions thrown out by my family, and the inside of Shohei's minivan was lively with everyone's gay voices.

"How was the food on the plane?" my mom asked.

"Ummm . . . it was okay."

"Auntie Kumi . . . I'll introduce you to my new boyfriend," said Aki.

"Wait a minute . . . what happened to your old boyfriend? The one you have been telling me about on the phone," I asked.

"Eh heh heh . . . he's history," Aki said.

"Kumiko-san. How was the weather over there?" Masako asked.

"It was cold," I said.

I had to think for a few seconds, but I tried to respond quickly so she would not think my memory was weak. All I could remember was it hadn't been raining. Hiding my true feelings wasn't easy. I tried to settle in and focus on being surrounded by my loved ones. They were a spiritual anchor.

Home again, home again, I thought, as we arrived at my parents' home around dinner time. Without any time to rest, I was wisked away to a Japanese restaurant where the rest of my family members were gathering to welcome me. Sitting in a *tatami* room with my beloved family, and savoring Japanese gourmet food, what more could I ask for? What I really missed about Japan were my family and Japanese food. I ordered assorted food—sweet fish grilled with salt, battered and deep-fried large shrimp and vegetables (lotus root, shiitake, eggplant), morisoba (cold noodle with dipping sauce), and crisply pickled cucumber and radish—all were artistically arranged on a black, lacquered wooden tray. I felt blessed. I rested well that night in my room, which my mom had been keeping for me since my marriage. Her keeping my room was my security blanket—I always had a home—and perhaps for my mom, the room was a sense of my presence.

The next morning after breakfast, using my mom's small bike, I rode around my parents' neighborhood. It always felt nostalgic to bike around my hometown. Older Japanese wooden houses had been demolished and replaced with modern concrete houses. In Japan, westernization is ubiquitous, but when I saw underwear on a clothesline hanging from the balcony attached to a contemporary-looking house, and colorful pink and green futons draped over the railings, it conjured up a third-world image. When I lived in Japan, I, too, hung clothes outside using two lines. The inner line was for intimate items and the outer one was for the other clothes. In the U.S., I hadn't seen clothes hanging outside to dry. Today many Japanese households have a dryer, but still there are many people who hang clothes outside because they either don't have a dryer or they prefer air-drying clothes so as not to damage the fabric. As for futons, if they have a balcony, Japanese like to air them in the sunlight during a time of day when the air is relatively dry. However, futons have been largely replaced with mattresses.

I then thought of the transformation of my parents' house, specifically the gigantic toilet my parents had installed in their bathroom. They finally quit using the old-style squat toilet with the flush lever on the front of the wall-mounted water tank. The replacement was the most luxurious Toto toilet, with all sorts of features: warm water, soft cloth seat, convenient control panel, and a heated seat with temperature control. This rivaled the cleaning cycle of a dishwasher. This made the downstairs' toilet too large for the room, and only my very slender parents could use the room.

The further along I rode, the more I was struck by the old Japanese houses standing like weeds amongst the new modernized buildings. I had mixed feelings about this picture. On the one hand it represented a loss of my origins. On the other hand, it should not have affected me, as I had immigrated to the U.S. In any case, the changes in those houses and buildings were attention-grabbing.

Whenever I was in Japan, my behavior automatically changed so I could fit in and not be treated as an outsider. In the U.S., I didn't act Japanese, although I had been maintaining a certain element of "Japaneseness." My internal conflict was that I wished to belong to one country, but in fact I didn't feel a strong sense of belonging to either. Fatalistically, I felt like my situation had evolved into a perpetually uncertain position. I had a strong desire to speak English like a native, as I felt I'd be more respected. But achieving an accent-free, native-like speaking ability was almost impossible when one immigrated to the U.S. after the age of thirty. This everlasting uncertainty would, I feared, plague me until I died.

On this trip, as usual, I found myself making some adjustments to be like the Japanese. Japanese people are very particular about how they dress, what kind of behavior is acceptable, and they use language that has many honorifics and parts of speech that show respect. For example, on one occasion when I visited my brother Kenji's house, I was embarrassed to hear Keiko (Kenji's new wife) say, "My goodness, you are young." She paused then added, "Your belly is showing." My shirt was not long enough and when I bent over backward, it slipped up an inch or so, exposing my belly for a second. I immediately realized her remark wasn't complimentary. Showing my belly was unseemly to her. She meant that I dressed like an adolescent. I said, "Oops. I put my shirt in the dryer too long."

I usually try to be aware of those things: 1) act my age; 2) dress my age; 3) use proper language, remembering to show respect and politeness. Consequently, while in Tokyo, I didn't wear tank tops, hooded shirts, or shorts, as those are considered attire for only young people. One nice thing about living in the U.S. is that you don't worry as much about how you dress and speak.

Since my mom had been encouraging me to go shopping, a few days after my arrival I took the Yamonote Line (commuter rail loop line in Tokyo) to explore the city. Frederick had been on my mind, but when I rushed through the bustling crowds in the center of Tokyo, my heart was instantaneously lightened. Changing my gait, I leaned a little forward to walk fast like the other Tokyo pedestrians. I needed to pay attention because the places I was once familiar with had drastically changed. I could easily get lost between all the new buildings. The city gave me a way to forget about my recent troubles and engage in the moment.

The large popular shopping districts like Ginza, Shinjuku, and Shibuya had numerous shops, upscale boutiques, and all sorts of restaurants. The popular trendy places were amusing to browse, and shopping diverted my glum mood. Boutiques and department stores in Tokyo carried what I wanted, since the clothes and cosmetics were designed for Japanese. To a degree, I still have a taste for the "cute" style many Japanese women prefer, such as an A-line dress, a large collar, an elegant ribbon blouse, or a fitted, flaring skirt.

But more importantly, I didn't forget to buy cosmetics to make my skin whiter. Fashions and fads are constantly changing, yet because of the desire of a great number of Japanese women to have porcelain, perfect skin, skin-whitening products have been in high demand for centuries. Asians' long-held attraction to white skin might be equivalent to the desire of Westerners for suntanned skin. I don't want to look too white, but I don't want my face to look too yellow, either. The problem is the huge selection of skin care products are pretty much the same, except for the packaging. That always confuses me. The strategy of the Japanese beauty industry is to bombard the market with similar products—which results in consumers looking alike. Nonetheless, the majority of Japanese people don't mind. Such a funny notion must seem absurd to Americans. Most Americans want to present themselves differently so as to demonstrate their individuality.

Japanese, in general, want to feel that they "fit in." They don't want to stand out the way Americans like to do. Americans love to show their uniqueness in ways such as displaying bumper stickers to explain who they are or with tattoos that show off the way they think. These are behaviors you see less of in Japan. Whenever I go to Japan, I always enjoy observing these two contrasting cultures.

Tokyo is a fun place. For hours I rambled through the most thriving hub of commercial districts in Tokyo. For lunch, I stopped at a long-established *ramen* restaurant. When Americans hear about *ramen*, what probably comes to mind is the cheap packaged instant version. However, if you eat a good ramen, the taste is quite memorable, and you'll want to go back to the restaurant many times. Japanese chefs take a long time to develop their skill for making delicious ramen. The ramen soup was indeed yummeeeee! My legs were then ready to take in the city again.

Around four in the afternoon as I headed home, I saw a horde of school students rushing onto the local train. I looked around at the passengers. Several young people were focused on their cell-phone screens, busily and dexterously moving their thumbs. I recalled my younger niece, fourteen-year-old, Rie, demonstrating her pink cell phone at my welcoming party. She had been using her cell phone since she was in elementary school, but her new phone included mobile Internet access and camera features. She showed me pictures that were sent by her school friends, played some downloaded music, and continued showing other features such as the alarm clock, games, and videos. I had been enthralled.

My thoughts jumped to my brother, Kenji, who already had a GPS device with a digital TV in his new pickup truck. I had never seen or heard of such a device, so it piqued my curiosity. I already knew that small consumer electronics took off faster here than in the U.S. A pretty voice navigated him precisely where to turn, even giving him traffic information that helped us avoid congestion. Tokyo was always crowded, so it was handy. But when he switched from GPS to TV for me, I asked, "Are you allowed to watch TV while driving?" My brother assured me he only watched when the car was parked. The Japanese government must trust people to use common sense, I reasoned. The instant I thought this, another example came to mind. In Japan anybody can buy liquor (beer and sake) and tobacco from vending machines. Well then, I supposed, having TV in the GPS unit wasn't so outrageous. Comparing technology, the norms, customs, and laws in the U.S. and Japan amused me.

Over the years when visiting family, my parents took me on an overnight trip to create a memory of each reunion. This time they suggested we go to Hakone. At once I called Hotel Green Plaza Hakone, a highly recommended *Onsen* (hot spring) hotel near Mt. Fuji, and reserved a room for one night the next week. Hakone is part of the Mt. Fuji-Hakone-Izu National Park, less than sixty miles from Tokyo. It was a perfect getaway place for us. I love to go on trips to rural areas, because it always reminds me I am still Japanese and the images of rural Japan touch my heart.

On the travel day, we left home around 9:00 a.m. The weather was sunny, warm, and beautiful, despite the fact it was in the middle of

January. After changing trains a couple of times, we arrived at Hakone-Yumoto station where we needed to take a *tozan* bus (mountain bus) to the hotel. After traveling on a scenic mountain road for a half-hour or so, we finally reached the Ubako stop, our final destination.

At the high elevation, nearly four-thousand feet, the winter air was noticeably cold. It was a half-mile walk from the bus stop to the hotel. While climbing the hill to the hotel, I saw steam rising from the ground. I walked closer to see. Hot spring water was running through the grass alongside the path. After five minutes or so, the hotel became visible in the distant mist. We entered the very contemporary-looking hotel, took off our shoes, and changed to a pair of slippers to step into the lobby. A striking, glittering chandelier hung from the center of the ceiling and under it set a grand piano. I saw a few employees carefully pushing tables with champagne glasses towards the entry door. They were preparing a complimentary cava for the guests who were returning from the trips.

There were both Western-style and Japanese-style rooms in that hotel, and we had chosen a Japanese-style room. Our room was on the second floor and was a bit of a walk from the lobby. We passed through a long glassed-in corridor with a view of bamboo gardens on both sides, then took an elevator to our room.

We took off our slippers at the little inlaid stone entrance and then opened the *fusuma* (sliding doors made of thick, decorative paper stretched over both sides of a wooden frame) to enter the room. The room was divided into two rooms by another *fusuma*. We walked into the main room that had a *tokonoma* (alcove in the wall where a scroll is displayed). On the window side, separated from the main room by *shoji* screens, there was a foyer with a pair of bamboo chairs and a table. When I stood in the foyer, I saw the stunning profile of Mt. Fuji through the window. I gazed at it for a while and murmured, "How beautiful Mt. Fuji is!"

We sat at the lacquered low table in the main room to have tea, which had already been prepared by the hotel. Serving green tea along with either Japanese confections or rice crackers is a typical welcoming gesture for most Japanese-style hotels and inns. We rested for a while, but soon decided to take a bath to kill some time before dinner.

Both the men's and women's open-air baths, separated by a bamboo fence, had a spectacular view of Mt. Fuji. I told my dad not to wait for us as my mom and I might take a long time, and then we parted. The outside air was cold, but once I was soaking in the hot mineral water after washing my body, I found it very relaxing. My mom looked very happy. I immediately noticed a long, rectangular tray filled with sake flasks and small cups sitting on one of the large stones surrounding the hot spring pool. I poured the sake into a little cup, and sipped it slowly while enjoying the conversation with my mom and the view of snow-clad Mt. Fuji.

Before we became too overheated, my mom and I came out of the pool and walked into the bathhouse to bathe and shampoo. The bathhouse also had a hot spring pool in the corner of the room with hot mineral water streaming from a pile of rocks. Opposite the pool was a row of washbasins in front of a wall-sized mirror. Each basin had a small wooden stool in front of it and was equipped with a handheld showerhead and a tap. My mom and I sat at the mirror next to each other. I washed my mom's tiny, bony back; she in turn washed mine. Without stopping her hands, she asked me in her utmost caring voice, "Have you lost weight?"

"Have I? Maybe I have," I responded, with little thought for her remark.

I was totally cherishing this precious moment with my mom. I had often wondered how I could possibly live so far away from her. I remember coming back from school once when I was in the fifth grade, and realizing my mom wasn't home. I had just stood in the living room and cried. *How could such a girl have left the country, and gone thousands of miles away from her mom?* Another thought popped into my mind. When I was a baby, around two or three years old, I used to run fearlessly into the ocean. My dad said, "You were unstoppable. You were not even afraid of big waves: you dashed into the water. Your mom and I always had to watch you. Sometimes I thought I would lose you, but you popped up like a buoy." I wondered if I had some innate risk-taking nature, something somewhere in me that must have been driving me to take chances.

Finally, it was dinnertime. As we entered the restaurant, a waiter in a tuxedo greeted us at the entry to the dining room, "Good evening, your dinner is ready."

"*Domo*," we said with a light bow, meaning *thank you.*

Soon a young waiter approached and escorted us to our table and pulled our chairs out for us, saying, "Your dinner will be served immediately."

"*Domo*," we said, bowing again.

At the first serving, a waitress carried in soy-base soup and cucumber and radish pickles. Soon small portions of the dishes on fine Japanese porcelain plates arrived one after the other: fried oyster, grilled red snapper, sashimi, tofu with crab sauce, seared scallops, spinach salad, and more. All were so decoratively presented that each dish was a work of art. Presentation is very important for Japanese. This traditional multi-course dinner was the highlight of our trip.

The next morning, after we had a buffet-style breakfast, we left the hotel. Hakone is a popular destination with tourists in Japan and has various attractions such as an open air museum, a botanical garden, lakes, an aquarium, an amusement park, and a shrine. We first went to Lake Ashinoko to ride a scenic boat across the lake. It was a sunny day, but when we stood on the bow deck, cold icy winds lashed our faces. We were chilled to the bone.

After the sixty minutes of cruising, we entered a snug noodle restaurant at the lakeshore, and ordered *Tenpura Udon* (two pieces of fairly large shrimp, battered and deep-fried in a thick wheat-flour noodle soup.) The hot *udon* revived us, so we could walk again and peek into each gift shop that stood at the lakeshore. We bought some *Onsen Manju* (red bean paste bun) as a souvenir for the rest of our family members. It was too cold for us to go other places, so we headed back to Tokyo a little earlier than we had planned.

During my stay at my parents' home, I wondered if my other family members had known about my breakup. No one brought up Frederick's name. To my relief even my parents, who knew my situation, did not breathe a word about it. Instead, they tried to make my stay as comfortable as possible. I was grateful none of my family members asked about him. They must have observed my forced smiles and my gloomy silences and tacitly understood that I did not want to talk about my failed relationship. Japanese are very good at reading minds—they use silence for communication as much as speaking.

One early afternoon during the second week of my stay, my mom asked me to go with her to my parents' bedroom. As we entered the *tatami* room, my mom calmly closed the *fusuma* and turned to me with an air of seriousness. I sat down on the Japanese floor cushion she had placed in front of the black, lacquered Japanese low table that was used for special occasions. I waited for my mom to sit down, but she instead approached the Japanese mahogany chest and opened the two swinging doors; she took out a tiny key from her wallet and inserted it into the keyhole of a hidden compartment in the rear of the inner drawer. She pulled a yellow cloth bag out of the drawer, placed it on the table, and then sat down in front of me. She immediately thrust her hand into the bag and pulled out two small see-through vinyl cases, each containing a banknote. I could see my name through the clear vinyl of each case. I kind of knew she was saving some money for me as I had once before heard her say something like, "Do not worry about money, I have saved some money for an emergency." But the amount was far more than I had imagined. I had never wanted to accept money from my parents, but this time my mom insisted. I thanked her from the bottom of my heart and told her the money would be saved. Poor as I was, I didn't want to use the money.

I still do not know why I didn't even say, "Thank you" to my dad. Perhaps, it had something to do with the fact that in Japan most wives manage family finances and often husbands are not even aware of how much they have in their bank accounts. It was very kind of my mom and dad. They did not even question what happened between Frederick and me, but supported me with tender care. I felt guilty about thinking only of my own contentment. I am sure my mom wanted me to live closer to her, at least not in a foreign country. Just thinking about how my mom worried about my misfortune made me feel worse. I tried to conceal my sad face in front of my family.

My aloof attitude and forced smile might have been what led my dad to suggest, "Kumiko, even though you think you are not in a good place to be cheerful, keep smiling because smiling will bring you happiness." He said this in a caring tone.

I feigned a smile and muttered to myself, "Yeah, right."

My dad smiled back at me and said, "It is true."

Once in a while, he imparted a little bit of wisdom. I always appreciated it, because he did it deferentially.

My family reunion bolstered my emotional state, but leaving them was heartrending. When my parents, Shohei, Masako, and Rie sent me off at the boarding gate, they each made a poor attempt at a smile. I always hated this time. As I dragged myself toward the departure gate, tears came to my eyes. But once I was on the airplane, I realized I had to get a grip on my emotions as I needed to worry about the huge sum of money my mom had given me. Unlike previous trips, this one was a bit cumbersome. I had to go through Vancouver, Canada's customs and immigration, because the direct flights between Portland and Tokyo had been canceled. The good part of this distraction was that it took my mind off my misery.

When I finally arrived at the Portland Airport, I saw Frederick standing impassively at the boarding area. It was a bit awkward, but we hugged each other and kissed lightly. We didn't separate with hate and our feelings still remained. Our relationship was like a broken glass, so it was better to be careful, yet feelings lingered.

He asked, "How were your parents?"

As he asked this, I felt his pain, and wondered if he might have felt sorry for my parents since they had thought we would marry.

"They were fine," I answered.

He said, "Good." Then he tried to say something more, but the noise of the crowed erased his words. Since he didn't repeat them, I didn't ask what he had tried to say. I realized conversation between us didn't flow easily.

Arriving at his house, I became more awkward at the sight of the boxes I had stacked up at the corner of the breakfast nook. On that night, we made love, but it was like a soda without fizz—there was no passion. I moved out of his house the next morning with his help.

XV

Communal House

How many times had I said "new home" since I left my country? My vagabond life . . . it seemed my friends weren't even surprised anymore to receive a Christmas card with a different address. One thing I had never neglected was to send holiday cards to keep in touch. My new home was located with convenient access to the junction of Highway 26 and Murray Boulevard, which led to three major cities: Beaverton, Portland, and Hillsboro—all accessible within thirty minutes. Two large supermarkets were within a ten-minute walk. Taking advantage of the opportunity to get more exercise, I walked to the grocery stores.

The first time I drove around the quiet and secluded residential area, I had a good impression. Each house, primarily old ranch-style homes, had mature trees like maple, plum, and other deciduous trees. Slowly passing by those houses, I saw how the owners had embellished their front yard landscapes with bushes and flowers, giving the neighborhood a tidy appearance. The vicinity looked a lot safer and more upscale than the area where I'd previously lived in southeast Portland.

I liked my new accommodations because the airy room had a southeast exposure where I could watch the sun rise from the comfort of my bed. The room was about the same size as my room in the previous house. I could fit in the small room without any mental adjustment. As long as the room was bright, size didn't matter much to me. Since my divorce I only owned a little furniture, which made my life easy. My life felt unsettled, nonetheless I was grateful to have my own place and not be under the care of anyone else.

Although I liked my room and surroundings, for the first couple of nights I had a hard time sleeping. The first night I woke up many times. Whenever I awakened, I tried not to become fully awake. But one time, I let my eyes open to glance around the dark room. My head rolled from side to side in my unfamiliar bed. The chilly air hit my face. Upon seeing the dark silhouettes of the not-fully-unpacked boxes, I thought of the unknown future awaiting me and anxiety attacked. I tried to shrug off my fear and closed my eyes tight in an effort to sleep, but my train of thoughts thwarted my efforts.

I must have dozed off finally, since the next time I opened my eyes it was dawn. The feeble light shining through the lacy white curtain that hung from the southeast window indicated that the world was still revolving. The sun progressively phased in and soon the room grew bright. I liked my room because of its sunniness and the feminine appearance of the white dresser with mirror, the single bed with a white and yellow-flowered bedspread. The pattern of the lamp shade was coordinated with the bedspread. *Cute*, I thought.

Early the next morning, I stepped into the kitchen. No one else was up yet. I took my bread out of the pantry, which had six shelves, one for each of the residents. All of my provisions and a few of my own dishes and cups were stored there. There were two refrigerators. None of the kitchen appliances and utensils matched, but they were abundant, indicating the house had been rented in this fashion for a long time. I made my usual breakfast: a piece of toast, a fried egg, and a cup of instant coffee. I sat alone with no particular thoughts except for the feeling of agitation about finishing the move so I could look for a job right away.

Settling down only took a few days. All my belongings were situated in the way which made the most sense for my tiny room. The house had a land phone with an answering machine system and fax feature, but I couldn't afford to miss any calls or to be misinformed by my housemates, so I purchased a simple phone with an answering machine system. In three days, I was already up for finding a job.

I looked in all the places I could call to mind: newspapers, online, the college career center, and employment agencies. It was 2003, and Oregon had high unemployment, so it was difficult to find a job. Although I sent many resumes, I received only a few responses.

During this time, I closed myself in like a clam so as to listen to my inner voice and become sensitive to my spiritual needs. I did two things in a ritualistic way. One was to take a walk around the neighborhood a couple of times a day. The other was to drive often into the country. I had a strong desire to go somewhere like the countryside, where there were no humans, only woods, lakes, rivers, and prairie in which horses, cows, sheep, and goats grazed. Sitting down in a grass field, I liked to watch pastured animals through the fence. Cows mooed at me when I came to close to the fence. They sounded annoyed, as if to say, "Go away, this is our green field!" Goats and horses were friendly—even friendlier if you gave them grass. I loved being in any meadow. I felt a sense of belonging to nature, especially because I didn't have a job or a special person in my life.

I took short excursions on the weekends so as not to miss any calls related to jobs. I packed a lunch, a ready-made sushi pack and some *Osenbei* (rice crackers), and made fresh green tea. The destinations were always spontaneous. Each time, I first glanced at the sky to see which direction the clouds were moving, then I decided whether I would go west to the Pacific Ocean or east to the Columbia River Gorge. Although Oregon winter weather could get pretty nasty, once in a while the thick clouds that covered the sky dissipated, revealing a beautiful sunny sky. Often I drove west, but didn't go far. Once I was on the road to the beach, I let my heart navigate. I rarely made it to the beach, but was drawn instead to the forest, and ended up driving down country roads.

One day I found my sanctuary. A few feet off a narrow country road, I came upon a tiny place surrounded by small trees and entwined bushes. I maneuvered my Honda Civic into the tight little spot. Suddenly I found myself camouflaged by the leaves. I turned the engine off. "Wow, how quiet it is!" I said. Skylarks trilled high above in the sky. All I saw was a vast field, not one human . . . just a brown field all the way to the horizon. I thought, *What if I die here? No one would find me. Well . . . after all, we all die alone.* I closed my eyes. In a few minutes, my mind was tranquil. This spot became my personal meditation retreat.

During my job-hunting, I had an interview that was so unpleasant, ridiculous, and bizarre that I cannot forget it. The job advertisement was listed in the free Japanese regional newspaper, which I picked up from the Japanese grocery store, Uwajimaya. It was a Monday, so I immediately called the company and received instructions on how to apply for the job via e-mail. I obtained their application forms along with translation tests, one from Japanese to English, and the other one from English to Japanese. The amount of work would be outrageous, but I decided to apply.

I started working right away on the translation from Japanese to English, but as for the other half—from English to Japanese—I did not know how I could manage without having the software that converts Roman letters to Kanji-Hiragana. Wondering who might have the software, I remembered my Japanese church friend, Naoko-san, and thought that she might have this.

Around one o'clock, I called her. In her usual affable tone, she said, "Please use my computer. I am glad if I can help you in this way." So I hopped in my car and drove to her house. Her three young children were in the roomy living room where her computer was placed, but Naoko-san quieted them down. I used her computer and typed away until I finished. Naoko-san's words, "Would you like to have some tea?" tempted me to stay, but I left her house so I could fax the test translation right away. The next day, the company called me in for an interview for the following day at five. My effort paid off.

I left my home at 4:25 p.m., giving myself plenty of time, even though the place was only twenty minutes or so away. But because the office was situated in an isolated area and the building numbering was not sequential, I got lost for ten minutes, and I arrived at five minutes to five. As I entered the lobby of the small office, a young Japanese lady greeted me politely and told me to wait for a second. I glanced around the office. The setup of the office indicated to me that the company had only a few employees.

Soon a young, slender, clean-looking American appeared and told me to follow him. He escorted me to a room that looked like a small warehouse in which a steel desk and two steel folding chairs were situated a bit awkwardly in the center of the room. We sat facing each other with a desk between us. His performance was scrupulous and efficient, but also friendly and pleasant. After thirty minutes of his interview, he politely said, "The president of this company, Mr. Suzuki, would like to interview you. Please wait here." Then he walked away. A few minutes later, a short Japanese man in his late forties or early fifties sat down in front of me. His face held no expression. I suddenly recalled how some Japanese men wouldn't even feign a smile, or joke in the workplace.

Mr. Suzuki was rather impudent. He said abruptly, "Your English translation was Americanized, and your Japanese translation was a bit inelegant."

His comment bewildered me, but I recovered and said politely, "I can be more sensitive to the tone of my translation."

He did not respond, but dropped his gaze to my resume and went on. "You have a master's degree in conflict resolution. Why do you want to be a translator?"

After wrestling with my thoughts, I responded, "I like both because they are equally challenging."

Once again, he didn't respond, but continued questioning me in his monotonous voice. He went on and on for an hour and at the end of the conversation he looked at me and said, "I will let you know the result of the MARRIAGE . . ." He suddenly lost his composure. For a moment, I didn't fathom what he had said, but I saw his face turn red. And then I was certain he had said "marriage." He started coughing uncontrollably. I felt awkward and didn't know what to say. He rushed for a glass of water, and then came back to me, rephrasing his sentence in a rushed, perfunctory manner. "I will let you know the outcome of the interview."

I walked out of the office with a strange feeling. I figured the interview was a failure. A few days later, a rejection letter followed. Sometime later, an employee of Mr. Suzuki told me that the position had been open for over a year. This made me certain he was searching for more than just a translator.

Every morning upon awakening, I felt the weight of depression. The word *uncertainty* came to my mind and dominated my thoughts, making it difficult for me to think straight. I mumbled, "How many times do I have to go through this?" I felt pathetic. I had to spur myself on, saying things like, "I can't afford to let my mind be so weak. *Ganbaranakucha* (hang in there!)" I tried to focus on my spirituality so as to receive the strength and courage to face my predicament. Walking helped me, so I did that twice a day, in the morning and evening. While walking around the neighborhood, I often mused. *What would it be like to own a nice house? Is there any chance for me to have a house in the future?* My train of thoughts became my companion. I responded to myself, *I cannot even foresee a week ahead, or even tomorrow. Well look up at the sky!* I liked seeing the sunset, because the sky glowed with the setting sun. I often stopped to view the sun going behind the hill. A brilliant red sunset fading into an afterglow entranced me. In that heavenly scene I always thought, *I am still living in a beautiful place.* Near the end of my walk, I would squeeze my eyes shut for a second, put my hands together, and pray I'd get a job soon. Walking meditation helped me to soften and soothe my mind and body.

Living with my housemates was a mental support, as many of them had circumstances similar to mine, in that they each needed a temporary place to start life anew. This communal house accommodated up to six people and the house was full most of the time, despite the frequency of turnover. Most residents didn't stay for a long time. One exception was Jacky, who had been there for many years. I heard this from the biggest gossiper in the house, Daisy, who had also lived there for many years. She was the one who informed me about the other housemates. She was the know-it-all when it came to disclosing information about others, including me.

When I was looking for a job, I avoided going to the communal rooms before five, so as to keep my mind in a job-search mode. I tried not to develop any indolent habits. Being confined in a tiny room all day took discipline, but in the evening, I watched cable TV and ate dinner with the other roommates.

Dining with housemates was like having guests at your table but without the need to prepare food for anyone other than yourself. Some people ate meals in their own rooms, but there were always a few people at the dining table around dinner time waiting for others to join them. Eating with people from different regions of the U.S., or even different countries (we had one lady from Ethiopia), was attention-grabbing as they cooked their food in different ways or ate different kinds of food, like fried peanut butter and banana sandwiches, apple-cheese quesadillas, rice with milk, or spicy roasted vegetables on flatbread. It was all an experience of discovery.

The housemates who ate at the dining table often lingered after dinner, conversing late into the night, especially on weekends. Some people were loquacious and shared their personal stories or just passed on gossip from the grapevine. One shocking story, which I heard from Daisy, was that our housemate, Mindy, had become pregnant after having been raped by her stepfather. Her stepfather and her mom took the baby away from her. When I heard this story, I was dumbfounded and all I could say was, "Wow!" Although this was hearsay, I kind of believed Daisy's words. Someone else said, "Mindy often suffers severe migraines, so she has to stay in her room without any lights." I rarely saw her, but whenever I did see her, her eyes were downcast. She carried a dark shadow. Even though she was twenty-something, she lacked the lively air of other young ladies her age.

Another story came from the person herself, Sandra. After I had known her for a few months, she started to open up, and shared her story: her husband had abused their son, who was their only child. She said she continued living with her husband for a long time in a state of denial, but finally couldn't take it any longer and left him. Her son was grown and suffering psychological problems, although he was able to support himself. I felt profoundly sorry for them both, and felt resentment toward her vile husband. It must have been difficult to move on with their lives.

I had thought my situation was dire, but my problems paled in comparison to theirs, and this gave me fresh insight. If I viewed my life in a negative light, I should correct my thoughts, I realized, and like my dad had said, smile. Perhaps the act of smiling could change my attitude.

At last, one afternoon toward the end of March, the employment agency called. The agent had found me a part-time position at a corporate office. In the phone conversation, she apologized for not being able to find the job I was looking for, but suggested I take the job until they could find a better one. I appreciated her gesture and took the job with the happy thought I could finally start my life again. Since I had returned from Tokyo, two months had passed without employment, so I was glad to be able to start working on the first of April.

The long-awaited spring arrived. Grateful to have a job, my innate cheerful nature returned, and I could laugh from the bottom of my heart again. Working at a corporate office with more than a thousand employees made me feel like I was a contributor to society. The pay wasn't good, but the steady income enabled me to make a plan: save some money, update my wardrobe, do things like take a day trip to a beach, and visit museums.

I felt like I had finally come out from the life of a ground mole. All of a sudden I was seized by the desire to get out of the house. On weekdays, I was already back home by 5:15 p.m. I waited for Daisy to come home so we could have dinner together. Sometimes Daisy and I strolled to a grocery store or took a long walk in our neighborhood. Our mindless rambling relieved my job stress. The advantage of living with other people was that you didn't get lonely, and if you were up for doing something fun, you could always find a few congenial housemates to go along. But because many housemates didn't stay long, a few with whom I had felt comfortable left and new ones took their places. Having a newcomer was amusing, because you just didn't know if she would be a disaster, or a real blessing. At any rate, the house was a center of drama and the drama entertained me.

One Friday evening in late June, Yolanda arrived in her vintage, two-tone Volkswagen van. Its white top and sky-blue body were highly polished. She parked in front of the kitchen, beside our picket fence.

I was watching out the window when a tall, sturdy-looking lady came out of the van, and gallantly strode toward our house. I immediately stopped washing vegetables and turned away from the window so she would not need to wonder if I was watching her. Soon I heard the door open. Yolanda appeared at the threshold of the kitchen where Daisy, Jacky, and I were busy fixing our dinner. She had a solidly built figure, dark cocoa skin, and a large head, with silver-gray hair mounded in curls. Had her hair been green, it would have looked just like a head of cabbage. She must have been in her early fifties. Her fleshy face and muscular body matched the image of her Volkswagen van—big, wide, and sturdy. She introduced herself in a thundering voice. "My name is Yolanda and I will be your new housemate." Her loud voice grabbed our attention. Her big round eyes, beefy nose, and protruding, tangerine-glossed lips made a strong impression. Despite her strident voice, it was a good impression, for she displayed sophistication in her conservative, but classy attire, and intelligence in the way she presented herself.

Yolanda moved into the room next to mine. Her predominant belongings were her art supplies and works. She had no furniture, only some dated clothes (late 1960s to early 1970s), a few cast-iron pots and pans, and a dozen jars of spices. Most people who moved into the house did not possess a lot, except for one person, Sandra, who crowded her eighteen-by-eighteen-foot room with knickknacks, leaving no space to walk. Sandra's space was like those antique shops that display many objects without any sense of order. Once in a while I had to knock on my housemates' doors to let them know of their phone calls. At such times I had a chance to sneak a peek into their rooms and I could see pretty much everything they owned. From their belongings I got a hint of their personalities.

Yolanda's creativity influenced me greatly in the artistic area. She worked part-time and changed jobs often. In her free time, she indulged in producing art. Once, soon after she had settled in, she showed me a couple of her oil paintings. I noticed that her portraits and still-life paintings all had dark backgrounds with luminous effects in the foreground. To me they gave an overall impression of a dark mood—but they were impressive.

"Do you like oil painting?" asked Yolanda.

"Yes, I do," I said, nodding my head slowly while wondering why all the faces in her portraits were pensive.

I glanced over to her still-life paintings which were also dark images—vases without flowers, mysterious images of mushrooms, snakes, mosses in the forest, and a chair in a deserted room. Much as I wanted to comment, I decided not to. Depressing was the only word that came to mind. Since I didn't remark about her work, she put the paintings back in her closet and pulled out a large cardboard box filled with various ceramic works.

The pots and vases were somewhat comical in design, having cavities and concavities. She showed me an artistic arrangement of succulent plants in a pot she had made. She sold her artwork through small local markets. I didn't get the impression she was making a lot of money selling her crafts, but she was an innate artisan and loved what she was doing.

One day, she asked if I wanted to make my own ceramic project. I said, "I want to make something small, such as a brooch or necklace. Something easy." She brought out a plastic bag with a mass of clay wrapped in a wet cloth and plopped the clay on the dining table. Slicing off a slab, she slid it over to me. She then cut off a lump for herself to show me how to knead and shape it, using her large selection of tools. With her skilled hands, she demonstrated techniques for slicing, smoothing, contouring and sculpting.

"Use this knife to draw the flower. Just the outline," Yolanda said. "Don't start from there. You're going to need a hole for the necklace," she added.

"How big should the hole be?" I asked.

"One quarter of an inch diameter, maybe. Use this awl," she said.

She guided me through the whole process from the beginning to end, even taking me to the shop where we could color and fire the final product.

I'd made a sharply sculpted iris on an oval-shaped pendant. The clay fired prettily and the purple petals, yellow anthers, green leaves, and white background glazed nicely with a soft luster. Yolanda was impressed with my work and I was pleased. Later, I glued a pin on the back of the pendant so it could be used also as a brooch.

Cooking was another of Yolanda's talents, and she displayed a touch of class in her cooking. Using chili peppers from a wreath she had woven, tossing in all sorts of fine natural and flavorful ingredients, and adding lots of olive oil, she cooked delicious Tuscan cuisine. I liked watching her cook and sampling her creations. When she had time, she made me a basil, tomato, and mozzarella sandwich. Since my divorce, my vagabond lifestyle had become well-established, and I didn't mind sharing things with other people or accepting their generosity. In fact, I appreciated it very much. Being in a communal house, there were times I was annoyed at not being able to have guaranteed quiet and absolute liberty, and once in a while I disliked the inconvenience of sharing a bathroom and the kitchen. Nonetheless, for the most part, I enjoyed living with housemates and sharing meals was one of the things I appreciated most.

Yolanda intrigued me, for she was well-read in science and art.

One day she asked, "You want to watch the video of Ito Takamichi? Do you know him? He is a Japanese contemporary sculptor. He does stainless steel kinetic sculpture that can be set in motion."

"I don't know of him, but it sounds interesting," I said, though modern art wasn't my favorite, especially abstract works, because I found it difficult at times to understand the artist's theme. It was, however, fun watching with her because she added her commentary. With her artistic mind, Yolanda brought me the joy of learning new things and I reveled in being with her. One of her foibles though, as I saw it, was a habit of showing her temper. Everyone in the house could easily tell when she was distressed, for she showed her anger not only in her face, but in her body. When her voice got louder, her body itself spoke volumes. I thought her volatility repelled people.

Five months after Yolanda moved in, a tense incident occurred between us. I must have offended her, as she cast her angry stare at me for a few days. I could not comprehend the grounds for such anger, but I didn't want to ask the reason, so I withdrew from her. A few days later, a note of apology was slipped under my bedroom door, saying, "I am sorry for my bad behavior. Please forgive me. I want to talk to you again." I knocked on her door with reservations. The door was opened in a moment. Seeing Yolanda's cheerful face, I forgot about whatever it was that had happened between us.

Sharing a house with five or six people was sometimes challenging, so everyone had to be accommodating in their behavior in order to live harmoniously. But cooking in the kitchen, eating at the communal dining table, or watching cable TV with others, I felt at home. In Yolanda's case, living harmoniously with others seemed to be difficult due to her fiery temper. That sort of personality would not be agreeable in our house setting for long, and I was worried about how this might play out.

One day Yolanda told me about her long pent-up grievance. When I heard her story, I kind of understood why she got upset easily. Her nasal muscles twitched as she talked about her dad who sold their house for a ridiculously low price when she was very young. When she said, "My family suffered from that for a long time," her face turned red. I suspected she had some deep-seated anger resulting from that childhood experience. I felt sorry for Yolanda because she was intelligent and had lots of talents, yet small things which would not bother most people easily vexed her. I believed her sudden mood shifts scared people.

Yolanda and Daisy were my buddies. Many evenings we gathered at the dining table and shared wine, snacks, and good conversation. Yolanda was generous about offering food, despite her meager income. Daisy was less generous, hiding alcohol in her metal coffee-mug with its black plastic lid. I often offered cheap wine. Our conversation took many paths.

In one conversation Yolanda asked, "Do you guys know about Einstein's first wife?"

"Did he divorce?" Daisy asked.

"Did he even marry? I thought he just had a girlfriend," I said.

"Einstein married twice and his secretary was a mistress. But anyway, his first wife was very smart and worked with Einstein," Yolanda said.

"Then what happened to his first wife?" Daisy asked. "You know I want to divorce my husband, but I don't have the money." Daisy digressed. "I hope I can do it soon, and marry a guy who makes money."

Our conversation tended to be carried along by our remorse, as we were all in the same boat: trying to forget our history and find happiness. We talked about all sorts of subjects, yet we most often ended up talking about how to find a new man.

One summer night, Daisy presented the idea of going on a singles' river cruise on the Portland Spirit, a cruise ship that operated on the Willamette River. Yolanda showed plenty of interest in the idea, and I, too, became excited. Even though it took a whole week to make up our minds, once we decided to go, we were of one mind to make the most of our party night. For days we talked about clothes, shoes, and hairstyles for that special occasion. Being on a tight budget, we were all frugal and eager to maximize our beauty. The measures we took were serious. Yolanda dyed her gray hair light blonde. When I saw her hair, I was shocked. *My goodness . . . she really changed!* I thought to myself. She was positively transformed and the new hair color softened her stern look, made her face warmer, and even added a bit of sophistication.

I commented on her changes saying, "You look great! You look a lot younger."

Yolanda grinned and looked a bit abashed, saying, "So you like my new hair color?"

I looked her straight in the eyes and nodded, "I do!"

She even changed her make-up to complement her new hair color. She looked beautiful.

On the morning of the day of the cruise, a Saturday, Yolanda took us to a consignment shop that sold quality used clothes, bags, shoes, and some jewelry at low prices. I was rather impressed. For fifteen dollars, I purchased a pair of black Italian-made, two-inch-heel sandals which had a delicate look. The sandals looked like they had never been worn.

We all tried to make ourselves as beautiful as possible. My goal was to project an image that was casual but chic. A bit dismayed, I realized my make-up set lacked color variation. I had only one color scheme of eyeliner, mascara, eye shadow, and rouge. I felt compelled to add a little color, so I purchased a wine-colored lipstick and nail polish, thinking it would be a striking-complement to my new black sandals. The day of the event, I wore a stylish, navy blue three-quarter-sleeved cotton shirt, a tight short white skirt, and a gold herringbone necklace. Usually I wore my hair up, but I wore it down, with a few strands hanging loosely around my face. Daisy attempted to project a smaller figure: she wore a pair of black slacks and a silky, white cotton blouse. We all invested tremendous energy in fixing ourselves up for the outing, hoping to attract someone on the boat.

Yolanda, Daisy and I left home after five and arrived at Waterfront Park an hour before the 7:00 p.m. departure. There were already a few people waiting for the boat to arrive. About a half hour before boarding, a large number of passengers in formal attire started to converge on the dock from all directions. All the women were lovely, and all the men were decent looking. The men presented a neat look with hair well-combed, faces shaved, clothes cleaned and pressed, along with a patient and calm demeanor. Many appeared to be bashful; they stood around, hands in pockets, but their eyes were busy sneaking quick glances at the pretty girls.

Finally, the triple-decked dinner boat arrived and employees of the cruise line came off to coordinate the boarding process. We stood in line, talking idly while focusing our attention on the passengers around us. I was particularly looking for men who were about my age, and anticipated someone would ask for a dance.

It wasn't a small boat. It had a capacity of four-hundred-fifty guests. The long line of people shuffled toward the boat, reminding me of the movie, *March of the Penguins*. Once we got on the boat we all hurried to search for prospective dates as if time were money. The boat cruised along the Willamette River for two-and-a-half hours. The destination was Oregon City, with a return to the Portland waterfront.

To start our journey, we each bought a glass of wine, and then moved to the stern of the boat so we could enjoy the view from the deck while waiting for someone to approach. Holding wine glasses, we posed as if we were enjoying our conversation. As time went by, we began to feel a little restless. Blue, orange, red, green and white lights from the city glowed in the night as the boat floated by. Those lights' reflection on the river was romantic, I thought, but I imagined many people weren't paying attention to the view, except for those few who were shy or out of luck and hadn't connected with anyone.

I went inside. There were some men who had not yet engaged anyone in conversation. It was a little awkward trying to catch their attention. When I self-consciously turned my eyes upon them, they reacted oddly. Some smiled back and some swiftly looked away. I didn't know exactly how I should behave, so I just milled around.

Finally, a tall, cute young man in his early twenties approached me. I thought to myself, "Hmm . . . I wish I were younger. If I were his age I wouldn't think twice about going on a date with him." I enjoyed a little small talk with him, but then excused myself to go back to my girlfriends.

When I went back to the stern, Yolanda and Daisy weren't there anymore, so I wondered if they had met someone. But soon I found them near the buffet, where only a little food was left. It was almost nine o'clock and our romantic fantasy was about to dock. We were quiet. Yolanda's and Daisy's faces showed their disappointment. We left the boat. Yolanda's eyes were hard. Without a word, she headed for the car. I felt the cold wind coming off the river as Daisy and I followed her in silence.

Another winter arrived. The last winter had worn heavily on me, coming out of the relationship with Frederick. Cold weather lowered my energy and made me moody. The cheerless scenery hit me hard. My two losses coincidentally happened in lonesome seasons. My divorce befell me when summer was about to turn to autumn. I remember one of my very sad moments. It was the end of October, a biting cold day. I stood at a bus stop waiting for a bus. The sun was shining, but strong, bleak winds were blowing, and mercilessly sweeping away the red-and-yellow leaves. I watched them whirling in the soft sunlight. The colors were as vivid as Van Gogh's autumn paintings. Watching the astonishingly bright leaves parting from their trees filled me with woe.

But this winter—almost one year had passed since my break-up with Frederick—was different, and the wintery scenery did not steal my soul. This recovery wasn't as bad as my divorce.

Two things had helped me getting out of my misery: My employment status had changed to full-time in September, enabling me to feel more financially secure. Secondly, I had acclimated to my new surroundings because of good housemates. My mind was less occupied with worries and that helped me be able to move on in my life. I even started listening to music again.

Music felt like a heartbreak remedy. Since the divorce I had become an avid music listener. Being alone for the first time in my life had scared me. Perhaps I had thought familiar songs would cradle me, so I made a habit of listening to the music on the radio. When I heard familiar songs like the 80s rock music—songs Thomas used to listen to—for example, Elvis Costello, Eurythmics, Eric Clapton, ZZ Top, Marvin Gaye, and George Michel, those songs diverted my mind. But to get over Frederick, I didn't need music because of my supportive housemates. In any case, when I felt like my life was coming together, I began to crave music.

This time it wasn't rock though, but country that appealed to me. Right after the divorce, when I heard Patsy Cline's song "She's Got You," I sobbed. Now I loved the lyrics. I could relate to some of the stories. Perhaps my illusion that there might have been a chance to reconcile finally died, and I could accept what had happened and feel all right, because many people fail in love. Well . . . maybe I *was* still licking my own wounded heart, but it was healing.

One evening just before Thanksgiving, when I came home from work, Daisy called me from the kitchen.

When I joined her in the kitchen, I asked, "What?"

"Yolanda left!" she said unhappily.

"What happened?" I asked.

"I've no clue. She was gone by the time I came home," she said. "The landlord just told me she had evicted her with the reason Yolanda was too distracting to the other residents."

Whatever the incident was, the consequence was immediate. All her belongings were already gone. It was unfortunate, because she had just started going to graduate school and she was very content. I worried about her. We meet so many people in our lifetime but we do not often connect at a level where we feel genuine concern. Yolanda continued to be one of those people I thought of on occasion, and I felt sorry she couldn't stay at the house until she was ready to move out.

But the communal house always welcomed newcomers. One left and another came. A week later, a new face appeared. Susan, perhaps somewhere between thirty and thirty-five, made a favorable impression on Daisy and me. She had pleasing green eyes, a charming smile—altogether an agreeable face—and her cheerful personality and genteel manners appealed to us. Since Yolanda had gone, Daisy and I were a little down, but Susan infused new energy into our spirits. We soon became a trio. As she had been an elementary school teacher before she moved into the house, she was naturally good at coordinating plans and people. She was the source of playful inspiration and took the lead. We went dancing, visited wineries, and discovered cool places to eat out.

One evening Susan and I sat at the dining table and talked about our ex-boyfriends.

"You and I are similar," Susan said, "in that honestly, it was better for us to leave our old boyfriends."

"You think so?" I said, rubbing my eyebrow with a fingertip.

She is right but I still have feelings, I thought to myself.

"My boyfriend and I were different. We dated for many years, and went through many rough patches. We argued over silly things," she said. Then, raising her voice she said, "I got tired of it."

Her voice calmed and she continued. "I wanted to change my life drastically, so I left. I drove miles and miles away, looking for a new home to rebuild my life. It was quite an interesting experience except for one incident when my car broke down."

Her stories soothed me, talking about our common subject. I liked Susan and admired her positive attitude. She had dropped out from the workaday world and decided to explore other possibilities, crossing the country from the New England states, to the West Coast.

Listening to her endeavors, my mind danced with many thoughts, as I compared my situation to hers, and I thought how difficult it must have been to end a long relationship like that. I had empathy, and was impressed at the same time by how brave she was to take such an action to make a difference in her life. The positive attitude she manifested was, I thought, a rare and magnetic quality.

Christmas was around the corner. Someone hung a big poinsettia wreath on the front door. Others put up decorations in every area of the house, inside and out. There were fun things about living with many housemates, especially during times like Thanksgiving and Christmas, when we didn't want to be alone. Our celebrations were sparked by the ideas of housemates who liked to decorate the house with items from Dollar Tree. The multicolored Christmas mini-lights were hung ostentatiously around the windows. A teeny-tiny artificial Christmas tree with a few figurines stood on the fireplace hearth. Red and green candles towered on the dining table which was covered with a paper tablecloth in a poinsettia print. Daisy put up plastic mistletoe between the dining room and the guest room. Little contributions from each of us made the house flashy but cheerful and festive. It looked cheesy, but for us, the house looked "pretty darn good."

All of us agreed to have a Christmas party. Five people cooked, but none of us created traditional Christmas food—no turkey, no ham, no cranberry sauce—but there were casseroles, meat dishes, and Japanese food. We had decided we could invite anyone who wanted to come to the party. I invited Frederick.

Christmas arrived with chilly but pleasant weather. As I entered the kitchen, I saw steam coming from pots and pans. The aromas permeated the whole house. That spurred me to do my share of cooking for this special day. The clock showed 7:30 a.m. Daisy, in a well-worn robe and holding a coffee mug, walked sluggishly into the kitchen from the dining room and then spoke to me with her distinctive tone. Because her eyebrows were so black and thick, and her pupils were atypically large, when she looked at me intensely I felt like I was being interrogated.

"So, Kumiko, what are you going to make today?" she asked.

"Well, as we decided, I am going to make Japanese food."

"Goooood," she said with a smile that changed her demeanor to one of geniality.

My mind was occupied with two things that day, cooking and Frederick, but predominantly Frederick, who had said he would come to the party. Someone put a boom box in the living room, and the Christmas songs of Nat King Cole, Frank Sinatra, and Dean Martin, all those honeyed velvet tones, flowed throughout the house all day.

Dishes of food were placed onto the formal table one by one, and as the day went by, the table was filled with everyone's contributions. By early evening we were ready and waiting for people who had said they might come.

Daisy's daughter, her son-in-law, Jacky's sister, and some friends of my housemates said they would come, but none of them showed up. Only Frederic joined our party around four o'clock, bringing his daughter and grandson. By evening, Susan and other housemates had left for their friends' or relatives' parties. Daisy, Jacky and I remained. I pretended to be a little aloof to Frederick, as his daughter was there, but when he noticed the mistletoe, he lured me there to kiss me.

When he kissed me, he whispered, "Can you meet me after dinner?"

"Well, I have to wash dishes."

"I'll wait," he said.

Occasionally, Frederick and I had coffee at Starbucks, and on some occasions we slept together.

After the party, I drove up to Frederick's house. My feelings for him had lingered and I couldn't say no to him. I wasn't proud of myself, nor happy either. In fact, I felt guilty and sinful. I consequently couldn't enjoy myself totally, although I could satisfy my ego with the notion that he still loved me.

Snow began falling on New Year's Eve and continued over the course of a week. The morning of New Year's Day 2004 was white. Susan, Daisy and I were as excited as children and prayed that the snow would continue to fall. Indeed, the snow kept falling. Thursday I was off work for New Year's Day, but Friday my office was also closed, and Monday it would be closed till ten o'clock in the morning. The weather reporters, including ones who weren't normally seen on TV in snow apparel, reported the snow conditions all day for a couple of days. Susan,

Daisy and I bundled up and went out to play. Five or six inches of snow lay on the ground. We made angels on the white sheet of snow, one small (me), one medium (Susan), and one big (Daisy).

On one of those snowy days, Daisy and I walked to the Thriftway supermarket that was about ten minutes away. In the snow we took a lot more time. When we got there from the back road, I immediately noticed a lot of SUVs filled the parking lot. The scene rendered me sentimental, not because I wanted to have such a big vehicle, but because I thought that husbands were taking charge of grocery shopping for their wives and thinking of their safety and this evoked memories of happy times with Thomas.

Inside, I saw more men than usual and the store looked different, like before Christmas when men show up in a department store on their shopping missions. Actually, I enjoyed watching those men as they held shopping lists in their hands while moving from place to place, searching intently for the items on the list, trying to finish their task as soon as possible. Some men used cell phones to ask their wives where to look for items. It was amusing to watch them move through the aisle from one place to another and back again like pacing animals in a zoo.

Time slipped by. Another event was on the way: Valentine's Day. One of our housemates left and another moved in. Connie, who had a distinctive personality, added character to our trio (Susan, Daisy, and I), and our activities became more active. She was perhaps in her late thirties or early forties, and had a small body with puffed-up tight muscles on her arms. Her small, cute face with big sparkling eyes and a cherry-like mouth was charming most of the time, but sometimes those eyes turned shifty and she seemed a little crafty at times. We viewed her with suspicion. Nonetheless, she was an interesting person to be with, and she suggested a lot of places and activities where single men might be found, although she didn't have a boyfriend at that time.

Another side of Connie was that she had been a professional house cleaner for more than ten years, so she knew many cleaning products and tips for cleaning. But there was a downside. She used our two washing machines for cleaning her dusting-rags that were covered with all sorts of nasty stains which emitted strong chemical odors. She used lots of bleach—so much that the smell almost suffocated me the instant I entered the laundry room. I detested it. But moreover, it was annoying that I had to worry about getting residual bleach on my clothes. That happened twice in the first month she lived with us. Cumbersome as it was, I had to rinse the washing machine before I used it, as I had no idea who had run the machine before me.

In February, Susan noticed an ad in the *Willamette Week* for a Valentine's Day Singles' Party being held at the World Forestry Center in Portland's Washington Park. Daisy, Connie, and I unanimously agreed to go. Susan said she'd drive.

On the party day, Susan dressed up in a moss-green cashmere sweater and blue jeans. Her V-neck showed a small pendant necklace. She knew how to dress well. Daisy wore a polyester satin blouse and black dress pants. She looked dandy. Connie had plenty of clothes for this kind of occasion, but she was a bit on the flashy side. Her many dresses were low-cut or had some shiny metallic fabric. I owned few clothes, as I had discarded many in the course of the divorce. I wore a simple silk sage-green blouse and a tight black miniskirt. I took time to polish my nails and do my hair with scrupulous care.

The World Forestry Center building had the look of a mountain lodge. The steep pitch of the roof gave it a romantic appearance. What a beautiful place to have a singles' party. The entry lights cast a warm glow on the building's natural wood interior. The place looked warm, cozy, and inviting from outside. We had high hopes as we entered.

Countless women! I thought, as I entered the room. *Are men hiding somewhere?* I estimated the ratio of men to women was at most 1 to 20. *Men don't like chocolate.* I thought if this party had been advertised like "Join us for a romantic single night with wine and beer!" then the place would have been overflowing with men. If not, at least there would have been more men than at this chocolate party.

Once inside, we decided when and where to meet at the end of the party and then spread out and went our own ways. I browsed. As men were indeed scarce, even the unattractive men could engage in conversation with pretty women. Of course all the good-looking men were already taken, so I shifted my attention to the food. The catering service had provided decorative party food along with drinks. Deli platters were prettily arranged with fresh fruits, vegetables, and fine cheese, hams, and colorful pinwheel sandwiches. There were, of course, lots of exclusive chocolates as chocolate companies had sponsored the party. I saw Daisy smacking her lips. I joined her.

For a while I ate, but I became bored just eating. I realized I could go to the second story museum since I had paid the admission. Daisy and I split up again and I headed upstairs to explore. The place was quiet. Since I was the only one there, I stopped to read each placard. At one corner, I checked out some indigenous plants. The placard was placed rather far from the wooden split-rail fence, so I needed to stoop over the fence to read the small placard. I then heard "Hi." Since I was focused on the small print, I hadn't immediately registered that someone was there. I was surprised, but soon resumed my action after saying "hi" to the man who had spoken to me. He looked like he was in his mid-thirties. I thought he was too young for me. We talked for a while but I felt our conversation wasn't engaging, and he, too, seemed to come to that realization. He said, "Well, I've got to go. It was nice talking to you," and parted from me with a gentle smile. I moved on to the next exhibit, but I'd lost interest in the displays, so I walked back downstairs. I found Daisy first, and then Connie, but we could not find Susan. Around the end of the party, Susan finally showed up. We didn't talk about what happened at the party, but Susan made a remark about how delicious the chocolate was. We ran to Susan's car in the crisp cold night. Once inside the car, we all agreed how good the food had been.

One Saturday in April, as spring breezes opened scented flowers and the world cheered up with myriad colors of flowers and a new season of fresh green, Susan suggested we go to the Woodburn Tulip Festival.

Yellow daffodils looked out through the white picket fence lining our yard and a cobalt sky made for delightful contrast. The day looked guaranteed to be gorgeous all day, and we definitely didn't want to stay in the house. Capricious spring weather forms all sorts of clouds, and I always liked the dynamic clouds with multiple shapes, however, on that day, the sun shone through little fluffy clouds and the temperature felt like early summer.

"Hop in the car!" said Susan.

"All right!" Connie said.

"Yeah!" Daisy and I yelped.

We took off in Susan's red Toyota. Inside the car, it became as noisy as a nest of hungry baby birds, becoming even noisier when we tried to talk over the blasting of air through the opened windows. We yakked non-stop. Once we reached the city of Woodburn, Susan followed the signs in the direction of the festival, joining a caravan of other cars headed in the same direction.

"We are here!" I exclaimed as I saw the tulip fields.

"Oh my goodness, they are so beautiful!" Susan said.

"Yes, they are," Connie agreed.

I saw acres and acres of tulips ahead of me. The farm was covered by a gigantic carpet of tulips—numerous shades of red, yellow, orange, purple, and even black. The brilliant colors looked stunning with the snow-tipped mountains of the Cascade Range as a backdrop. I was overjoyed at being in such a beautiful land with beautiful people.

We walked along the skinny foot paths between tulips.

"Stay there. I'll take a picture of you guys," said Susan as she stood amidst rows of yellow tulips.

"Look, Kumiko. Have you seen black tulips?" Daisy asked as she stood still for the picture.

"Aren't they deep purple? Or are they truly black?" I asked.

"I think when the sun begins to set, the color gets blacker," Daisy said.

"I see," I said.

"You guys want to go to the fair?" Connie asked.

We walked back to the fair, where there were vendors of crafts, drinks, and foods.

"Let's get wine," said Connie.

"I'll go with you." I followed Connie as she headed toward the wine vendors.

The rest of our crew started browsing. Connie was by no means shy. In fact she had the nerve to ask the vendor to pour her one wine after another. Each time she swirled, sniffed, and then smacked her lips several times with the air of a wine connoisseur. The vendor eagerly poured all the sample wine and chatted for more than thirty minutes. He even gave her a second sample when she said, "Good! This has a nice bouquet and I like it very much." But at the end, Connie only paid three dollars for the wine, thanked him, smiled, and moved on.

Susan and Daisy had disappeared. Connie and I finally left the area of vendor tents and then Connie wandered in another direction. So I walked alone for a bit, but finally spotted Susan and Daisy and caught up with them. When we saw Connie, a guy was talking to her engagingly as if they were having a first date. When he parted from Connie, I walked up to her. "Do you know him?"

"He is a local newspaper editor," said Connie.

"Hum . . . you seemed to be enjoying the conversation."

"I was," she readily replied.

I didn't think they had already exchanged phone numbers, but asked with curiosity, "Are you guys meeting each other sometime?"

"He's supposed to call me Monday."

"Whoa, you are so good!" I was a little shocked at the speed with which they connected, but a realization hit me *this is Connie, I shouldn't be surprised.* I smiled at her and she grinned back, for she was in a good mood.

We were having a great time at the fair, but we couldn't stay longer as we had another plan. Connie was going to take us to her friend's party that evening. Once we returned home, we hurried to dress up for the party and took off without resting. However, Connie evidently didn't know exactly how to get there, so she drove around the area many times until we finally had to say, "Let's give up!"

Nonetheless, that day remains with me as a wonderful day.

Especially after Susan moved into our house, my life became active and full. I had a job that paid the bills and friendly housemates who entertained me. Life was good. Then, a few weeks after the tulip trip, Frederick called me at my office to tell me he had a girlfriend. After I hung up the phone, I sat staring at it for a few moments, then covered my face with my hands.

Susan stood by me. Everyone else was supportive and caring, too. I felt thankful to have good people around me. I had survived the vicissitudes of life and I had always bounced back, so I knew I would be all right, but I had to go through the familiar pain again. I assured myself that our relationship had been dead. *Why was I feeling the loss then?* I knew it was time to move on. I realized I hadn't seriously tried to find a boyfriend. A few weeks later I placed my profile on yahoo.com.

XVI

New Beginning

I sat at my computer desk for a long time, thinking about what I wanted to put in my profile. Finally, I wrote:

"In all important trials in life we have to take a leap in the dark. Whatever life throws our way, if we strive to make a meaningful life in good faith, the consequences will be rewarding; this I have learned from my major life changes. I hope I can utilize this knowledge in finding the right person. I am Japanese and have a different thinking style. Even so, I have practiced thinking in similar ways to Americans' low context cultural thinking. I still have some Japaneseness in being able to reason that peoples' rational thinking is not always as important as emotions. I am a very caring person. I am a flexible, healthy, loyal, honest, youthful, considerate, 5' 4', 97 lbs, 51-year-old who has been divorced for seven years and has no children. I am active and enjoy living life to the fullest. I am open-minded, and intellectually curious. I am looking for that one special person who can appreciate who I am in the same way as I appreciate who he is. A passionate, caring and spontaneous relationship requires great efforts and patience. Therefore, I would like to have a person who has the maturity to build a good relationship. I enjoy visiting art museums, going to movies, spending time at the beach, and going on picnics. Actually, I can enjoy anything if I am with the right person. I like to paint in oils, watercolors, or ink. I also like reading, cooking, and watching good movies. I am a romantic and fun person to be with."

How I described my ideal match:

"Looking for someone who is honest and has the energy to make some adjustments in order to nurture a good relationship. Although my approach to a better way of living is eclectic, I still have deeply rooted Japanese cultural attitudes and beliefs, so I would like to be with someone who is a man of sensibilities in this regard. He would be healthy, active, positive, affectionate, romantic, and internally handsome."

How could I possibly have written this lengthy profile as if I were a perfect person? I remember one person who sent me an email saying, "Are you for real? Do you really think you can find such a person as you describe in your profile?" He lectured me. I realized I wasn't realistic or practical, although I truly wanted to find a person with such attributes. I sent an email reply back, saying, "Thank you very much for your email. I know what you mean, but I am a dreamer." But his words—*are you for real*—stuck in my mind, so I considered changing my profile to be less demanding.

But before I changed my profile, I came across a person who had written a detailed profile like mine. In his e-mails, I found sincerity. His profile picture reminded me of a passport picture. Usually men photographed themselves in front of an expensive car, a big sailing boat, a beautiful house, or at least some charming background. His picture looked unpretentious and honest. This sincerity appealed to me.

On my first date with him, which took place at a teahouse, I seemed to talk a lot. He listened to my spiel without interrupting and only spoke when I ran out of things to talk about. I must have liked him, though when he called me that night, I couldn't remember his face or anything about him physically, except his sincere-looking blue eyes. We arranged another date.

On the second date, the early June weather was sunny and balmy. Portland was packed with people lining the streets waiting to watch the Rose Festival parade. We rambled around the crowded city all day, and our conversation was engaging. His soft-spoken voice and extremely laid-back attitude tamed my nervousness. His knowledge of a wide range of fields drew my attention.

As we walked, I asked millions of questions about his past. Steve's life had been colorful. As a student, he did a foreign-exchange program in Germany for two years. His venturesome father, who had completed a ten-year odyssey across the Pacific Ocean in a fifty-foot boat he had built, encouraged Steve to share his joy of sailing. His father wanted him to see the world. In less than a month, Steve made a big decision. Quitting his job, he took his two young sons and his wife on a year-long cruise in the Indian Ocean. He also lived and worked as an engineer in Singapore for two years. His adventures revealed that he was a motivated person and I liked that.

Though my initial impressions of Steve were appealing, I needed to know more about his other attributes, such as, what kind of circumstances or situation he was in; what kind of relationship he had with his family and his friends; and what kind of lifestyle he lived. I had learned from my previous relationship with Frederick that opinionated friends and family members can tear apart a relationship. I did not want to repeat this bitter experience. This time, I was determined to be more diligent in finding out about these matters before committing.

Picnics, walks, and going to the beach were our favorite get-together activities, with our focus on talking with each other rather than being entertained. I soon met Steve's two sons, Raj, the oldest (twenty-three) and Marco, the youngest (twenty-two). His adventurous son, Raj, lived in Hawaii, and occasionally would come to the mainland to visit his dad. On Raj's birthday, we threw a party, inviting family, friends, and old neighbors, as well as my friends. At the party, a couple of my friends said, "I would like to introduce Steve's son to my daughter." Both Raj and Marco were considered desirable catches for son-in-laws. These complements, coming from my friends, were particularly flattering. In fact, Raj and Marco were adored by everyone I met, as they both had remarkably calm, gentle, and affable natures.

On other occasions, dining with his mom, his siblings, or his close friends, I received warm and good vibes. Steve's mom often brought me flowers from her garden. Even his dad and his stepmom in Colorado asked on the phone, "When do we get meet you?" Encouraged by the people closed to Steve, I felt more confident about getting into a deeper relationship with him.

After four months of dating, I had a reassuring dream. I was in my dad's workshop, holding a baby in my arms. I asked myself, "Whose baby is this?" In that instant, I saw Steve working near the window where my dad used to work. Then I answered myself, saying "It must be our baby." I gazed at the tiny newborn baby's face to see if the baby was a boy or girl. As I woke up, the first thing to enter my mind was, "He'll be my husband." This dream seemed to foretell our future together.

When six months had passed, he suggested I move in with him. The invitation didn't sound as immoral to me as it once had. I must have learned from my previous relationships that mutual compatibility wouldn't be really proven unless a couple lived together for some time, though a one-year trial period was my limit. In mid-December, I moved into his house, which was located in an unincorporated community. The home sat in a pastoral setting, where herds of cows and flocks of sheep grazed in the fields. There were many horse lovers in this area, and some residents owned goats, llamas, and chickens. On a nice clear day, to the north, a tiny tip of Mt. Rainer was visible. Often Mt. St Helens, Mt. Adams, and Mt Hood lined up grandly in the eastern sky. It was a beautiful place to live.

Steve's house stood on a two-acre plot of land. In spring, the cherry, apple, and pear trees embellished the yard with their dazzling blooms in pink and white. My three additional new companions were his handsome twenty-two-year-old second son, Marco, an obedient, thirteen-year-old Labrador retriever, Mango, and one age-unknown adult cat named "Boat." I effortlessly bonded with the whole good-natured crew. His oldest son, the adventurous twenty-three-year-old Raj, lived in Hawaii. He and I had hit it off well from the first time we met.

I enjoyed the rustic life on weekends, but weekdays were a different story. My long-distance commute took a toll. The arterial road over Cornelius Pass in the Tualatin Mountains, known for its high accident rate, was quite treacherous in winter. My wimpy '87 Honda Civic had a hard time climbing the hills, and its body was rather low, so on-coming cars' headlights blinded me. Vile weather, like a foggy, rainy, snowy, or icy day, made the drive unnerving and fatiguing. But as spring and summer approached, the pass transformed into a verdant green forested corridor, providing cool shade throughout the summer.

After six months of living together, we married in June.

We began mapping our future life. One of our first dreams was to build a house by ourselves. To buy a new plot of land became our weekend task. Finding our ideal property was a slow process. Weeks, then months, passed, but we saw no place we wanted. Our enthusiasm began to fade.

Nearly a year had passed when, fortuitously, our future land presented itself. One day I had taken a day off from work because of heavy snow. We were taking a long walk on a snow-covered road when I saw a beautiful property on a hillside. Snow blanketed the land, the house, and the shed. The scene looked like a Christmas card. Actually, I had passed it several times before, but without the snow, it had looked dilapidated and uninviting. We spotted a snow-covered post with a for-sale sign. Right away we made an offer and in short order had purchased the plot.

Steve had left the corporate world two years earlier, and had started working in the remodeling business, but after we purchased the land, he dedicated himself full-time to building our new house. We planned to do everything by ourselves, including designing, building, plumbing, electrical work, and painting, so we worked like geared-up squirrels.

The house where we were living was placed on the market, as Marco had already moved out to be closer to school in Portland. The old house on the new property was demolished. The project entailed myriad tasks. It was also my job to make sure the house we were trying to sell stayed neat and clean, lest it be unappealing to potential buyers. On weekends, after my weekly cleaning was done, I rushed to the worksite to help Steve as sweeper, organizer, lunch-deliverer, and general gofer. Beyond that, we frequented the building centers to buy lumber, flooring, windows, tiles, and other materials.

Even with a full plate, we kept our social life going. I often saw all of Steve's family members and his close friends and I learned a great deal about his past life. Steve had happy memories of his late wife. My past didn't shine like his. Who wants to hear about an ex-husband or ex-boyfriend, right? I had no children and my family was far away. Since I had moved from place to place like rootless duckweed, leaving my old friends behind, no one really knew about me, or my past. In spite of my contentment, a sense of aloneness started to befall me. It was as if a significant chunk of my life was covered by a veil. I knew this was no one's fault. This was me, feeling sorry for myself.

Spring arrived and the house building was well underway. We had made good headway. This thought lifted a bit of weight from my shoulders. One day, I got up an hour early and found myself writing poetry. Writing poems was good for my soul, and I liked sharing them with my husband. A few months later, Steve suggested I write a book. The thought flashed through my head: *I'll write my memoir.* I surprised myself, but as I thought more about it, I realized this would be one way I could unveil my history. Steve not only understood my urge, but supported me. With his understanding, I felt ready to portray my past in a meaningful way.

I became busier than ever, but writing my story fulfilled me. I remember how, when I sat at my desk pondering how I should begin my book, my mind immediately traveled back to the day I moved to the U.S. How eventful my life had been! Now I could laugh about everything, but how many times had I fallen down, and how many times had I bounced back like a *daruma*? A traditional daruma, or wishing doll, is shaped like a balloon with no arms, no legs, and no eyes. This tumbling doll is made of papier-mâché, but weighted on the bottom, so that no matter how many times you kick it down, it always stands up again. The Japanese proverb, "*Seven times down, eight times up,*" is another way to say "Never give up hope." In the spirit of the proverb, I realized I'd always kept moving forward with hope and determination, and had grown in strength and in compassion for others. In writing this memoir, I have come to see that perhaps I do have a story worth sharing—indeed, we all do.

www.ingramcontent.com/pod-product-compliance
Lightning Source LLC
Chambersburg PA
CBHW071305110426
42743CB00042B/1182